TENNESSEE: THE VOLUNTEER STATE

Tennessee

THE VOLUNTEER STATE

by Mary French Caldwell

CONSULTING EDITOR
R. R. Vance,
Former State Director of Instruction,
Tennessee Department of Education

RICHTEXT PRESS
A BRANCH OF CHILDRENS PRESS

CHICAGO, ILLINOIS

ILLUSTRATION CREDITS

Grateful acknowledgment is made to the following organizations for permission to use the illustrations in this book:

The Bettmann Archive: pp. 8, 10, 15, 16, 19, 22, 33, 46, 53, 56, 58, 61, 86, 88, 90, 95, 100, 104, 105, 109, 126, 133, 162; Eugene Derdeyn (pp. 2, 3, 129, 145, 163, 165, 169, 171); Executive Department of the State of Tennessee: p. 154; Library of Congress: pp. 13, 51, 111, 112, 114, 116 (top), 122; Tennessee Department of Conservation: pp. iii, viii, 4, 14, 37, 52, 71, 72, 75, 79, 80, 82, 91, 107, 115, 116 (bottom), 123, 131, 134, 143, 146, 147, 149, 150, 151, 152, 153, 155, 156, 157, 158, 159, 160, 166, 167, 168, 175, 176, 177, 178, 182, 184, 185; Tennessee State Library: pp. 102, 103, 179 (top); Tennessee State Museum: pp. 43, 63, 70, 101; Terry Tomlin: pp. 55, 97, 164; Wide World Photos: p. 139; University of Tennessee: pp. 6, 7, 179 (bottom).

Cover and Body Design by Margrit Fiddle

Library of Congress Catalog Card Number: 68-31301

2 3 4 5 6 7 8 9 10 11 12 13 14 15 16 17 18 19 20 21 22 23 24 25   R   75 74 73 72 71 70 69

Contents

The Tennessee Walking Horse perpetuates one of Tennessee's oldest traditions, the raising of fine horses. Developed by southern plantation owners who wanted a horse that could carry people comfortably over long distances, the breed has a smooth and easy gait, a pleasing combination of walking and running. It is one of the most popular breeds in the United States for pleasure riding.

The Land and the People

THE FACE OF THE LAND

This is the story of Tennessee, a state blessed with bountiful natural resources and rich in romance, adventure, and human accomplishments. From the store of legend, song, story, and facts, the past will be told. From it, coming generations may gain inspiration and courage.

What do we know about this land? It may be assumed with reasonable accuracy that when the first human being came to live upon it, the land was somewhat like it is today. There must have been the same mountain ranges with their rich vegetation and the same deep valleys watered by the streams which formed its great rivers.

The face of the land had been altered long ago, however, by great internal upheavals. The strata of different geological ages **were** brought to the surface. With the passage of many many years these strata were weathered by the heat of the sun, the cold of the age of glaciers, and the impact of winds and waters. Very slowly, the rocks were pulverized and converted into rich soils. In turn, these soils began to support varied species of plant and animal life.

GEOGRAPHY

Tennessee's 42,244 square-mile area lies between some of the tallest peaks of the Unaka Mountains in the east and the Mississippi River in the west. Approximately 115 miles from north to south and 480 miles from east to west, Tennessee is in the shape of a long rhomboid.

It is bounded on the west by the Mississippi River; on the north by Kentucky and Virginia; on the east by North Carolina; and on the south by Georgia, Alabama, and Mississippi. Across the Mississippi River from its western border are Arkansas and Missouri.

Geographic Regions There are three major geographic regions in Tennessee: East Tennessee, Middle Tennessee, and West Tennessee. Today, these regions also happen to be the three major civil or political divisions of the state. These natural regions, or physiographic provinces, are created by the topography of the land. There are eight natural regions. From east to west, these are: the Unaka Range; the Great Valley of East Tennessee; the Cumberland Tableland; the Highland Rim; the Central or Nashville Basin; the Western Valley of the Tennessee River; the Plateau of West Tennessee; and the Mississippi Bottoms.

The Unaka Range forms a natural barrier along the Tennessee-North Carolina border. Many of the peaks rise to between 5,000 and 6,000 feet. The highest point in the state, Clingman's Dome, 6,642 feet, is in the southwestern part of this range, in a section known as the Great Smoky Mountains because of the blue haze which hangs over the peaks. These mountains present a formidable barrier, and for a long time prevented the white men from entering Tennessee from the east.

The Great Valley of East Tennessee is part of a valley which extends from New York to Alabama. This Great Valley, also called the Appalachian Ridge and Valley

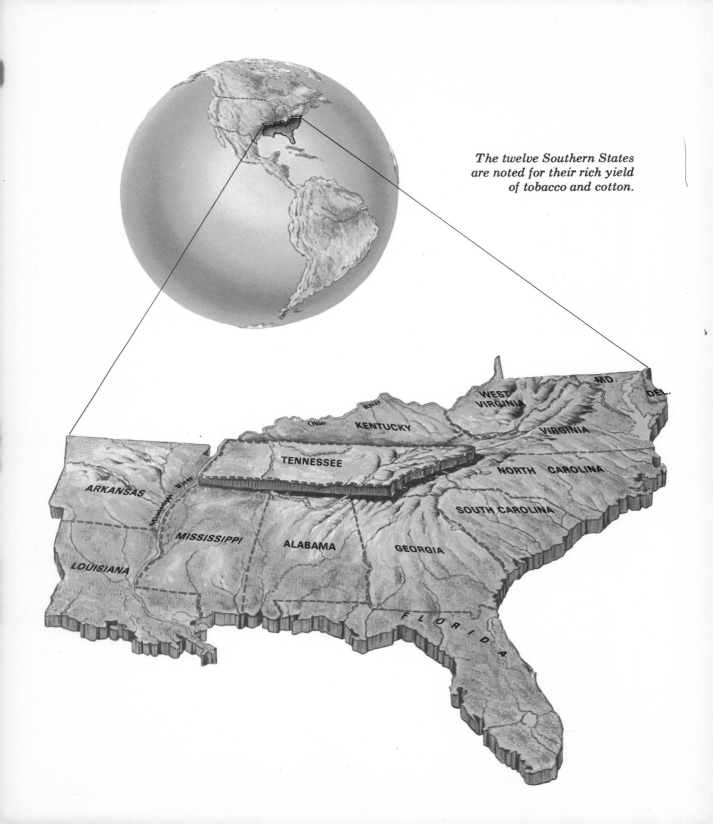

The twelve Southern States are noted for their rich yield of tobacco and cotton.

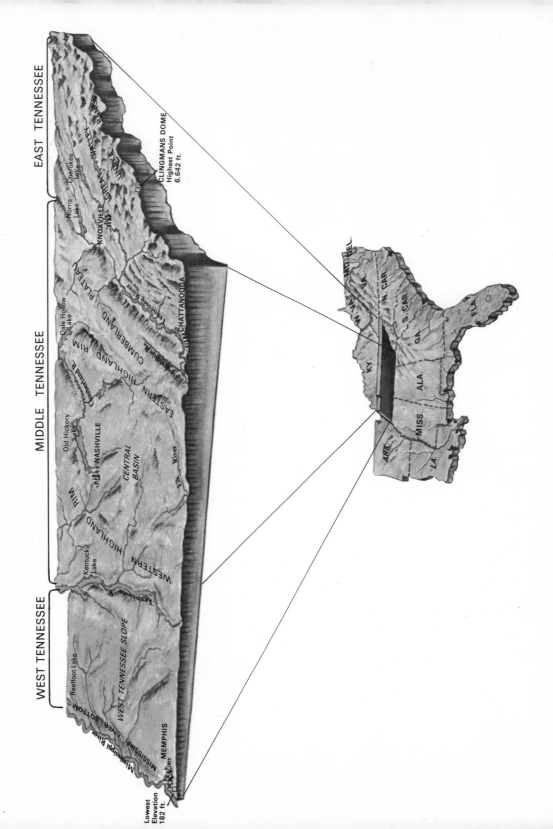

Tennessee covers an area of 42,244 square miles and has three large river systems, the Mississippi, Cumberland, and Tennessee. The many lakes formed by dams on these great rivers are called "The Great Lakes of the South."

The Great Smoky Mountains were once called "The Land of the Thousand Smokes" by the Indians of the region.

Region, is about 75 miles wide. Beyond the Great Valley is the Cumberland Plateau or Tableland. This plateau rises as much as a thousand feet above the surrounding countryside.

The next region to the west is the Eastern Highland Rim. The land then drops down to the Central or Nashville Basin, only to rise again to the Western Highland Rim. The Central Basin, which is almost completely surrounded by the Highland Rim, is sometimes called the "Garden of Tennessee."

The Western Valley of the Tennessee River is part of the Gulf Coastal Plain which extends from the Gulf of Mexico to southern Illinois. The seventh region, the Plateau of West Tennessee, is also part of the Gulf Coastal Plain. It slopes toward the Mississippi River, ending in a steep bluff overlooking the lowlands. These lowlands, known as the Mississippi Bottoms, are mostly swamplands. This area averages less than 300 feet above sea level, and is the lowest part of Tennessee.

Rivers Tennessee's rivers have always been one of the state's major assets. They provided the Indians, and later the white men, with an easy means of transportation as well as rich alluvial lands for farming.

The Tennessee, Cumberland, and Mississippi are the principal rivers of the state. The Mississippi and its tributaries, including the Hatchie, the Forked Deer, and the Obion, drain most of West Tennessee. The Tennessee and the Cumberland rivers, both of which rise in the Appalachian Mountains and flow into the Ohio, drain almost all of the remaining part of the state.

The Tennessee River, more than 600 miles long, is formed by the junction of the Holston and the French Broad near Knoxville. It follows a great U-shaped course, flowing southwest through eastern Tennessee into Alabama, then north through western Tennessee into Kentucky, where it joins the Ohio River. Its major tributaries include the Little Tennessee, the Hiwassee, the Big Sandy, the Buffalo, the Elk, and the Duck rivers.

The Cumberland River describes an arc through north central Tennessee. Rising in eastern Kentucky, it flows southwest into Tennessee, through Nashville, and then northwest into Kentucky to join the Ohio just above that river's junction with the Tennessee River. Among the major tributaries of the Cumberland within the area of Tennessee are the Harpeth, Stones, and Caney Fork rivers.

PREHISTORIC PEOPLE

There is a close relationship between the nature of a land and the character of the people who inhabit it. A way of life, customs, progress, and individual characteristics are influenced by the land. The people who first saw the territory now called Tennessee and chose it for their home were fortunate. For centuries, nature had been making it suitable for human habitation.

Who were these first people who came to live upon the land? Though there are many theories about their origin, no one really knows. One theory states that they belonged to an Asiatic race which migrated to the North American continent by way of Bering Strait. Another theory states that they are descendants of a lost tribe of Israel. But despite all the studies that have been made, their origin still remains a mystery.

Archaeologists term these earliest inhabitants Paleo-Indians. These ancient people were an extremely primitive group of wanderers. Many traces of them have been found in the area of the lower Tennessee River.

Some ten thousand years ago the Paleo-Indians gave way to another group known as Archaic Indians. These Indians were of a more advanced culture. They lived a settled life in villages and knew how to shape and

An early engraving of the French Broad River, whose beauties attracted many families.

polish stones and the bones of animals to make weapons and tools. Their village sites have been discovered in Benton and Henry counties in north central Tennessee.

These Archaic Indians may have been the first of the mound builders in Tennessee. Actually, however, there were many groups of mound builders who built many different kinds of mounds. One group, known as the Woodland Indians, built burial mounds. Another group, called Mississippians, constructed temple mounds. These mounds consist of many layers of ceremonial buildings or temples. When such buildings had outlived their usefulness they would be torn down and covered with dirt. New buildings would then be built on top of the old ones.

There are a great many burial and temple mounds throughout Tennessee. In fact, the state capital, Nashville, is located in the center of an area known for such mounds.

All of the mound builders and other early Indian groups are called prehistoric Indians because we have no written records of them. The Indians inhabiting the land when the first white men appeared are termed historic Indians, because the white explorers provided written records concerning them.

THE SOUTHERN INDIANS

A number of historic Indian groups or tribes lived or hunted in Tennessee. From the accounts of early explorers it is evident that these tribes had been long established. Their pattern of life had not changed in generations, and even their most ancient legends threw no light upon their origins. They had neither a written language nor a calendar. Passage of time was measured by moons, and distance by the days required to traverse it. The years faded into a shadowy, legendary past, marked only by events which lingered in the memory of old men, or in the stories which had been handed down from generation to generation.

Food and Shelter   The Southern Indians were especailly fortunate, for they lived in a temperate, or sub-tropical climate, with rich, well-watered soil which supported bountiful vegetable and animal life. Almost every species of animal and plant life known from Canada to the Gulf of Mexico could be found within the borders of their nations. Not only were their populations small, but they were kept so by disease, wars, and the hardships of daily life in a savage wilderness. When excessive hunting in one region destroyed or drove away the wild game, the Indians simply moved on to new hunting grounds. The major tribes had reasonably permanent boundaries, but, on the hunt, as well as on the war path, they ranged far afield.

The Southern Indians had worked out a reasonably comfortable way of life. They lived in small villages, made up of cabins and communal houses, which varied with the thriftiness, the energy and importance of the tribe.

The Cherokees, contrary to the popular ideas about Indians, lived in neatly plastered cabins, not wigwams. Near each dwelling was a small garden. At a suitable distance from the village, were fields planted and tilled by the women.

Clothing   Indian dress, before it was influenced by the wares obtained from white traders, was a product of the land. All clothing was made by the women, for the men considered such labor degrading. In the winter season the women gathered the coarse, curly, brown hair of the buffalo, spun it as fine as possible, and wove it into cloth. Many

These arrowheads, found in Henry County, Tennessee, date from about 5,000 B.C.

*This sandstone figure,
an example of pre-historic Indian artwork,
was found in Wilson County, Tennessee.*

of them, as they wove, worked small beads into the fabric. Usually they followed a uniform pattern, but sometimes this varied according to the artistic abilities of the weaver. The result was a garment which was beautiful, as well as warm and durable.

Turkey feather blankets were another interesting product of skill and ingenuity. The long, soft feathers of the neck and breast of this large fowl were taken and woven into fine nettings made either of hemp or the inner bark of the mulberry tree. The snow-white feathers of the swan, the glistening green

ones of the little Carolina parakeets, and the feathers of many other species of birds which were found in the greatest abundance were also woven into blankets, robes, crowns, fans and various kinds of ornaments. The Natchez women were especially adept at making such things, and were known also for the long, white robes which they made from the bark of the mulberry tree.

Bearskins were used for rugs and blankets. Deerskins, beautifully cured by the skillful Indian women, were made into moccasins, leggings, and hunting shirts. Raccoon skins, with their tails retained for an ornament, were made into caps, and the horns of the buffalo became convenient receptacles for precious gunpowder.

Government Most of the Southern tribes had a reasonably well-established form of government when the white men first came among them. These governments granted a considerable degree of individual freedom and, in the choice of leaders or determination of important affairs, permitted a democratic exercise of opinion.

Chiefs were chosen for their prowess in war, for their eloquence, or for their adroit statesmanship. Their power continued only as long as they pleased the majority of the people. An unpopular chief was not necessarily displaced; the people simply transferred their allegiance to another leader whose policy, at the moment, was more to their liking. This characteristic of Indian government was responsible for their constant vacillation in loyalty between the French and English, and for their swift changes from peace to war.

The freedom enjoyed by the Indians, however, was the undisciplined freedom sought by all wild things. Theirs was a loosely organ-

Indian women did all the menial tasks while the men hunted and fought.
This copper engraving from about 1650
shows women preparing food in an Indian village.

ized society, one which had not, in the countless years of its existence, approached anything like the civilized concept of a free and
responsible form of government. Nor had the
Indians themselves progressed beyond their
ancient barbaric state. Savage brutality was
always ready to burst forth at the slightest
provocation, not only against the white man,
but against enemy tribes and offenders within their own nations. Indian women, toiling
peacefully in their fields, or at their crude
looms, would be transformed into shrieking
furies when prisoners were turned over to
them. Yet, now and then, pity and love, and
humane consideration for the unfortunate,
came to the surface.

TRIBAL AREAS

The eastern approach to the great wilderness
empire of the Southern Indians was by way
of Charleston, South Carolina, and the first
tribe encountered on this route was the
Catawba. The Cherokees, who adjoined
them, inhabited lands which began on the
eastern slopes of the Great Smoky Mountains and reached eventually to the Chickamauga villages at the site of the present city
of Chattanooga.

Farther to the northwest were the
Shawnees, or "southerners," whose name was
given to the chief river of their country, now
known as the Cumberland River. The
Shawnees were a wandering nation which

had come north from the Savannah River area to the Cumberland. They finally were forced to leave their Cumberland River territory when both the Cherokees and the Chickasaws, who had formed an alliance, marched against them. After a series of devastating wars all of the tribes left the Cumberland country. It was because of these Indian wars that the first white settlers in this section found the country free of Indians.

South and west of the Shawnees were the great tribes of Creeks, or Muskogees, the Choctaws, the Chickasaws, the Natchez, and many lesser tribes.

All of the tribes east of the Mississippi were connected by a great network of trails, as well as by waterways. Streams which have their beginnings in the southern peaks of the Appalachians flow into the upper reaches of the country once held by the Creek and Chickasaw nations. Then, gathered into the Mississippi, they continue southward to touch upon the western boundaries of the Choctaw and Chickasaw country, finally reaching the region of the ill-fated Natchez and lesser tribes which once lived on the Gulf of Mexico. This great system of waterways afforded a means of contact among the southern tribes.

The Cherokees It is from the ancient Cherokee town of Tanase, on the Little Tennessee River, that the Tennessee River and the State of Tennessee take their names. Like all mountain people, the Cherokees looked upon their land with a fierce devotion. They were a proud people, brave and relentless foes to all those with whom they had a quarrel. Their history, from 1700 until the great removal in 1838, is one of the great American epics—tragic, but of such magnifi-

cence that pity has no place in its contemplation.

James Adair, a Scotsman who spent nearly thirty years trading with the Cherokees, saw their country in its primitive beauty. In his *History of the American Indians* he gave a comprehensive description of the Cherokees in their native setting about the middle of the eighteenth century.

"The country," he wrote, "lies in about 34 degrees north latitude, at the distance of 340 computed miles to the north-west of Charlestown,—140 miles west south-west from the Katahba nation,—and about 200 miles to the north of the Muckohge or Creek country.

"They are settled, near in an east and west course, about 140 miles in length, from the lower towns where Fort Prince George stands, to the late unfortunate Fort Loudoun. The natives make two divisions of their country, which they term *Ayrate*, and *Ottare*, signifying 'low' and 'mountainous'....

"The eastern, or lower parts of this country, are sharp and cold to a Carolinian in winter, and yet agreeable; but those towns that lie among the Apalache mountains, are very pinching to such who are unaccustomed to a savage life....

"Formerly, the Cheerake were a very numerous and potent nation. Not above forty years ago, they had 64 towns and villages, populous, and full of women and children. According to the computation of the most intelligent old traders of that time, they amounted to upwards of six-thousand fighting men; a prodigious number to have so close on our settlements.... But they were then simple, and peaceable, to what they are now....

"The Cheerake mountains ... are of prodigious extent, and frequently impassable by an enemy. The Allegeny, or 'great blue

An old engraving of Outacite, an early Cherokee chief.

ridge,' commonly called the Apalache-mountains, are here above one hundred miles broad . . . In the lower and middle parts of the mountainous rugged country, the Indians have a convenient path, by the foot of the mountain: but farther in . . . they are forced to wind from north to south, along the rivers and large creeks, to get safe passage: and the paths are so steep in many places, that the horses often pitch, and rear on end, to scramble up."

Today, only a small, stubborn remnant of the Cherokees remains in the picturesque land over which their nation once reigned supreme.

The Creeks   Most warlike of all the southern tribes were the Muskogees, or Creeks. They waged frequent wars against the white settlements until they were subdued by Andrew Jackson in the wars of 1813-1814.

This victory in the Creek country not only paved the way for expulsion of the British from the southern coast, but led to treaties which opened the vast territory between the Tennessee River and the Gulf of Mexico to white settlement.

Chickasaws and Choctaws   One of the most important factors in the destiny of the Tennessee country was the unswerving friendship which the Chickasaws, smallest of the major southern tribes, bore toward the English. This nation more than any other influenced the development of the Cumberland settlements and the rich territory they once inhabited in what is now West Tennessee.

It was in the Chickasaw country that the first explorations of the Spanish were halted and De Soto met his death. And it was the Chickasaws who, in their unceasing war against the French, helped defeat French plans for establishing a chain of forts and settlements from the mouth of the Mississippi to Canada.

Although the Choctaws were closely related to the Chickasaws in physical appearance, as well as in language, custom, and tradition, the two tribes were constantly quarreling. Because of their proximity to New Orleans on the one hand, and the Chickasaw nation on the other, the Choctaws became a useful tool for French intrigues.

AN ENCHANTED LAND

The first white men who crossed the Appalachian mountain ranges and made their way into Tennessee were enchanted—some so powerfully so that they actually believed themselves to be bewitched. There is a story that the waters of a spring, at the watershed on the western side of the mountains, had powers to bewitch the drinker and to hold him in captivity. About 1730, some traders, hunters, and explorers who had begun visiting the country beyond the mountains declared that anyone who drank these waters would not leave the country for a period of seven years.

The spring was a center of great curiosity, not only because of its supposed powers of enchantment, but also because it was the beginning of the "French waters," which was the name given to the area under the control of the French.

Before these white men stretched a new land, fertile beyond their most extravagant dreams. To the west, the Mississippi flowed southward to the Gulf of Mexico and to ships from the Old World. From the mountain springs of its watershed to the great rivers, a network of waterways united to serve the land.

Today, much of this land lies within the boundaries of the present state of Tennessee, but portions of it are also in Kentucky, Virginia, the Carolinas, Alabama, and Mississippi. In reality, this land drained by the Tennessee River and its tributaries cannot be confined by man-made boundaries.

The first white men who explored the Tennessee waters, and followed them to the distant Mississippi and the Gulf of Mexico, had to battle for years before they actually possessed the land. The Indians who held it used all their strength to repel the white man's advances. At last, the curiosity, courage, ingenuity, determination, and even the greed, of the white man prevailed—but not without a struggle which forms one of the most dramatic chapters in American history.

Spain and France in the New World

SPANISH EXPLORATION

The Spaniards wrote a brilliant **but, in the end**, ineffective chapter in the story of western exploration. Their efforts mark the earliest attempts of the white man to reach the Mississippi Valley in the heart of what is now the eastern half of the United States. Following the discovery of America by Christopher Columbus in 1492, the nations of the Old World began to send out explorers to find and claim the riches of this new land. Spain was then the most powerful of the European countries and took an early lead in this search for gold.

The Fountain of Youth In 1512 Juan Ponce de León, an aging, but still vigorous soldier of Spain, entered upon a voyage of exploration. His primary objective was not gold, but an even more coveted treasure—the fountain of eternal youth. With three ships, outfitted at his own expense, he hoped to restore his youth and add to his fortune and prestige.

His squadron sailed for Puerto Rico on March 3, 1512, and on Easter Sunday, March 27, sighted land. Because of the abundance of flowers and vegetation, he named the land Florida.

Rough weather prevented an immediate landing, but early in April he went ashore a little north of the site of St. Augustine and claimed the territory for Spain. After a futile search for the magic fountain, and numerous encounters with hostile Indians, he set sail for home with the news of his discovery. In 1521 Ponce de León returned to Florida as the Spanish governor and attempted to establish a colony. When his party was attacked by Indians, and he himself wounded by a poisoned arrow, he returned to Cuba, where his death soon followed.

A few years after Ponce de León's failure, Pánfilo de Narváez was granted the unexplored land in Florida. Narváez landed in Florida in 1528, but found the natives sullen and uncooperative. Against the advice of his lieutenants, he undertook to explore the country. He was soon cut off from his ships and lost more than half his men in battles with the Indians. The remainder then built crude boats and attempted to escape into the Gulf of Mexico. Caught by seasonal storms, Narváez and all but three or four of his men were lost.

One of the survivors was Alvar Núñez Cabeza de Vaca, who was cast ashore somewhere on the coast of what is now Texas. He and three companions were enslaved by the Indians, but eventually escaped and made their way to Mexico.

DISCOVERY OF THE MISSISSIPPI

One man, in particular, Hernando De Soto was impressed by the stories Cabeza de Vaca told upon his return to Spain. In 1539 he led an expedition to Florida, landing somewhere near Tampa Bay. Some six hundred men and between two and three hundred horses were put ashore upon Florida soil. To discourage the weak ones who might be tempted to turn back, De Soto ordered his ships to return to Havana. De Soto then headed north in search of gold

DeSoto discovers the Mississippi. (From an old engraving of the painting by Powell.)

and other treasure. A Spaniard who had been held captive since the earlier expedition of Narváez was rescued, but even when he told them that he had seen or heard nothing of treasure, De Soto still refused to turn back.

Indian guides, in slave collars and chains, became sullen under harsh treatment and continually led the party astray into the swamps. Horses and men died. Provisions began to run out. But De Soto still pushed on through Georgia and South Carolina.

Early in the summer of 1540, the expedition approached the Cherokee country at some point which may or may not have been within the boundaries of the present state of Tennessee. Parties sent northward to explore were discouraged by the denseness of the vegetation, ruggedness of the mountains, and poverty of the natives. By late fall, De Soto was in the country of the Chickasaws. Supplies were dwindling, and the loss of men and horses was appalling. But stubborn pride outweighed common sense, and the expedition drove forward to its tragic end. Quarters in a Chickasaw village in what is now the northern part of Mississippi, offered little protection from the snows and cold of an unusually severe winter.

In the spring of 1541 De Soto was prepared to move forward again and demanded of the Chickasaws two hundred men to carry baggage and perform other menial labor. The answer was a bitter attack in which the Spaniards lost several men, as well as a great

The Chucalissa Indians lived along the east shore of the Mississippi River hundreds of years before the white men came to America. Villages like this one were first encountered by DeSoto in 1541, but were found deserted by French explorers in 1673.

amount of equipment and many horses. De Soto then pushed westward and northward through the wilderness until he reached Indian settlements near the Mississippi River. Somewhere in the vicinity of the present city of Memphis, Tennessee, he first saw the mighty "Father of the Waters." To De Soto this great river was but one more obstacle in the path of his impatient search for wealth and fame. It necessitated a halt while rafts were built to carry men and horses to the western bank. Once over the Mississippi, De Soto journeyed up the Arkansas River, but found no gold. During these final wanderings, the Spaniards visited several tribes west of the Mississippi. Finally, completely discouraged they turned back to the Mississippi.

De Soto was stricken with a "malignant fever" and died in May, 1542. To conceal his death from the Indians he had so ill-treated, his body was wrapped in a mantle and, in the stillness of the night was silently sunk in the middle of the river he had discovered.

FRENCH EXPLORATION

It was the French who first made extensive exploration of the Mississippi Valley and eventually came into the Tennessee country. Their missionaries and soldiers fought in the conquest of the vast watershed of the Mississippi. The French claim to this rich territory was based directly upon their explorations and construction of forts, trading posts, and missions. The priests, armed only with their zeal for converting heathens, were often more powerful in the conquest of the Mississippi than either statesmen or soldiers.

During the period of Spanish explorations, the French were not idle. But whereas the Spanish approached the American Continent from the south, the French did so from the north. In 1608, Quebec was founded on the banks of the St. Lawrence River in Canada. French explorers, fur traders, and priests moved out into the surrounding territory. Wherever they went they heard of a great river to the south and west, a river which went all the way to the sea. French authorities were determined to discover if this were true, for if so they would be in a position to control most of North America.

FATHER MARQUETTE AND JOLIET

Louis Frontenac, the governor of New France selected Louis Joliet, a French explorer to head the expedition. Father Jacques Marquette, a Jesuit missionary was appointed to accompany Joliet.

The expedition set out in May, 1673, and the voyagers soon arrived in the Illinois country. Here they were received with great ceremony and were entertained for six days. Upon their departure, the sacred calumet, a symbol of peace among the Indians, was presented to them and under its protection, they pushed southward.

Soon they passed the river now known as the Ohio, but then called the Oubache or Wabash. Then came the peaceful villages of the Shawnees and still farther on, the Chickasaw nation. Here they observed that the natives bore firearms, a fact signifying that they had encountered the English or Spanish settlements.

A little farther south, they came to the mouth of the Arkansas River. After visiting the Indians in this vicinity, they decided to return to Canada with the valuable information they had obtained. Convinced that the Mississippi flowed into the Gulf of Mexico and not into either the Atlantic or Pacific, they thought it best not to continue farther south for fear that they might be captured by the Spanish. Marquette, too, was satisfied to return. Risking their lives, he and his party had carried the word of God to strange tribes and had discovered new fields of conquest.

Joliet returned to Quebec to carry news of the expedition's success. Marquette remained to preach the gospel to some Miamis and other tribes in the vicinity of Chicago. Here, Marquette labored for two years until his death.

Marquette and Joliet explore the Mississippi with their Indian guides. (Taken from an old engraving by Darley.)

La Salle and Hennepin on the Mississippi. This print is taken from the original sketch by Father Hennepin published in his book "Description de La Louisiane" in 1683.

ROBERT CAVALIER DE LA SALLE

The report Joliet carried back to Canada was well received, especially by Robert Cavalier de La Salle, who lived on a vast grant at the outlet of Lake Ontario. La Salle, who had renounced his inheritance and embarked for New France, had become familiar with the Indian trade and was rapidly acquiring both wealth and fame.

With the assistance of Frontenac, La Salle returned to France and obtained noble rank. He was then established at Fort Frontenac, named for his benefactor, on the condition that he maintain the fort. With the magnificent grant, he had also obtained the exclusive right to trade with the Five Nations, as the Mohawk, Oneida, Onondaga, Cayuga, and Seneca tribes of the Iroquois Confederacy were known. La Salle began his activities among the Indians in 1669. Within ten years, through his own explorations and from stories told to him by the tribes he traded with, La Salle gained much valuable information.

At the French court and in New France, La Salle became known as a great navigator and trader. His success, however, inspired much jealousy. Because of this, it was difficult for him to secure cooperation for his expedition on the Mississippi.

He had begun preparations for the trip in the early winter of 1679. With Henri de Tonti, Louis Hennepin, two other Franciscan priests, and about thirty followers, he set out for the Illinois country. They reached Lake Peoria early in 1680, but were delayed when their supply ship, the "Griffin," failed to return. Their delay necessitated the building of a fort on the Illinois River. From Fort Crevecoeur (Broken Heart), La Salle dispatched exploring parties in various directions, and he himself set out on foot for Fort Frontenac to secure supplies.

Meanwhile, Indians from the Iroquois nation descended upon the men he left behind. When he returned to the Illinois country, La Salle found the post deserted. The voyage down the Mississippi was delayed another year while he located and reorganized the survivors who had found refuge among friendly tribes. He reinforced his party with men and supplies that he had brought from Fort Frontenac and, early in the year of 1682, they finally embarked.

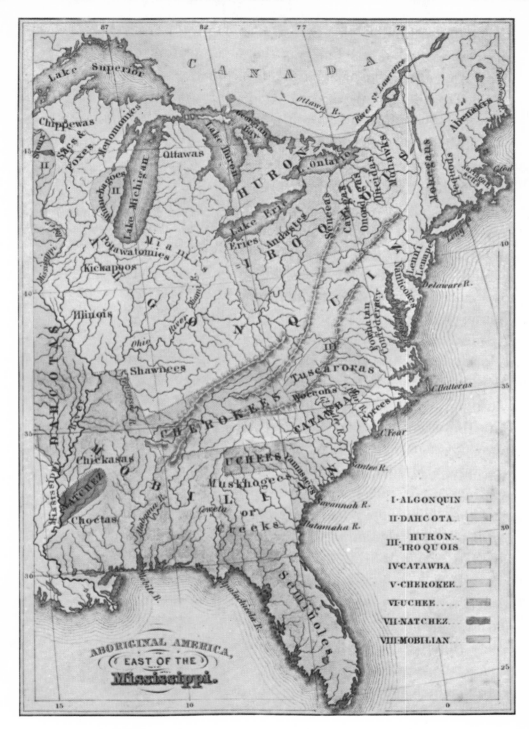

At the time of the first explorers, each Indian nation had its own territory.
This map, published in an early history of the United States,
shows the tribal boundaries of the nations east of the Mississippi.

Beyond the Ohio, the party floated southward until it came to the Chickasaw Bluffs. Here, a landing was made and the first fort, Prudhomme, was erected by white men in the Tennessee country.

In the Arkansas country, La Salle planted the French flag. The party observed with interest the Indian customs and the general nature of the country.

"They have cabins made with the bark of cedar," Tonti recorded. "They have no other worship than the adoration of all sorts of animals. Their country is very beautiful, having an abundance of peach, plum, and apple trees; and vines flourish there; buffaloes, deers, stags, turkeys are very numerous. They have even domestic fowls . . ."

When the village of the Taencas was reached, La Salle sent Tonti to inform the chief of their arrival.

Tonti noted that the cabins were made of mud and covered with cane mats. The women and old men wore large white cloaks made from the bark of the mulberry tree.

Beyond the Taencas, in the Natchez nation, La Salle was well received by their great chief, whose village was situated on a hillside near the river. Farther south, however, at the village of Quinipissas, the Indians were hostile and shot arrows as the party attempted to land. La Salle, who was determined not to fight any nation, at once pushed southward.

A few more days of sailing brought the voyagers to their goal, the sea. Camping on the right bank, they planted the French flag and named the land Louisiana in honor of the French King, Louis XIV.

But the party did not remain in Louisiana. First, they retraced their journey up the Mississippi. When provisions ran short, the men attempted to secure food and were attacked again by the hostile Indians. The Natchez Indians, although afraid of firearms, carried food to the Frenchmen, who ate with guns in their hands. Fearing other attacks, the friendly chief of the village begged La Salle to leave at once.

Some time later, La Salle and his party reached Fort Prudhomme, where La Salle fell dangerously ill. Tonti, pushing onward, arrived at the "River Chicagou" about the end of June and reached Michilimakinac about the middle of July. La Salle, having recovered meanwhile, joined Tonti in September. Pausing only long enough to build Fort St. Louis and to establish Tonti as its commanding officer, La Salle planned his return to Quebec and his departure to France.

A TRAGIC RETURN

At the court of Louis XIV, La Salle's stories of the great territory he had claimed for France were well received. Soon, preparations for planting a French colony at the mouth of the Mississippi were underway. In July, 1684, a fleet of four vessels carrying 280 persons, including 100 soldiers under the command of Joutel, set sail for the New World.

The voyage, though free from mishaps, was marked for disaster. Beaujue, an arrogant naval commander, refused to yield to the judgment of La Salle. The first serious difficulty arose in January, 1685, when the fleet must have been close to the mouth of the Mississippi. Unfamiliar with the approach by sea, La Salle was not sure of their position. Meanwhile, headstrong Beaujue kept moving westward. Soon convinced that the course was wrong, La Salle urged the commandant to turn back, but his pleas were ignored. When the fleet reached the Bay

An early illustration of La Salle claiming the Mississippi for France.

of Matagorda, La Salle decided to land, believing that he could follow streams of this region to the Mississippi. Again, disaster followed him. A heavy storm shattered the vessel which carried their provisions. La Salle managed to retrieve some of the cargo and saved enough of the vessel to serve as a crude shelter after it was roofed with buffalo skins.

When the remaining vessels set sail for France, they left behind some 230 people. Their efforts to found a colony were doomed to failure, but they were successful in establishing French claims to lands far west of those La Salle had actually explored on his voyage down the Mississippi.

La Salle then set out to lead the remaining men up the Mississippi to Canada. With him were Joutel, his two nephews, and several others including the rebellious Duhaut and L'Archeveque. During the journey, one of the nephews failed to return from a deer hunt, and La Salle went to search for him.

To get a response from the missing nephew, La Salle fired his gun and thus revealed his presence to the dangerous Duhaut and L'Archeveque. They answered his inquiries with a gunshot. La Salle fell, fatally wounded, and the murderers left his body unburied there. Joutel, the remaining nephew, and several others recovered La Salle's body later and buried it in a wilderness grave. They then continued their journey to Canada.

But, Louis XIV's elaborate plans for establishing a colony at the mouth of the Mississippi had been wrecked. More than a decade was to pass before the French were to make another such attempt. La Salle's death was mourned in France. His knowledge of the country and the Indian tribes, as well as his wisdom and courage, were to be missed. For the English, however, the end of La Salle's expedition provided a further opportunity for their occupation of the Mississippi Valley.

England in the New World

ENGLISH EXPLORATION

English activity in the New World began with John Cabot's voyage to Cape Breton Island in 1496, but it was not until more than a hundred years later, in 1607, that the first permanent English settlement in America was established at Jamestown, Virginia. For the next hundred and fifty years England contented herself primarily with establishing additional colonies along the Atlantic seaboard. Thus the English, whose southern colonies were the closest to Tennessee, were the last to approach it.

For more than a century, the English settlers along the eastern seaboard knew nothing of the land beyond the southern Appalachians. For a still longer period, their knowledge was vague and indefinite. When stories of the land's beauty and fertility were finally related by traders and hunters, the information was resented, rather than welcomed, in colonial official circles. The idea of a new country on the other side of their own frontiers was disturbing.

The British colonial policy in America did not plan to build settlements beyond easy reach of established colonial governments. Nor did it favor development of trade from the Mississippi to French or Spanish ports on the Gulf of Mexico—in direct competition with British interests.

Eastern colonies benefited from the Indian trade and from the rich furs brought for shipment from Virginia and the Carolinas. These pelts, along with tobacco, cotton, and other products of the colonies, were wanted by England in return for manufactured articles.

Disturbance of the *status quo* was, therefore, actively opposed by the colonial governors. Selfish motives, rather than respect for French claims to the Mississippi Valley, caused the British officials to accept the designation of the entire western watershed as "French waters" and to oppose settlement of it by men from their colonies.

These were the conditions surrounding the Tennessee country about the time when white men were beginning to make serious and continued efforts to penetrate its interior.

INTO TENNESSEE

The first white men to penetrate the Tennessee country were probably James Needham and an indentured servant, a boy named Gabriel Arthur. In the spring and summer of 1673, they explored tributaries of the Tennessee River and possibly reached Chota, or other Cherokee towns near the mouth of the Little Tennessee River. Their expedition was sponsored by Colonel Abraham Wood who had established himself in a fort and trading post at the Falls of Appomattox. Wood was interested in learning something definite about the unknown lands beyond the Appalachians.

Needham and Arthur were accompanied by eight Indians. At the beginning of their journey, they were supplied with four horses. Horses were a novelty to the Cherokees, for it was not until early in the eighteenth century that they were introduced to them. But, the horses were not trained for mountain travel, and only one survived even the first stages of the journey.

The fur trade brought wealth to Spain, England, and France but caused many conflicts between them. In this old engraving, explorers trade tools and arms for furs.

After a few weeks in the Cherokee country, Needham returned to Fort Henry to report to Colonel Wood. He left young Arthur with the Indians, instructing him to learn something of their language and ways.

In September of 1673, Needham left Colonel Wood's fort on his second journey. He was accompanied this time by a party of twelve Indians and carried supplies for a long stay in the Indian country. The party had scarcely passed the Yadkin River when Needham was killed by "Indian John," an Occaneechi who accompanied the party.

Still in the Indian country, Gabriel Arthur was marked for a similar fate, but he was rescued by a Cherokee chief. The boy remained under the protection of his benefactor for a year. During this time, he went out with warriors and hunters on expeditions to the Spanish settlements in Florida; to Port Royal, in South Carolina; and to the region where the great Kanawha joins the Ohio. He returned from the last expedition by the Warriors' Path through the Cumberland Gap and is thought to be the first white man to set foot on Kentucky soil. In May, 1674, the Cherokee chief returned Gabriel to Colonel Wood at Fort Henry.

BRITISH AND FRENCH CONFLICTS

During the last part of the seventeenth century and the first half of the eighteenth century, England was engaged with France and Spain in a world-wide struggle for empire. Each clash in Europe and other parts of the world led to warfare on the American continent. There were four major conflicts, known collectively as the French and Indian wars, which took place in America between 1689 and 1763. Hostilities involved not only attacks by regular French and British troops and their colonial counterparts, but all the savage terror of Indian border raids as well. Both sides made considerable use of Indian allies in their bid for supremacy.

The first of these wars, King William's War, lasted from 1689 to 1697. It ended with the Treaty of Ryswick, under the terms of which both France and England returned all the American territory they had taken. For the moment the fighting was over, but mutual distrust was still strong.

Excluding the brief exploration of young Gabriel Arthur and the ill-fated Needham, it appears that the first white men who traveled extensively in the Tennessee country were French. A few of them, as early as 1698 or 1700, were making their way from the Mississippi to the Carolina settlements, by way of the Tennessee River and its tributaries.

In February and March of 1701, nineteen or more Frenchmen arrived in South Carolina from Canada, by way of the Mississippi River. The question of what to do with them was raised in the South Carolina House of Commons. The Governor wanted to know how these men should be disposed of and whether they should be allowed to come into the settlement.

It was decided that the Frenchmen be treated as friends, but that they be ordered back as soon as possible. They were encouraged not to return with any furs in the future.

Stronger measures than resolutions of legislative bodies would have to be invoked, however, before the progress of the French in the Mississippi Valley was halted. The formal expeditions sent out by the French king were not the only forces to be combated. The activities of small groups of renegade Frenchmen, probably survivors of military and exploring parties, also posed a threat to the English government.

One such renegade, Jean Couture, was probably the leader of the group in South Carolina in 1700. Born in Rouen, France, Couture was a carpenter by trade. Known to La Salle in 1684 as a "coureur des bois," or trapper, he was with Tonti's party when it made a vain attempt to join La Salle's ill-fated colony in 1686. Couture was one of the six men chosen to hold the fort built at the mouth of the Arkansas River by Tonti. Four of the men, becoming discouraged, returned to Fort St. Louis. Couture who was commandant and one other remained until they were found by survivors of La Salle's party in July, 1687. It was not until Couture's return to Fort St. Louis that Tonti received news of La Salle's death.

Many years later, Couture transferred his allegiance from New France to the English and settled in South Carolina. Here he became widely known as a trader and prospector for mines.

A second war with the French, known as Queen Anne's War, broke out in 1702 and lasted until 1713. Once more the frontier became a blood bath, marked by savage attacks such as the massacre of the English settlers at Deerfield, Massachusetts, in 1704. Hostilities ended with the Peace of Utrecht. Under the terms of this agreement, France gave England the Hudson Bay region, Newfoundland, and Acadia.

By now, scores of hunters, trappers, and traders from French and English settlements were in the western wilderness.

Some of these Frenchmen, undoubtedly, penetrated the Cumberland country and found the Great Salt Lick at the site of the present city of Nashville. The Great Salt Lick had attracted great herds of wild animals and flocks of birds. By 1715, a French trader named Charles Charleville had established a trading post at this spot.

Although these adventurers left few traces of their passing, the stories they returned with must have inspired others to engage in similar activities. It is not strange then that leaders in the eastern colonies began to look to these lands and these "western waters" with an increasing interest. At long last the British government began to think seriously of its claims to this vast territory.

EXPLORERS FROM VIRGINIA

For years the most important men of colonial Virginia had done little more than talk about the country on the western side of the Appalachian Mountains. There was a definite tendency to limit settlement to the eastern slopes in order to preserve the Indian country as a market for English traders and a rich source of furs. This policy was doomed by constant French aggression and by the determination of individuals from the English colonies to occupy the potentially rich western country.

In the year 1716, there was one, however, who undertook an extensive personal exploration of the west. Governor Alexander Spotswood of Virginia did not penetrate the country beyond the mountains, but he and his "Knights of the Golden Horseshoe,"

Types of early rivercraft used by Indians, explorers, and pioneers.
Upper left, the keelboat; lower left, the raft; upper right, dugout canoe; lower right, flatboat.

were successful in making additions to the meager knowledge of the country and in locating ". . . an easy passage over the great Ridge of Mountains w'ch before were judged impassable."

During this period, Virginia strengthened her hold on the Indian trade and sent an increasing number of men into the western country. But Governor Spotswood's policy of exploration was not followed, nor was any effort made to fortify the Appalachian country for years to come. Even Governor Spotswood, who had traveled farther west than any of his associates, had touched only the fringes of the mountain country. Little was known of the obstacles to be confronted in its occupation.

MISSION TO THE CHEROKEES

About the time of Governor Spotswood's explorations for Virginia, Colonel George Chicken, a Scotsman who had arrived in Charleston about 1700, was sent into the Cherokee country to promote the interests of South Carolina. On his first journey in 1714 and 1715, Colonel Chicken testified to the presence of Frenchmen among the Cherokees.

Ten years later, in 1725, Governor Middleton of South Carolina ordered Colonel Chicken to undertake another mission to the Cherokees. On this journey, he was accompanied by his son, a secretary, and two interpreters, Eleazar Wiggin and Joseph Cooper. Both Wiggin and Cooper were already established in the Indian trade and knew the language and habits of the Cherokees.

The party reached the Overhill towns (as the Cherokee villages on the western side of the mountains were called) late in July after a few days delay due to heavy rains. Colonel Chicken recorded in his journal, ". . . the Shower being over, we set away and about one o'Clock in the Afternoon we Arrived at Tunissee (Tennessee) where the King of the Upper people lives, and some time after my arrival there, I had the whole Ceremony used before me . . ."

At the conclusion of this sacred ceremony, the Indians were informed that Colonel Chicken had come to give a "beloved talk" to the heads of all of their towns.

Standing before the assembled chiefs, Colonel Chicken spoke of the friendship and love that the English bore to the Indians and to the advantage of their being friends and trading together. Then being the shrewd Scotsman that he was, he advised them that if Frenchmen should come among them, they should capture them and take their possessions. Although they had not yet entered the towns, he told them, the Frenchmen had come a long way with other Indian tribes, planning to destroy the Cherokees.

The Indians replied that the English Governor had told them the same thing about the French. They also assured Colonel Chicken that they would do as he had told them, because "they never had any Value for the French nor never will . . ."

THE CROWN OF THE CHEROKEES

Sir Alexander Cuming was the next to visit the Cherokee nation. In 1730, he had the Cherokee leaders agree to submit to the British Crown. To prove that they were sincere, Sir Alexander brought seven Cherokee chiefs and an interpreter with him to London.

Within three weeks after they landed, Sir

Alexander was introduced to the King, George II. In the presence of the Court, Sir Alexander knelt and declared that he had received full power over the Cherokees; the chiefs knelt with him to indicate their agreement with what he had said. Then Sir Alexander laid the Crown of the Cherokee nation at the King's feet. The King was pleased to accept the crown which had five eagles' tails and four Indian scalps.

The seven chiefs, however, became uneasy. Late in the night, they plotted to kill their interpreter, Cheesto Kaiehre, "the old rabbit." They charged him with betraying them in the Court by answering with the strong assent — *To e u hah* — the talks of the British King. When they returned home, they themselves were tried by the national tribunal for having betrayed the public faith and for selling their country. After much deliberation, they were acquitted.

RENEWED CONFLICT

In 1744 England and Spain renewed their conflict in Europe. This was quickly followed by hostilities with the French in America in a struggle known as King George's War. Again there was considerable border warfare, all of which was inconclusive. The Treaty of Aix-la-Chapelle in 1748 brought the formal fighting to an end, but not the struggle to control the frontier. Soon the rivalry with the French for the western lands, especially the upper Ohio Valley, would lead to another major conflict.

By the middle of the eighteenth century, men in Virginia and the Carolinas began to consider the practical aspects of their colonization. In 1747, the Ohio Company was organized by several leading men of Virginia; Christopher Gist, who lived on the Yadkin River in North Carolina, was employed to examine and locate their lands. In 1749, the Virginia Provincial Council authorized the Loyal Company to enter and survey 800,000 acres of land north of the dividing line between North Carolina and Virginia. Dr. Thomas Walker was selected to settle occupants on this land within a period of four years.

Dr. Walker, who had already begun his exploration of the western country, found that the gap discovered by Governor Spotswood in 1716 was the lowest and best passage through the Appalachian range. Walker named it "Cumberland Gap," in honor of the Duke of Cumberland, son of King George II. He gave the same name to the Cumberland River, whose headwaters he had found in his early travels, and to the range of mountains he had crossed. Dr. Walker's explorations and the expeditions he conducted to the west between 1748 and the early 1760's were of great value in learning the nature of the country and in encouraging responsible men of the east the promote its settlement.

Following the Warriors' Path used by the Indians, in 1750 the Walker expedition examined rich lands within the boundaries of the present states of Tennessee and Kentucky. Near the present city of Kingsport, at the Great Island of the Holston River, Dr. Walker selected lands for his friend and associate, Edmund Pendleton, and for others. Although they did not actually develop the land, these men gave substantial support to the western movement.

THE FRENCH AND INDIAN WAR

From the earliest days, English colonial authorities had been aware of the activities of

*The country's mountainous and rugged terrain made exploration
and settlement difficult. Cut off from the colonies
on the coast by wilderness, early forts and settlements were difficult to defend.*

the Spanish and the French to the south and west of them. They recognized the danger in such activities and also knew that the Spanish and French would try to cause an uprising among the Southern tribes.

In his document, "The Colony, It's Climate, Soil, Population, Government, etc.," Governor Arthur Dobbs of North Carolina described the Indian country.

". . . There are no French or Spanish settlements near this Province. The nearest at present is a Stockaded fort called l'Assumption lately erected upon the Tenasse or Cherokee River which is a great check to ye Chickasaws our most valuable Indian allies, and has had a great influence upon the Cherokees . . . The other Forts which affect the Southern Provinces belonging to the French are the Alabama fort situated upon a branch of the Mobile, and another called

Fort Tombeebee higher up on the Mobile River . . . These are also stockaded forts and have about 100 men in each fort.

"The only Spanish Fort which affects our colony of Georgia is St. Augustine, the Garrison of which is about 300 men . . . these are at constant war with the adjoining Indians and do not extend their plantations. Their Forts of Sta. Rosa and Pansacola on the Florida Coast in the Bay of Mexico are no Detriment to our colonies but a Confinement to the French at Mobile.

"The grand Settlement of the French upon the Mississippi and Mobile are the only places dangerous to our Colonies as they will always spirit up the Creeks, Choctaws, and Cherokees to molest our Southern Colonies and embroil us with the Indians . . . ."

As English explorations progressed, the English approached French settlements and felt the French influence in the Mississippi Valley. The pressure of events finally forced the eastern colonies of the Carolinas and Virginia to face the western question and to plan for defense of the "western waters." In 1754, Governor Dinwiddie of Virginia was concerned enough to send someone to the west; for this mission, he chose a youthful Virginian—George Washington.

On his arrival at the Ohio, Major Washington found that the French had a fort on that river. He also learned that they had four forts on the Mississippi, besides their strong settlement at New Orleans where they had over 1,400 men. Washington also learned that by means of the Oubasch (Wabash) River, the French communicated between Canada and the Mississippi. Forts on the river covered and protected this communication. Governor Dinwiddie wrote to Governor Glen of South Carolina to inform him of Washington's findings.

ENGLISH FORTS
IN THE CHEROKEE NATION

In 1755, Governor Glen held council with Attakullakulla and other Cherokee chiefs. At this time, a treaty was made which permitted the building of two English forts in the Cherokee nation. The first of these, Fort Prince George, was erected near the source of the Savannah River, about three hundred miles from Charleston. With this as a stepping-stone, plans were made for another stronghold deeper in the heart of the Cherokee country.

The site chosen and agreed to by the Indians was in what is now Monroe County, Tennessee, near the junction of the Little Tennessee and Tellico rivers, but the long-awaited plan was hampered by bickering and delay. First, Governor Glen waited to obtain funds from Governor Dinwiddie. Dinwiddie had been granted a sum of £10,000 by the Crown to carry on joint military activities with South Carolina. Displeased at not receiving more than £1,000, Glen accepted the money, but made no attempt to execute the plans or supplement the fund.

At the suggestion of the Virginia House of Burgesses, Governor Dinwiddie named Major Andrew Lewis and Captain Samuel Overton to head an expedition to the Cherokee country to build a fort. For this, Virginia provided £2,000 in addition to £8,000 from the fund donated by the Crown.

Lewis erected a fort near the sacred town of Chota, on the Little Tennessee River. As neither Governor Dobbs of North Carolina nor Governor Glen of South Carolina would cooperate in manning the new fort, Virginia took steps to provide its own garrison. After discussing the situation with Major Lewis, however, Dinwiddie did not execute the plan.

Never named or manned, the fort was a menace to the Cherokees themselves. There was a dangerous possibility that the northern Indians might seize and occupy the fort, gaining a strong position on the Cherokees. Therefore, the Cherokees destroyed it.

FORT LOUDOUN

While the Virginia fort was under construction, South Carolina still debated and delayed any action. Finally, a number of Cherokees headed by Attakullakulla arrived in Charleston. They demanded that there be no further delay in the building of a new fort. The Cherokees' demand, and the fact that unless the English established themselves at once the entire Cherokee country would go over to the French, at last forced Glen into action. Even though he was awaiting the arrival of his successor, William Henry Lyttelton, Glen headed a military expedition to the Cherokee country. The party was in the upper part of South Carolina when a messenger brought news of Lyttelton's arrival and an order for Glen's return to Charleston.

Left in command of the expedition was Captain Raymond Demere, who reluctantly accepted the responsibility. The group assembled at Fort Prince George and prepared for the final days of the journey into the Cherokee country. In September of 1756, they set out.

The party was divided into two sections. The first, led by Attakullakulla, was composed of twenty soldiers commanded by Sergeant William Gibbs. The second was under Demere and moved more slowly because it carried the swivel guns for defense and supplies for construction of the fort.

Having at last reached the Overhill country with supplies for both defense and construction of the fort, work progressed; but it was accompanied by serious disputes. There were bitter arguments over the site, the height of the fortification, and minor details of every description.

DeBrahm, one of the builders, became enraged when he was forced to reduce the height of the towerhouse. Demere reported that DeBrahm offered him one of his pistols, telling him to shoot him through the head. After this episode, DeBrahm left, declaring that only three more days of labor would be necessary to complete the fort. Old Hop, still the most powerful chief of the Cherokees, although he was old, sick, and lame, called DeBrahm the warrior ". . . who ran away in the night . . ." After DeBrahm's departure, the fort was completed under the command of Captain Demere.

The fort was named in honor of the Earl of Loudoun who had arrived to take command of all the British military forces in North America. Fort Loudoun stood at the fork of the Tellico and Little Tennessee Rivers. Its thick walls were surrounded by a deep ditch and a space cleared for the distance of a rifle shot; this offered excellent defense against weapons used at the time. The thorns from a hedge of young locust trees were to impede the progress of Indian warriors and a deep well within the walls of the fort was to provide water in case of seige.

Early in the autumn of 1757, the fort was ready for occupation. Settlers as well as soldiers, were invited to its seven hundred rich acres. Many thought it was a foolhardy venture, for even when the Cherokees and the English were at peace, its support was difficult. If they were at war, or if the Cherokees were overrun by a stronger tribe, its protection would be utterly impossible.

Quick to absorb the benefits of civilization, the Indians sought artisans of all sorts. Blacksmiths and gunsmiths showed them the mysteries of metal-working and the power of weapons deadlier than their arrows and feeble blowguns.

A small settlement grew up about the fort, and for the first time, the flaxen hair and blue eyes of the English children were seen west of the mountains. Here, too, were the Indian wives and half-breed children of traders and soldiers who had come to live in the Indian nations. The stage was now set for the last act of a cruel drama.

Between the first occupancy of Fort Loudoun in 1756 and its destruction in 1760, the small settlement went about the everyday business of living, unmindful of the storm which was gathering. Men experienced in frontier warfare saw the growing strength of the French. Yet the Fort Loudoun settlement was permitted to remain in the wilderness.

By the time the work on Fort Loudoun was finished, the chain of French forts in the Mississippi Valley was nearing completion. Although they were situated at great distances from each other, and no attempt toward settling the interior was made, they served as a barrier to the English and strengthened the hold of the French Crown upon this territory.

For the French, a fort in the Cherokee country would have filled the long gap between Fort Duquesne and Fort Toulouse, in the Alabama country. Assistance from the Cherokees would have counteracted the influence of the Chickasaws, who since the Natchez wars had been implacable enemies of the French. But the establishment of Fort Loudoun delayed and eventually prevented the success of the French plan.

In 1757, the Earl of Loudoun sought the support of the southern colonies and their Indian allies in the war against the French. A number of Cherokee warriors who had been persuaded to join the English, made their way through the frontier settlements of Virginia and the Carolinas.

Clashes between some of the Cherokees and settlers along the Virginia frontiers continued through 1758 and reached a climax when the great chief, Attakullakulla, and nine warriors were deprived of their arms and placed under surveillance of British soldiers. Despite this indignity, Attakullakulla remained friendly. A large portion of his nation, however, was infuriated.

Throughout this critical period, the Cherokees were insulted by blundering colonial officials, British military men, and various individuals who happened to be in the Indian country. Finally, Governor Lyttelton organized an expedition against the angry Cherokees. He proceeded to Fort Prince George, where he assembled a force of over a thousand men. Meanwhile the Cherokee chiefs had been told to follow the armed force closely and were promised full protection and safe conduct back to their nation. After reaching Fort Prince George, however, Lyttelton went back on his promise. Instead, he had them "closely confined in a miserable hut without permission to see their friends, nor even the light of day."

This unfortunate condition was deplored by statesmen and military men who struggled to create a better Indian policy. Through their efforts, a powerful element of the Cherokee nation was persuaded to fight with the English during the French and Indian War.

In December of 1759, Lyttelton tried to extricate himself from his embarrassing

INDIAN VILLAGES, FORTS, AND PIONEER SETTLEMENTS IN TENNESSEE IN THE EARLY EIGHTEENTH CENTURY

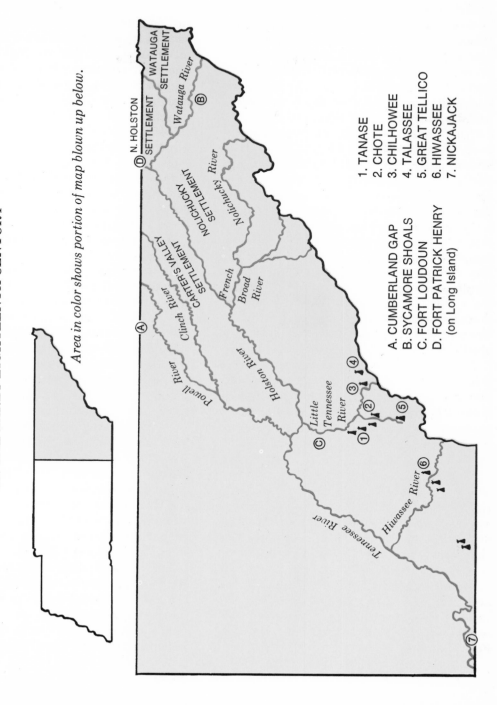

Area in color shows portion of map blown up below.

1. TANASE
2. CHOTE
3. CHILHOWEE
4. TALASSEE
5. GREAT TELLICO
6. HIWASSEE
7. NICKAJACK

A. CUMBERLAND GAP
B. SYCAMORE SHOALS
C. FORT LOUDOUN
D. FORT PATRICK HENRY
   (on Long Island)

situation. He sent for Attakullakulla and informed him of the recent fall of Quebec. He also reminded him of the 1730 agreement in London when the Cherokees promised to submit to English rule. Then he demanded that twenty-four Cherokees be killed in exchange for twenty-four settlers recently killed by the Cherokees.

Upon Attakullakulla's request, warriors were to be substituted for the chiefs Lyttelton had been holding as prisoners. These warriors were immediately chained in irons, Attakullakulla's party was so frightened that it fled, and the influential chief himself hurried back to his nation. On his way, however, he was overtaken by a messenger from Lyttelton who persuaded him to return to Fort Prince George. There Attakullakulla signed a treaty which provided that the chiefs already imprisoned be held as hostages until the murderers were delivered. The warriors that had recently been imprisoned were to remain prisoners.

Lyttelton returned to Charleston as a conqueror, and his "victory" was celebrated by bonfires and wild acclamations. Three months later, he left South Carolina. Bull, his successor, was to suffer the consequences of his folly.

THE CHEROKEES ATTACK

In January, 1760, Fort Prince George was besieged by Cherokee warriors who demanded the release of their imprisoned chiefs and warriors. South Carolina was soon to realize that Lyttelton's expedition had done much more to arouse the Cherokees than it had to quiet them. When the siege of Fort Prince George proved unsuccessful, the Cherokees turned their wrath on Fort Loudoun.

News of the attack was carried to the settlements by the few civilians who managed to escape. Half-hearted attempts were made to send relief expeditions. North Carolina took no action at all. South Carolina relied upon Virginia to send relief. The Virginians under Colonel William Byrd III, marched northward to the Great Island of the Holston, where they built a fort. However, no further attempts were made to relieve Fort Loudoun.

Meanwhile, the settlers in the doomed fort were being slowly starved out. For weeks they ate lean horses and dogs for meat. Often, however, their sufferings were greatly relieved by the help of friendly Indians.

In June 1760, the Indians pretended to give up the siege. Taking advantage of the lull, one of the two physicians in the fort and another man attempted to go on a hunt. They were killed near the gates, and the fifty soldiers who had attempted their rescue were driven back by heavy enemy fire. Now, hope for rescue was dimmed.

Two months elapsed, however, before it was finally decided to surrender. On the seventh day of August, 1760, Captain Stuart and Lieutenant James Adamson went to Chota where they offered Captain Demere's terms of surrender to the Indians.

Captain Demere agreed to surrender the fort and its cannons and gunpowder to the Indians, provided that the Indians would permit the garrison to march for Virginia or Fort Prince George and that they be provided with an Indian escort, who would also hunt for provisions on the march. In addition, the Indians were to provide as many horses as possible and agree to take care of sick and lame soldiers until they were able to return to Fort Prince George.

The forts of the region were always in danger of attack by the Indians.
In this old illustration, Indians attack a garrison house where troops are quartered.
Protected by the smoke screen caused by burning the dry grass in the "fire wagon,"
the Indians are trying to set the wooden building on fire by ramming the wagon into it.

To this agreement, the two Indian chiefs, "Cunni Catogue" or Standing Turkey and "Oconostota" made their marks and Captain Paul Demere, "Commanding His Majesty's Forces," signed his name.

The day after the terms of surrender were agreed upon, those able to make the journey prepared for their departure. The next day they left the fort, accompanied by Oconostota and other chiefs. They marched about 15 miles before they camped for the night. Throughout the day, however, various chiefs had deserted the party. On the morning of August 10, men on the outposts reported that they were completely surrounded by Indians in war paint. The weak band prepared to make its last stand, but little time was allowed them. The Indians attacked them almost immediately.

Four officers, including Captain Demere, twenty-three privates, and at least three women were killed. Many others were wounded and most of the survivors were brought to the Indian towns.

Captain Stuart, one of the survivors, was rescued by Attakullakulla and kept as one of his family. The sympathetic chief arranged to carry him on a hunting party, from which he would either be permitted to escape or would be delivered safely to his friends. Fearing death at the hands of hostile Cherokees, Attakullakulla and Stuart left the beaten trails and traveled through the wilderness, guided only by the sun and moon. On the eighth of September, they met 300 soldiers from Colonel Byrd's regiment, commanded by Major Andrew Lewis. The soldiers had been sent out to search for survivors of the Fort Loudoun massacre.

Colonel Byrd warned the Cherokees with the following message:

"My good brother Attakullakulla has delivered me Captain Stuart and three other of my countrymen . . . I am building forts all the way and propose soon to be in your Nation, when I will not leave an Indian alive, one town standing, or one grain of corn in all your country, if I do not find all the white people well when I get there . . ."

Byrd also demanded that Fort Loudoun and its ammunition be delivered to Virginians who expected to occupy the fort; that Virginians should be free to build at other strongholds in the Cherokee nation; and that Attakullakulla should be recognized as Emperor.

In the meantime, Attakullakulla's own house had been plundered by his warriors, and Fort Loudoun, at the command of Oconostota, had been destroyed by fire.

THE FINAL BATTLE

The struggle for the possession of the Mississippi Valley was approaching an end. Fort Duquesne had surrendered in July, 1758, and French intrigues had failed. The English were victorious over the French at Quebec. But despite temporary victories, neither France nor England was to hold the Mississippi Valley or to inhabit the Tennessee country.

For their attack and victory at Fort Loudoun, the Cherokees paid a heavy price. Their French allies, defeated at Duquesne and Quebec, were powerless to aid them. The colonies of Virginia and South Carolina, aroused by the sufferings of their countrymen, sent out a large body of troops. Once again Virginia forces, under Colonel Byrd, encamped at the headwaters of the Holston, which they called Fort Attakullakulla in honor of the friendly Cherokee chief.

News of this powerful expedition traveled swiftly into the Cherokee nation. Thoroughly alarmed, the Cherokees sent the friendly Attakullakulla to ask for peace. But only after their defeat in a great battle near the town of Etchoe was peace granted.

The Cherokee granaries and corn fields were destroyed and the Cherokee families driven to the barren mountains. When Attakullakulla said, "I am come to see what can be done for my people, who are in great distress," peace was finally ratified between the parties.

"The peace which followed this victory over the Cherokees, and the expulsion of the French and Spaniards from the borders of the southern provinces, brought with it a remarkable increase of population and prosperity. Multitudes of emigrants from Europe and the middle provinces came out in rapid succession to the interior, sought out their sources, and planted their little settlements on the sides of lofty hills or valleys."

BRITISH SUPREMACY

It is not difficult to understand the white man's belated approach to the Tennessee country when events of the two centuries preceding it are recalled. Even accessible lands on the eastern seaboard, along the Gulf of Mexico, and in Canada, were explored slowly and occupied only after the greatest of hardships. Not until these settlements were secure and had increased in population did men begin looking toward the remote and dangerous interior of the continent. Even then, ambitious and adventurous men were restrained by governments which through lack of foresight sought to restrain emigration and the development of the land beyond the mountains.

The French policy, which advocated only fortification of the Mississippi Valley, was never effective, although it was responsible for discovering and making that rich part of the continent known to the world. Spanish efforts to reach and occupy the interior were even more futile. The English, seeking to preserve the mountains as an unbroken frontier from Georgia to Canada, openly forbade settlers to cross the Appalachian ranges.

While frontiersmen built their first rude cabins in this western wilderness, the European countries struggled with one another for supremacy on the continent of North America, on the high seas, and in India. Britain, emerging triumphant from the Seven Years' War in Europe and the French and Indian War in America, claimed victory on all three fronts.

France, by the Treaty of Paris in 1763, relinquished the entire St. Lawrence Valley and all territory east of the Mississippi River to Great Britain. Spain lost Florida to the English, but retained Cuba, the Philippines, and portions of Louisiana west of the Mississippi, ceded to her by France. Spain had difficulty in taking over the French in Louisiana, and Britain's own colonists were beginning to prove a greater threat to her supremacy than any of her ancient enemies.

Westward Expansion

PRELUDE TO REVOLUTION

While the west beckoned with promises of wealth and freedom, oppression in the eastern colonies was goading men to desperation. In both the Carolinas and Virginia there was a surge of resentment against petty abuses of local colonial governments as well as against the major infringements of the English upon American freedom.

In this critical period, Virginia was soothed, but not subdued, by Lord Botetourt, who arrived, with great pomp and ceremony in 1768, to be its governor. With this display of courtly trappings, England sought to impress the Virginians with the power and dignity of the Crown. But neither the members of the legislative bodies nor the citizens themselves were moved to give up their firm resolutions. Botetourt was received with the greatest courtesy, but members of the House of Burgesses declared for their body the sole right of imposing taxes.

While Virginia was engaged in asserting her rights, groups in South Carolina were driven to drastic action. Here people suffered under a judicial system which provided that processes might be served and fees collected anywhere in the province, but that courts were to be held only in the capital city of Charleston. This left remote districts at the mercy of dishonest officers and denied their citizens recourse to the courts. They met the situation by taking matters into their own hands and "regulating" their own disputes and business. From this attempt to provide necessary local self-government, they became known as "Regulators."

Similar groups became active in North Carolina, where the unscrupulous Governor Tyron, aided by his notorious officials, went to even greater extremes. Titles to property were questioned and exorbitant fees were charged for recording new deeds. Juries were packed; men were arrested and imprisoned upon the slightest provocation; the cost of any lawsuit became prohibitive. To already heavy taxes were added the illegal collections.

To combat these evils, the Regulators of North Carolina arose. Revolt flamed high in Orange, Rowan, and Mecklenburg counties where countless citizens were outlawed and forced to flee for their lives. They, their families, and their friends formed the backbone of the western movement.

Meanwhile, western expansion still continued to be a debated subject. American colonial leaders, notably Benjamin Franklin, and a few of the more liberal representatives of the Crown advocated it; but the royal edict of 1763, forbidding movement west of the Appalachians, though little heeded, was still in effect. Settlers along the western borders of the colonies had already proved to the British government that they could be rebellious.

THE FIRST ADVENTURERS

British opposition, along with the inability to obtain legal titles to the land, helped discourage western expansion. The hostility of Indian tribes was also a disadvantage. But, the adventurous settlers did not wait for assurances of safety and security. A hardy few, in defiance of all restrictions, moved themselves and their families to new

*Pecan tree on the Natchez Trace,
a famous overland route.*

homes beyond the mountains. These first adventurers were not a lawless mob. At their earliest opportunity they worked out their own way of providing law and order. They also attempted to secure titles to their lands by direct purchase from the Indians, although such negotiations were forbidden.

Their problems were too urgent to permit them to comply with ancient rules and regulations. Many of them had been declared outlaws and a price placed on their heads. Others, fleeing poverty, oppression, and worn-out lands, were seeking new opportunities in a new country. All of them looked forward with eagerness to a spot where they might enjoy the fruits of their

labors and where their children might have a chance to build a better life for themselves.

Through treaties with the Cherokees at the frontier outpost of Hard Labour, South Carolina, in October, 1768, and with the Six Nations at Fort Stanwix in New York the following month, vast tracts of western land were ceded to the British Crown. (The Five Nations, or Iroquois Confederacy, became the Six Nations about 1722 with the adoption of the Tuscarora Confederacy, which had been driven out of North Carolina by the British. At one time the Iroquois Confederacy controlled territory as far south as the Tennessee River.) These negotiations were followed by a great rush toward the western boundaries of the Carolinas and Virginia. Here restless and adventurous men and women waited for a pretext to claim estates in the western country. Many had already chosen sites for homes. For more than a decade, they had known this land through the glowing descriptions of explorers, hunters, and colonial soldiers.

When a family reached the west, it usually went to some site selected by the head of the household or some of the older sons who had been out with hunting parties. Here, they sometimes found crops and a crude shelter provided by men who had gone out the year before to prepare for them. Often these sites were too remote to be occupied at once; common safety usually demanded that settlers remain close together, within or near a fortified position. At first, however, isolated cabins were not attacked by the Indians.

William Bean One of the first men, if not the first, to cross the mountains, build a cabin, and take possession of the land was William Bean. Bean chose a site for his home when he had been out on a hunting trip with Daniel Boone. When they were camping at a beautiful spot on Boone's Creek, a tributary of the Watauga River, Bean decided that because of the abundant game and generally desirable location, he would make his home there. It was there that he brought his wife Liddy and built their cabin in 1769. Liddy Bean was to be not only the mother of the first white child born in Tennessee—her son Russell Bean—but also one of the great pioneer heroines of the west.

No easy task faced this first adventurer. He knew that certain dangers and inescapable hardships lay ahead. Yet he stood straight and tall, breathed deeply of the mountain air, and shook from his back forever the burden which he and his kind had carried from the beginning of time. Danger? Yes, but none great enough to force him back to the old life which he had left behind.

After descending the first western slopes, Bean raised his home in the wilderness and was free. By this simple act he inaugurated a new era and began to enjoy the liberty which man had always hoped to achieve.

Bean may have been preceded in settlement of the western country by a man named Honeycut, with whom James Robertson spent the winter of 1770-71. Little is known of him or of the details of his residence in this locality. Fortunately Bean himself was only a little ahead of the many other settlers who came westward during the years of 1770 and 1771. A single cabin would not have endured long against the dangers which were soon to be experienced.

George Washington   One western explorer of this period was George Washington. He was deeply interested in the claim to 200,000 acres of western land which had been awarded to the officers and men who had served with him in the French and Indian War. In 1770, Washington set out on a tour of the Ohio country to investigate this land and protect the rights of his men. His services in this capacity were valuable to the entire west, for he was not only a good surveyor, but also a superb woodsman and a competent judge of land. The experience gained on this journey was useful in later years. It provided him with a full understanding of the nature of the western country and its value to the nation.

Shortly after Washington's tour the subject of Virginia's western frontier and indeed, the whole western question, had reached a crisis. Benjamin Franklin's influence with British leaders, added to that of the Virginians, was undoubtedly an important factor in preventing the closure of these frontiers.

"No one," the historian Bancroft declares of Franklin, "had more vividly discerned the capacity of the Mississippi Valley, not only to sustain commonwealths, but to connect them with the world of commerce. And, when the Ministers would have rejected the Fort Stanwix Treaty, which conveyed from the Six Nations an inchoate title to the immense territory southwest of the Ohio, his influence secured its ratification . . ."

Daniel Boone   By 1760 or earlier, Daniel Boone was hunting and exploring in eastern Tennessee. Later, while Washington explored the Ohio lands, Boone was pushing into the Kentucky country. Inspired by John Finley's descriptions of his trip of 1768, Daniel Boone was determined to see the country with his own eyes. In May,

An old engraving of Daniel Boone, the great hunter and explorer. Boone and others built the Wilderness Road through the Cumberland Gap and encouraged settlement of the region.

1769, leaving his wife and children at home in North Carolina, Boone set out for Kentucky. With Finley as his guide, he began to search for a new home for himself and his family. In his footsteps came many others who roamed the wilderness which was to become the states of Tennessee and Kentucky, exploring every stream and seeing in every cove or hilltop a site for a future home. These explorations during 1769 and 1770 not only paved a way for actual settlement, they created a widespread interest in emigration and encouraged financial backing, without which colonization schemes could not have been carried out.

Other Adventurers During this time, James Robertson of North Carolina—who was soon to take a leading part in the building of the west—was making his way into the wilderness. He explored the Holston River and its tributaries and, in 1770-1771, stayed for some time in the little settlement which was being formed on the Watauga.

An early portrait of James Robertson. His work in the founding and settling of the Tennessee Country earned him the title "Father of Tennessee."

While Washington was in the Ohio country, Boone in Kentucky, and Robertson on the Watauga, another group had pushed farther west to explore lands watered by the Cumberland River and its tributaries. Early in June, 1769, John Rains, Kasper Mansker, Abraham Bledsoe, John Baker, Joseph Drake, Obadiah Terrill, Uriah Stone, Henry Smith, Ned Cowan, Robert Crockett, and possibly others whose names have escaped the historians, banded together and explored the country in the great bend which the Cumberland River makes in the fertile basin of Middle Tennessee. These men left Fort Chiswell, on the New River in Virginia, and traveled across the headwaters of the Holston, Clinch, and Powell rivers, through Cumberland Gap, and into a still undiscovered portion of southern Kentucky.

While the hunters were scattered in separate directions somewhere on the headwaters of Roaring River, Robert Crockett was killed by marauding Indians. During the eight or nine months the party hunted over this vast territory of forests, canebreaks, and dense vegetation, they found no sign of human habitation. Neither the Indian tribes nor the white man held this fertile paradise.

In April 1770, members of this party, like Boone and Robertson had done, returned to their homes east of the mountains where their narratives produced a remarkable sensation. Ramsey says:

"A spirit of further exploration was thus excited in the settlements on New River, Holston, and Clinch, which organized an association of about forty stout hunters, for the purpose of hunting and trapping west of Cumberland mountains. Equipped with their rifles, traps, dogs, blankets, and dressed in the hunting shirt, leggins and moccasins, they commenced their arduous enterprise, in the real spirit of hazardous adventure, through the rough forest and rugged hills. The names of these adventurers are now not known. The expedition was led by Colonel James Knox. The leader and nine others penetrated to the Lower Cumberland, making an extensive and irregular circuit and adding much to their knowledge of the country. After a long absence, they returned home. They were known as 'Long Hunters.' "

THE WATAUGA SETTLEMENTS

By 1772 the trickle of population which began in 1769 had become a steady stream. There were now four flourishing settlements in Tennessee, known collectively as the Watauga settlements. One was on the Watauga River, a second north of the Holston River, a third west of the Holston in Carter's Valley, and a fourth on the Nolichucky River. Settlements on both the Holston and Watauga were strengthened daily by refugees from eastern oppression. Conservative wealthy men began to see the tremendous possibilities of western lands and they too entered into schemes for its colonization.

The situation of the North Carolina Regulators had by this time become desperate. For Governor Tyron, viewing their boldness and increasing numbers, had determined to put them down. Commanded by experienced officers, his well-equipped forces met them on the Alamance on May 16, 1771. Though somewhat superior in number, the Regulators were poorly armed and were defeated. Most of their leaders escaped, however, and fled to the west.

Although the defeat of the Regulators on the Alamance temporarily silenced the spirit of resistance, discontent remained and caused the voluntary exile of thousands of freemen to the west. Far from the seat of power, and free from the oppression of English officers, these patriots were warmly welcomed to the Watauga settlements.

During this period the Virginians had also pushed westward and, until the Treaty of Lochaber extended their boundaries, they were, in some cases, actually living on Indian lands. Emigration was greatly encouraged by Virginia's liberal policy. Four hundred acres were granted to every settler who had built a cabin and had cultivated a small amount of ground in this region. A later act enabled the settlers to buy 1,000 acres ajoining their home tracts for scarcely more than the amount required to survey it. These generous provisions and the additional advantage of living within the boundaries of Virginia attracted scores of families from the oppressed sections of North Carolina.

Watauga In 1770, James Robertson and a group of friends from North Carolina settled on the Watauga River a few miles east of William Bean's cabin. The Wataugans were soon confronted with difficulties. According to the line run by Colonel John Donelson in 1771, their settlement did not fall within the Virginia boundaries. They found themselves trespassing on Indian lands. To remedy this situation, James Robertson and John Boon were chosen to negotiate with the Indians. For merchandise valued at approximately five or six thousand dollars, these men were able to lease all the lands on the waters of the Watauga for a period of eight years.

The settlers were still rejoicing over this solution when a tragic incident occurred.

At the close of that treaty, a great race was to be run at Watauga. Pioneers from all the adjacent settlements came to participate in the athletic amusements of the frontier people. Mischievous white men, from the neighborhood of the Wolf Hills in Virginia, lurked about the place where the race was to run. They waited for an opportunity at the close of the day and they killed one of the Indians. This inhuman act produced much alarm. The inhabitants felt not only that it was wrong, but that it would expose them to the vengeance of the outraged Cherokees.

At this crisis, Robertson's wisdom and courage saved the settlement. He journeyed 150 miles to the Indian nation to apologize for this barbarous act.

Robertson's courage in going alone and unarmed to the Cherokee nation impressed the Indians, and his attitude of humility and regret pleased them. Assured by Robertson that the murderer would be caught and punished as he deserved, the Cherokees agreed not to take retaliatory measures against the Watauga settlers.

Carter's Valley   After the establishment of the Watauga settlement, several families settled north of the Holston River, about 18 miles from the present town of Rogersville. This settlement, taking its name from John Carter, its leading spirit, was known as Carter's Valley.

The Carter's Valley settlers, being north of the Holston River, thought at first that they were also in Virginia. When it became known that they were outside the line, they cast their lot with the Watauga and Nolichucky settlements.

North Holston   This settlement was located between the south fork of the Holston River and the Virginia line. Here Evan Shelby, who was also to play an important part in the winning of the west, built his home at Sapling Grove in King's Meadow, site of the present city of Bristol, Tennessee-Virginia. Another leader in this settlement was Colonel Arthur Campbell who took a lively part in both military and civil affairs. These settlers, being within the Virginia line, enjoyed formal titles to their lands and were included in the government of that colony.

Nolichucky   Jacob Brown migrated from North Carolina and settled with his family on the Nolichucky River. He set up a small store and by encouraging the Indian trade, worked himself into the favor of the Cherokees. Having established friendly relations, Brown was soon able to negotiate a private treaty with them for the purchase of lands on the Nolichucky.

From the standpoint of the British authorities, these private treaties with the Indians were highly irregular, but they served the immediate purpose of keeping peace and allowing the young settlements to become strong enough to protect themselves.

THE WATAUGA ASSOCIATION

All of these settlements were being reinforced by the steady stream of emigrants from Virginia and the Carolinas. These people, regardless of their colonial origins, came west and after long and arduous experiments in government, finally established the State of Tennessee. Actually, they became Tennesseans as soon as they set foot on the soil of Tennessee.

Some semblance of allegiance to Virginia was shown in the North Holston settlement, but the others from the beginning were openly and admittedly independent.

The Nolichucky River, the site of one of the first settlements in Tennessee.

They themselves best described their situation and their early accomplishments in government:

". . . Finding ourselves on the Frontiers, and being apprehensive, for want of a proper legislature, we might become a shelter for such as endeavored to defraud their creditors; considering also the necessity for recording Deeds, Wills, and doing other public business; we, by the consent of the people, formed a court for the purpose above mentioned, taking (by desire of our constituents) the Virginia laws for our guide, so near as the situation of affairs would admit. This was intended for ourselves, and was done by the consent of every individual; but wherever we had to deal with people out of our district, we have ruled them to bail, to abide by our determinations (which one, in fact, leaving the matter to reference, otherways we dismissed their suit, lest we should in any way intrude on the legislature of the colonies . . ."

The court referred to above was formed in 1772 and was composed of five members. It functioned according to provisions of the Watauga Association which was established to meet the everyday needs of an unassuming people. That they in this Association had created the first independent government on the continent, however, did not seem to have occurred to them.

LORD DUNMORE'S WAR

In the fall of 1773, Daniel Boone, his family and four or five other families that Boone had convinced, joined the advance toward the Cumberland Gap. Before this, no white female, much less a family, had attempted to cross the Cumberland range. The small group was joined at Powell's Valley by forty well-armed hunters; together they formed a caravan of eighty persons. One day, as they were filing through a narrow passage on their march, they were startled by the terrific yell of the Indians. As the Indians attacked, some of the men rushed to the protection of the women and children, while others rushed to fight. After some confusion, the Indians retreated, surprised at the fierce resistance of the men.

Six men were killed and one was wounded by the attack from the ambuscaded Indians. Among the dead was the twenty-year-old son of Daniel Boone. Realizing now that further progress would be foolhardy, the Boones and their friends turned back to the nearest settlement, where they remained until after the conclusion of Lord Dunmore's war a year later.

This attack upon Boone's party and others along the Virginia frontiers made it evident that stern measures were necessary. Lord Dunmore, who had succeeded Botetourt as governor of Virginia, began to organize an expedition against the hostile Indians of the Ohio country.

Dunmore was the last of the royal governors of Virginia. His task was difficult, not only because of the popularity of his predecessor, but also because of the growing tension between the British Crown and the colonies. His conduct of the campaign did nothing to improve his reputation, for, in spite of the seriousness of the Indian attacks along the frontiers and the widespread demand for action, his preparations had moved slowly. It was midsummer in 1774 before the campaign started, and early October before contact was made with the enemy. In spite of this delay, however, Dunmore raised and equipped an army of some 3,000 men and served as commander of its right wing. The left wing was commanded by Colonel Andrew Lewis.

According to the plan, the left wing was to follow the Great Kanawha River to its junction with the Ohio. The right wing, under Dunmore, was to strike the Ohio somewhere in the neighborhood of the present city of Wheeling and proceed down the Ohio to form a junction with Lewis.

The Holston settlements supplied a company of more than fifty men, commanded by Captain Evan Shelby. They left their homes on August 17, 1774 to join the regiment of Colonel Christian at New River, and from there proceeded to Green Brier, where they united with the rest of Lewis' army.

"... On the 11th of September," Ramsey says, "the army set out for the designated point. The route lay through a trackless wilderness, down the rugged banks of the Kanawha—through deep defiles and mountain gorges, where a pathway had never been opened. Twenty-five days were consumed in slow and toilsome marches. On the 6th day of October, the army reached the site of the present town of Point Pleasant..."

The Battle of Point Pleasant Expecting to meet with Dunmore's men, the left wing made no effort at fortification or digging entrenchments. The camp lay in this unprotected condition when, just before daybreak

A settler's cabin on the French Broad River. Although treaties were signed, the Indians felt that the white settlers were invading their tribal lands.

on the morning of October 10, James Robertson and Valentine Sevier of Captain Shelby's company, having been sent out to kill game, suddenly came upon a large group of Indians. The two hunters fired upon the Indians and then fled toward the encampment to give warning of their approach. The Indians halted temporarily, unable to judge the size of the firing party in the darkness.

Immediately after Robertson and Sevier had given the alarm, detachments under Colonel William Fleming and Colonel Charles Lewis, brother of the commanding officer, were ordered to meet the enemy. They had scarcely passed their own senti-

nels when 1,000 Indians of the western confederacy, led by the Shawnee chief, Cornstalk, fell upon them.

The attack began on the section held by Colonel Charles Lewis and some 300 men. He and his aide, Hugh Allen, received fatal wounds and under the fierce assault, this portion of the line gave way. Swift action by Colonel Fleming against the enemy's right turned the tide of the battle. The Indians, inspired by their gigantic chieftain, who mingled among them chanting "Be strong!" "Be strong!" kept fighting desperately until early afternoon. From then until sunset, they confined their efforts to firing from be-

Cornstalk, the chief who led the Shawnees against the settlers at Point Pleasant.

hind trees and other concealed places. At nightfall, they retreated across the river, carrying their dead and wounded with them.

Final Surrender The day following this battle, runners came with a message from Dunmore. Colonel Lewis was to join Dunmore on the Scioto, near the Shawnee towns, some 80 miles from his present encampment. Despite his weakened condition, Lewis left a small garrison at Point Pleasant and made his way through a completely unbroken wilderness to the banks of Conge Creek. Here, within striking distance of the Shawnee towns and not far from Old Chillicothe, the principal town of these Indians,

Lewis joined Dunmore. No sooner had they advanced toward the villages, when they were met by a white man named Ellis, bearing a flag of truce. Defeated by Lewis at Point Pleasant, the Indians had had enough, and Dunmore accepted their offer of peace.

Lewis' division of the army, which included men from the Virginia frontiers and the Holston settlements, was difficult to restrain. They were eager to punish the Indians for their attacks on the frontiers. It was only after Dunmore had drawn his sword upon its commanding officer that the division was held in check.

A peace was negotiated by Dunmore and Cornstalk, in which Cornstalk relinquished the claim of his tribe upon the lands south of the Ohio. This, however, was more or less an empty gesture. The Shawnees had been driven off these lands by the Cherokees and other southern tribes—none of which had apparently been strong enough to hold it.

After the treaty Dunmore and most of his army returned to Virginia. The Shelbys, Seviers, Robertsons, and their companions in arms, hastened back to their homes. They had participated in the last of the colonial wars, and their next campaigns would be against the British and their Indian allies. Even then, Dunmore was laying groundwork for the conspiracy which brought the southern Indians to the side of the British in the Revolutionary War.

TREATY OF SYCAMORE SHOALS

Meanwhile, plans which would lead to occupation of lands south of the Ohio were being made. Richard Henderson of North Carolina, the leading spirit in this movement, had associated with himself, such men as Thomas Hart, John Williams, James

Hogg, Nathaniel Hart, David Hart, Leonard H. Bulloch, John Luttrell, and William Johnston. This group raised funds to cover the expense of acquiring the lands and establishing the initial settlement. At a meeting held at Hillsborough, North Carolina on August 27, 1774, matters pertaining to the proposed settlement were discussed and agreed upon.

Henderson, with Nathaniel Hart and the Indian trader, Thomas Price, set out at once for the Cherokee country. There they interviewed the leading chiefs and prominent men. The influence of Attakullakulla was secured, and early in 1775 leaders of the nation were summoned to "talks" at the Sycamore Shoals in the Watauga settlement. Accordingly, on March 14, 1775, some 1,200 Indians and every white man within reach of the treaty grounds, several hundred in number, assembled.

Little was accomplished on the first day beyond the usual preliminaries and the questioning of the Indians concerning their rights to the lands under consideration. On the second day, the Indians offered to "give up some lands which they said Colonel Donelson had agreed to give them five hundred pounds for, and had not paid them."

To this, Henderson replied that ". . . it would not be worth his while to talk about buying that only, as he had a House full of Goods for them, and should be a yet greater Expence for the Beares and Rum to entertain them upon . . ."

At this point, an element of the Cherokees composed largely of the younger chiefs and warriors, opposed cession of the vast tract sought by Henderson and complained that there were not enough goods for the number of persons assembled. Dragging Canoe, their leader, leaped forward into the council circle and stamping his foot, pointed toward the Kentucky lands, saying:

". . . We give you from this place . . . but there is a dark cloud over that country . . . it is a dark and bloody ground . . ."

After an impassioned speech, in which he opposed cession of greater tracts of land, he and some of his followers left the treaty grounds. On the third day, the Indians agreed to sell land as far as the Cumberland River, but Henderson still insisted upon having ". . . Cumberland River and the Waters of the Cumberland River . . ." Finally, the Indians agreed, but only after telling him, ". . . . they were their Hunting Grounds, and their children who were then growing up might have reason to complain, if they sold that land, an argument they frequently made use of, from the time they offered to sell the land below Kentucky. Also observing that it was a bloody Country, and if he went to it they would not hold him by the hand any longer, and he must do it at his own Risque, and must not blame them if anything happened to him . . ."

On the fourth day, March 17, 1775, papers were completed and read, sentence by sentence, by the interpreters to the prominent men of the Cherokees. Complete understanding and agreement had been reached, and the great empire called Transylvania passed from its ancient owners to the hands of the white man.

The Watauga Purchase All of the western leaders were vitally interested in the proceedings at Sycamore Shoals. The Seviers, Shelbys, Robertsons, as well as Carter, Brown, and others represented friends and kinsmen east of the mountains who were eager to follow them into the west, once the way was open for them.

The situation of the Wataugans regarding the lands they held through their previous negotiated lease was complicated at one stage of the "talks," when it appeared that Henderson was on the point of including them in his purchase. Charles Robertson, representative of the Wataugans, succeeded in a separate treaty held on March 19, 1775, with ". . . Oconostota, Chief Warrior and First Representative of the Cherokee Nation or Tribe of Indians, and Attakullakulla and Savanucah, otherwise Coronch, for themselves and the rest of the whole Nation, being the aborigines and sole owners by occupancy from the beginning of time, of the lands on the waters of Holston and Wataugah Rivers . . . in consideration of the sum of one thousand pounds, lawful money of Great Britain, in hand paid . . ."

This purchase began ". . . on the south or south-west side of Holston River, six English miles above Long Island, in said river; thence a direct line near a south course to the ridge which divides the waters of Wataugah from the waters of Nonachuckah; thence along the various courses of said ridge nearly a south-east course to the Blue Ridge or line dividing North Carolina from the Cherokee lands; then along the various courses of said ridge to the Virginia line; thence west along the Virginia Line to Holston River; then down the meanders of Holston River to the first station, including all the waters of Wataugah, part of the waters of Holston and the head-branches of New River or Great Canaway, agreeable to the bounds aforesaid . . ."

Jacob Brown, on the Nolichucky, also made a private treaty through which he obtained much of the best land in Washington and Greene counties.

In the Carter's Valley settlement, Indians had robbed the store of Parker and Carter, who went to the Sycamore Shoals Treaty seeking repayment. The Indians, apparently admitting their guilt, agreed to give them certain lands provided an additional sum be paid them. This was done by Carter, Parker, and Lucas. It was found later that the lands in question were within the boundaries of North Carolina and the transaction was unsuccessful.

All of these negotiations were in opposition to the British policy which forbade private purchases or treaties with the Indians. Henderson and the Transylvania Company had already been seriously disapproved of by Patrick Henry and other leaders who believed that the western lands should be reserved for public control.

Richard Henderson and his associates were practical men, but they also had their dreams. Not the dreams of Daniel Boone and the others who loved the space and freedom of the wilderness, but a dream in which the fertile country would be tamed and turned to the uses of civilization. Indeed, they saw in Transylvania a new and separate state.

The important consideration was not the legality of the transaction, but rather the practical value of the land to the west. In the first place, the purchases satisfied, at least temporarily, the largest and most powerful part of the Cherokee nation. They also revealed the break between the older chieftains and the seceders who followed Dragging Canoe to the Chickamauga towns. Above all, the purchases gave some semblance of permanence to the western settlements and encouraged further emigration. Had posts on the frontier not been manned by these sturdy settlers, the war for American freedom might well have been lost.

The American Revolution in the West

DRUMS OF WAR

In the late spring and early summer of 1775, events rapidly led to the final break with Great Britain. News of the Battle of Lexington, which took place on April 19, swept through the colonies like wildfire. Even though Thomas Jefferson and other colonial leaders still hoped for a reconciliation, they faced the situation with a stern realism. Arsenals, fortifications, arms, ammunition, and supplies were seized. Troops were raised and on May 10, George Washington was chosen by the Continental Congress as Commander-in-Chief of the army of the United Colonies.

A month after the Battle of Lexington, May 19, 1775, citizens of Mecklenburg County, North Carolina met to consider the situation. After much deliberation and discussion they declared themselves free and independent of Great Britain.

Warfare in the Settlements In the lands west of the mountains, men who had already established an independent government kept in close touch with the rebelling colonies. Before many months had passed, they sought the privilege of sharing in ". . . the glorious cause of Liberty . . ." Some time before August of 1776, they described their situation, their type of government, and offered to share the burdens of the eastern colonies.

In their petition to the Provincial Council of North Carolina, these men had chosen to call their settlement "Washington District." They were the first to so honor the Commander-in-Chief of the American Army.

It was not a surprising choice, for many of the westerners had known George Washington in person in the field and in the legislative halls of Virginia. It was a great domain which bore his name, for Washington District, soon properly annexed to North Carolina, stretched from the Appalachian Mountains to the distant Mississippi River.

The petitioners of Washington District soon had an opportunity to prove their sincerity. Fortunately, there had been a brief lull in Indian hostilities following Lord Dunmore's War of 1774. During this time, the Holston settlements were strengthened and Daniel Boone's party began a permanent settlement in the Kentucky country. Only a few months passed, however, before the hostilities which were to last nearly twenty years broke out.

In the late spring and early summer of 1776, men on the western waters fought Tories and prepared to defend their families against the combined attacks of the British and the Southern Indians. As the Revolutionary War progressed, they participated in most of the major campaigns in the southern colonies. At the same time, they waged a bloody warfare on their own side of the mountains.

The first contribution was in May, 1776, by a small, but effective group of western riflemen. These men helped repel the British fleet commanded by Sir Henry Clinton and Sir Peter Parker when they attempted an invasion of Charleston, South Carolina.

At this time, young Felix Walker was appointed lieutenant in Captain Richardson's company and was to furnish money for recruiting. Walker came back to the Watauga, raised his quota of men, and returned with his platoon to participate in the defense of Charleston. An entire company under the command of Captain James Robertson was also preparing to go on this expedition. But as the Watauga petitioners pointed out, the threat of an attack on their own frontiers made it necessary for keeping these men at home.

Walker's platoon remained in South Carolina, however, and participated in the successful repulse of the British fleet during the latter part of June, 1776. It remained on the seaboard for several weeks, but news of the outbreak of Indian hostilities beyond the mountains caused them to hurry home.

CHEROKEE INVASION

It was fortunate that only Walker's platoon had been allowed to leave the western settlements, for while Clinton and Parker were threatening Charleston, a great Cherokee invasion got underway in the west. The British, fully aware of the importance of these western outposts, had conceived an elaborate plan for wiping them out and reducing the three southern colonies in two great blows. Had either the British attack on the seaboard or the invasion by the Cherokees succeeded, the cause of the American Revolution would have been seriously threatened.

The Cherokee invasion of the west was, perhaps, the greater threat of the two. Had the Indians ever been able to get a foothold in the sparsely settled frontiers of the southern colonies, they could have been reinforced until the British forces from the north and east united with them. The small, heroic groups of western riflemen who went to the aid of the eastern colonies were "The Rear Guard of the American Revolution," and should be recognized for their important contribution.

On the eve of the Cherokee invasion, John Sevier and a fairly large group of settlers were at the yet uncompleted Fort Lee on the Nolichucky River. Warning of the impending attack was brought to Sevier by four traders who had been informed by Nancy Ward. Sevier immediately gave the alarm and sent a messenger to alert the officers of Fincastle County. If not for Nancy Ward, "Beloved Woman" of the Cherokees, Sevier and the settlers at Fort Lee would have been wiped out by the surprise attack and even the stronger forts on the Watauga would probably have fallen. The settlers at Fort Lee, alarmed at news of the Cherokee attack, abandoned Fort Lee and hastened to join the forces at Watauga. This action saved the people of the weaker settlement at Fort Lee and strengthened Watauga for the impending attack.

The Cherokee invasion was well planned and strongly supported by both the British and the Indians. A force of about seven hundred, mostly Cherokees and a small number of Creeks, were divided into three sections. One, under Old Abram, of Chilhowee, was to attack the Watauga and the Nolichucky settlements. Another, under The Raven, was to fall upon the Carter's Valley settlements. The third, headed by Dragging Canoe, was to attack the settlements near the Long Island. Accomplishing this, they were to move into Virginia for further attacks.

Long Island Flats The major engagement took place near the Long Island. On being informed that the Indians were approaching, the men at Long Island decided to march out to meet them, rather than permit them

An engraving representing the beginning and completion of a typical farm settlement.

to attack the fort and the nearby cabins which it protected. This battle is known as Long Island Flats because it took place on the level land near the island.

The unique battle formation of the Indians in this encounter—a cone-shaped center, with wings curving outward—was a near disaster for the white men.

Dragging Canoe fought brilliantly and mingled with his warriors, encouraging them and assuring them of victory. But when their leader was carried from the field, wounded and with a broken thigh, the Cherokees broke off the battle and retreated.

Fort Caswell Old Abram's attack on Fort Caswell on the Watauga was the most serious threat to the settlements. The fort was commanded by Colonel John Carter. Serving under him were Captain James Robertson, then thirty-four years old, and Lieutenant John Sevier, not quite thirty-one. Both Robertson and Sevier would serve the western country for almost forty years after this historic battle was fought.

The Watauga attack came in the early morning of July 21, 1776. For nearly ten days the settlers had gathered in the fort and were preparing as best they could to defend themselves. Increased by the arrival of the little garrison from Fort Lee, the number of men available for the defense was now about seventy-five. Women, were also present in considerable numbers. They not only cared for their children and performed their daily work under siege, but proved valuable aides during the battle.

News of the siege, with Sevier's plea for help, was carried by the fastest runners to Virginia. Rangers prepared to aid the frontiers and Colonel Evan Shelby of the North Holston settlements set out with one hundred men. Before Shelby or the Virginia rangers arrived, the Indians, unable to capture the fort, had retired.

Invasion of Carter's Valley The raid led by The Raven, and directed against the Carter's Valley settlement, was carried out by not more than one hundred warriors. The section was sparsely settled, and the families which were able to do so fled to the stronger forts, or back to Virginia.

The Raven broke his force up into small bands, which moved in fan shape, the westernmost flank harassing the settlements on Clinch River in Virginia, while others attacked settlements in the neighborhood of Wolf Hills, now Abingdon. Others made a trail of death and destruction as far up the Holston as the Seven Mile Ford.

EXPEDITION AGAINST
THE CHEROKEES

In September, 1776, Colonel William Christian of Virginia arrived at the Long Island of the Holston with a considerable body of men, to carry out an expedition against the Cherokee nation. Here he found Lieutenant-Colonel William Russell. Russell had built a fort named Patrick Henry in honor of the Governor of Virginia, and had it ready for Christian's troops.

Protection of the frontiers had become a necessity for both the eastern colonies and the western settlers. By the early summer of 1776, plans for accomplishing it were well under way. Authorities of Virginia, Georgia and the Carolinas had anticipated that the Cherokees, under the influence of John Stuart, his brother Henry, and Alexander Cameron would cooperate with the British.

On October 1, the forces under Colonel Christian started out for the Cherokee country, leaving behind at Fort Patrick Henry about one hundred men under the command of Captain William Witcher of Pittsylvania County, Virginia. Christian was reinforced by men from the Nolichucky and Watauga settlements commanded by Captain James Robertson, and a company of cavalry under Captain John Sevier. Two chaplains—the Rev. Charles Cumings and the Rev. Joseph Ray—the first of many who were to follow western fighting men, joined the expedition.

This army, now reinforced by three or four hundred North Carolina militia commanded by Colonel Joseph Williams, Colonel Love and Major Winston, numbered from eighteen hundred to two thousand men. They were well-armed with rifles, tomahawks and knives. As they moved for-

The French Broad River. The junction of the Holston and the French Broad forms the Tennessee River.

Colonel Christian crosses the French Broad River in pursuit of the Cherokees. Encountering no resistance, he burned several villages.

ward, sixteen spies were sent forward toward the place where the crossing of the French Broad River was to be made.

Swampy lands near the French Broad River and the Indians' warning not to cross this stream, made progress slow and cautious. The army, however, successfully passed through a heavy canebrake and camped for the night near the mouth of Lick Creek.

At this encampment, Alexander Harlin brought in the information that a body of three thousand Indians stood ready to dispute the passage of the French Broad. His statement was verified by Colonel Christian's spies. At the bend of the Nolichucky, the spies had found recently abandoned camps indicating the presence of large numbers of Indians. Harlin was sent back to the Indians with the message that Colonel Christian intended not only to cross the French Broad, but to push on to the Tennessee River and the Cherokee towns on that stream.

The next day's march was taken up with great caution. Since the country was entirely unknown to the military commanders, the well-known trader among the Cherokees, Isaac Thomas, was chosen as guide. Before they had forded the river, they were met by an Indian trader named Fallen, who had a white flag on his rifle. Colonel Christian ordered that the trader be left alone. Fallen left and it was later learned that he rushed back to the Indians and told them that the white men, ". . . as numerous as the trees . . ." were marching into their country.

The Cherokees Vanish Learning of the force moving against them, a thousand Cherokee warriors had dashed to the Big Island of the French Broad to offer resistance. The Warriors' Trail led across this island and it was considered a gateway to the best part of their country. After Fallen's message had been received by the warriors assembled here, a trader named Starr warned them that the Great Spirit had made them of red clay and the white man of white clay and that he intended that the palefaces should invade, overrun and occupy their country. He advised them to make no resistance, but to retreat to their villages and the fastnesses of their mountains.

Whether due to Starr's persuasive powers or to Fallen's warning that the approaching white men were as numerous as trees of the forest, the Cherokee warriors decided to abandon their position without making a stand.

Meanwhile, unaware that his opponents were retreating, Colonel Christian made careful preparations for his crossing of the French Broad. During the night, he sent a large detachment down the river to another island. It was ordered to cross during the night and to come upstream on the southern bank in the morning when it would help the remainder of the army make a daylight crossing.

The following morning, the remainder of the army crossed in battle formation, but the enemy had fled and there was not even a trace of the recent encampment. Puzzled and still cautious, Colonel Christian paused for one day to dry the baggage and supplies which had gotten wet in crossing the river. Then he pushed on toward the Cherokee towns.

Following the valley of Boyd's Creek, down the Ellejay to Little River, and then to the Tennessee, still not a single Indian was seen. The total disappearance of the enemy increased Colonel Christian's suspicions. Expecting a strong resistance at the Tennessee River, he ordered his men as they approached the crossing of that stream ". . . to follow him at a run until they came to the river."

Still, no enemy greeted this approach. The army, its packhorses, its bullock-drivers, and its supplies passed through the town of Tamotlee. The following morning the march was continued to the Great Island Town, which was also entered without resistance.

Certain villages, like Chota—the city of refuge—had not been guilty of making war and were exempted. Many other villages were left in ashes. During the invasion of these towns an occasional warrior was discovered and killed. No prisoners were taken.

Peace Colonel Christian succeeded in bringing together enough warriors to make a temporary peace. The leaders of the nation were to be brought in for a formal treaty at the Long Island in the following May. The camp at Great Island Town was broken up. The army marched through Chota, crossed the Tennessee, and returned to the settlements. In the campaign that lasted three months, no white man had been killed and the few who became sick because of hardship and exposure later recovered.

Neither the expedition nor the peace talks produced anything of permanent value. The Indians had no respect for the motives which inspired Colonel Christian's mercy. Even his demand that Cameron and Dragging Canoe be turned over to him failed, for they had fled. Cameron had gone to the Alabama country and Dragging Canoe down the Tennessee River to the rapidly growing Chickamauga towns. Reinforced with British goods supplied by Cameron, he and a renegade band would continue to harass the settlements.

From a military standpoint, Christian's campaign and his "soft peace" left much to be desired. It subdued the older Chero-

Cragfont, near Gallatin, home of the Revolutionary War leader General James Winchester, was used as a fortress against Indian attacks.

kees temporarily and gave the settlers an opportunity to strengthen themselves. There were, however, certain long range effects of the Cherokee invasion and Christian's campaign into their country.

Spring came and passed, but the Cherokees still failed to make the treaty they had promised Colonel Christian. Colonel Nathaniel Gist, who had returned to Virginia and proved his worth to George Washington, was sent to use his influence with them. He arrived at Fort Patrick Henry late in March, but it was the end of June before the treaty talks got under way. Significantly, it was a treaty with the old men. Attakullakulla and Oconostota, now aged and growing feeble, were seated in the council's place of honor. Old Tassel was spokesman for the Indians and Waightstill Avery for the white men. But even the old men were uneasy. They resented the encroachment already made by the Watauga and Nolichucky settlements and feared further negotiations.

The arguments continued and the treaty was finally concluded on an unsatisfactory note. While it gave the white men certain additional lands, it was apparent that the chiefs attending the "talks" did not have the power to enforce its terms. They admitted that Dragging Canoe, now founding towns of the seceding Cherokees on Chickamauga Creek, would not be bound by it. They also blamed him for the constant attacks on the settlements and said they were unable to prevent them.

THE CHEROKEES RETURN

In an effort to save the situation, the North Carolina Commissioners appointed James Robertson as temporary agent to the Cherokee nation. Robertson was directed to go to Chota with the warriors returning from the treaty, and to stay there until ordered otherwise by the governor.

While in Chota, Robertson was instructed to discover, if possible, the attitude of Dragging Canoe toward the treaty, as well as others who had not attended. He was also to find out the conversations between the Cherokees and the Southern, Western and

Dragging Canoe and other Indian leaders continually led attacks against the settlements. In this old woodcut, a woman defends her home.

Northern tribes of Indians. He was to search in all the Indian towns for persons disloyal to the American cause, and to have them brought before a justice of the peace to take the oath of fidelity; in case of refusal, they would be dealt with as the law directed. Any traveler into the Indian nation without a pass, such as the third article of the treaty required, was to be arrested.

Robertson was to inform the government of all occurrences worthy of notice and to obtain the favor and confidence of the chiefs. In all matters to which he had not been particularly instructed, he was to use his own discretion, always keeping in view the honor and interest of the United States in general, and of North Carolina in particular.

Inspired under the leadership of Dragging Canoe, the Indians harassed the settlements continually. Cabins were burned; horses and goods were stolen. Each day the Chicka-

mauga towns, reinforced by restless young warriors, increased in strength and warlike spirit. Stuart and Cameron, agents for the British, kept them well supplied with goods and weapons.

Many renegade white men sought refuge in the Chickamauga towns. There were also Indians outlawed by their own tribes who joined the Chickamauga towns to share the British goods and goods carried off from raids on the white settlements. There were also a few Frenchmen and Spaniards among them. For almost two decades, this mixed population menaced the settlements on the Holston, Watauga and Nolichucky rivers, as well as those which were soon to be formed at the bend of the Cumberland River.

Similar dangers confronted the Kentucky settlements. The fort which Daniel Boone built in the spring of 1775 was subjected to constant attack. Minor attacks continued throughout the years of 1775 and 1776. In the bloody year of the "three sevens"— 1777, the existence of Boonesborough and the younger settlement at Harrodsburg were threatened. The forts at these points were attacked simultaneously by large bodies of Indians on April 15, 1777; for several weeks they were under siege. During May and June the Indians made every effort to destroy both strongholds. Despite repeated efforts, however, they failed to scale the sturdy walls or to set fire to them.

On July 4, 1777, two hundred Indians attacked Boonesborough with great fury. After two days and nights they were repulsed. One man of Boone's garrison and seven Indians were killed. Although the Kentuckians had exhibited great military skill in defending their position, their situation had become desperate.

Captain William Bailey Smith, who had lived in the Watauga settlements, carried news of the critical position to old friends and neighbors. A company was organized and under Smith's command, set out at once to the rescue—exhibiting again the volunteer spirit of the west. They reached Boone on July 25 and on August 20, a body of one hundred Virginians under Colonel Bowman arrived.

From that time on, as Boone related, the fort became stronger and stronger. For about six weeks there were skirmishes with the Indians in one quarter or another almost every day.

CLARK TAKES KASKASKIA, CAHOKIA, AND VINCENNES

George Rogers Clark, who was in Kentucky during the attacks on Boonesborough, felt that it would be necessary to put down the Indians and eliminate British influence in the Ohio country in order to ensure the future of the Watauga and Kentucky settlements as well as the success of the Revolution.

Convinced of the necessity of reducing the hostile forts in the Ohio country, Clark submitted a plan for this purpose to Virginia in December, 1777. His scheme was highly approved, and Governor Henry and his council were so interested that all preliminary arrangements were soon made. Two sets of instructions were given to him. One was public, ordering him to proceed to the defense of Kentucky; the other private, directing him to attack the British at Kaskaskia. His force consisted of only four companies. But, as records of their achievements show, their services were out of all proportion to their small numbers.

Early in the spring of 1778, according to plan, Clark received an invaluable addition to his forces—Simon Kenton, one of the boldest pioneers of the west.

Leaving the Falls of the Ohio, Clark proceeded to the mouth of the Tennessee River where he met a group of hunters who were familiar with the country. These men volunteered to serve as guides, and also gave Clark important information concerning the condition of the garrison at Kaskaskia. They stated that they believed a surprise attack against it could be successful.

The expedition then moved down the Ohio to a point on the Illinois shore where they concealed their boats and began their march through the wilderness to Kaskaskia. On the evening of July 4, 1778, they arrived near the town, undiscovered by any of the people. Before midnight the town and the garrison were in possession of the Kentuckians.

The British commander, Philip Roche-

George Rogers Clark, Revolutionary War hero.

blave, was surprised in bed and taken prisoner. His wife, whom the polite Kentuckians would not disturb, secured or destroyed most of his papers. Enough papers were found, however, to show that the British were inciting the Indians to hostilities. There was no bloodshed in this conquest. In a few days, Clark's wise policy secured the respect of the French settlers and they accepted the government of Virginia.

An equally successful move was made against the important British supply post, Cahokia. Soon, the important post of Vincennes was captured and the flag of the young American republic floated over its ramparts.

Clark, who by now had been promoted to the rank of colonel, continued his successes in his dealings with the Indians. During the autumn of 1778, he negotiated with the various tribes in the vicinity. This state of affairs ended abruptly on January 29, 1779, however, when Colonel Clark was informed that Governor Hamilton had marched a force from Detroit and now occupied Vincennes. The day of bloodless conquest had ended. Clark was now confronted not only by the present disaster, but by

the certainty that a large force would attempt to retake Kaskaskia in the spring. Prompt attack was his only hope. Accordingly, in February, 1779, the little band of one hundred and seventy-five men waded into icy waters and appeared, once more, before Vincennes.

An inhabitant whom they had taken was sent in with demands for a prompt surrender. The people were greatly alarmed, believing that it was a new expedition of fierce fighters from Kentucky. Some of them reported later that they could not have been more astonished if the armed men had dropped from the skies—for it seemed impossible that they could have come through the icy waters which then flooded the country.

Governor Hamilton refused to surrender without resistance, so a siege began. After fourteen hours, the town and the fort were surrendered. Governor Hamilton and members of his garrison were captured and later carried to Virginia as prisoners of war. The British colors were lowered once more and the Stars and Stripes hoisted to take their place.

The importance of Clark's expeditions cannot be overestimated. Had they failed, the British plan to unite the Indians and wipe out the Kentucky and Watauga settlements, and then fall on the western frontiers of Virginia, the Carolinas and Georgia, might well have succeeded.

CHICKAMAUGA TOWNS SUBDUED

Dragging Canoe's warriors were a constantly increasing menace. Three years had passed since he had walked out of the "talks" at Sycamore Shoals and withdrawn to the country of Chickamauga Creek. Each day brought more recruits to his ranks and greater strength to his rapidly growing towns.

As Superintendent of Indian Affairs, Captain James Robertson was instructed to take steps to counteract the intrigues of British agents. Accordingly, he carried a conciliatory talk to The Raven at Chota.

But these conciliatory talks did not repress the warlike attitude of Dragging Canoe and his hostile tribe, the Chickamaugas. This tribe of Cherokees had now extended their villages on both sides of the Tennessee.

Few white men were then familiar with the country to which Dragging Canoe had fled, but strange stories were told by Indians. It is said, that they themselves moved some of their earlier villages because they feared witches and other spirits.

Early in 1779, it became apparent that the settlements on the Holston and its tributaries would have no relief from hostilities until the Chickamauga towns were subdued. Patrick Henry, then governor of Virginia, who had already put George Rogers Clark in the field, took another step designed to strengthen him. At the same time, he planned to relieve both the Holston and Kentucky settlements.

Writing Governor Caswell of North Carolina, on January 8, 1779, Governor Henry stated that he had ordered Colonel Isaac Shelby to raise three hundred men and to go at once to Chickamauga and "totally destroy that and every other settlement near it which the offending Indians occupy." His suggestion that North Carolina raise two hundred men to join the expedition met prompt response in the General Assembly, which was then in session. The sum of £9,000 was voted for supplies and a resolution was passed providing that two hundred men under a lieutenant-colonel and four captains be taken from the Washington County militia by voluntary enlistment.

Major Charles Robertson, who represented Washington County in the North Carolina senate, was advanced to the rank of Lieutenant-Colonel and placed in command. Major Jesse Walton, then serving in the lower house, was placed in charge of supplies and ordered to return home at once with Robertson to prepare for the expedition. There was no difficulty in obtaining volunteers.

Virginia provided some £200 to build Colonel Shelby's boats. The large ones were probably built at the Long Island under his direction. Smaller craft were made in the Indian fashion, by hollowing great poplar trees. These were constructed by the backwoods volunteers who had been instructed to bring their axes and their adzes, as well as clothing and rifles to the rendezvous. Some of the troops probably met at the Long Island, but the main rendezvous of Robertson's and Shelby's troops took place at the mouth of Big Creek of Holston, the home and fort of James Robertson.

Robertson and Shelby carried out the first phase of the campaign—reduction of the Chickamauga towns. The second—reinforcement of George Rogers Clark—was to be commanded by Colonel John Montgomery. Montgomery had been with Clark at Kaskaskia and had been sent back to Virginia with the captured commandant and the papers revealing British plans for uniting the northern and southern Indians. Then a captain, Montgomery had been instructed to recruit troops for Clark. As a result of success in both missions, he had been elevated to the rank of lieutenant-colonel.

No funds were furnished Shelby for the

subsistence of his troops, so he had to purchase supplies on his own credit. The individual soldiers usually left home well supplied with clothing and as much dried meats and other food as they could carry. Once in the field he was as skilled as an Indian in fending for himself.

A Surprise Attack   On April 10 the fleet began the descent of the Holston. It then followed the meanders of the Tennessee River into the enemy country. A spring flood had made the Tennessee waters turbulent. Expert seamanship was necessary for the management of the slender canoes, as well as for the larger craft. But the western pioneers were skillful on water; they were also skillful in their landings at the Chickamauga settlements, for the swift currents of the western waters made speedy retreat upstream impossible.

One morning about the middle of April, the fleet reached the mouth of Chickamauga Creek, entirely undetected by the Indians. Turning into this smaller stream, the advance units discovered an Indian asleep at a fish trap. With him as their guide, the troops waded out through a flooded canebreak and entered the town of Chickamauga. The town was nearly a mile long and was governed by two important chiefs, Dragging Canoe and Big Fool. The Indians, about five hundred strong, were so astounded at the invasion of their town by water that they fled to the mountains without resistance. Meanwhile, the soldiers burned the town.

John McCrosky of Sevier County took a party to follow the Indians across the river and dispersed a camp of them which he found on Laurel Creek. Little Owl's town and others were taken and burnt.

With the fall of the Chickamauga towns, the Americans took valuable military supplies, twenty thousand bushels of corn, a large number of fine horses, and other valuable goods. These were disposed of in public and carefully recorded private sales, instead of being distributed among the troops. Most of these goods had been supplied by the British in preparation for their proposed attacks with the Indians on the western frontiers and the southern colonies.

The destruction of the Chickamauga towns having been accomplished, Colonel Montgomery's men assembled their portion of the supplies and floated down the Tennessee to join Clark. The remainder of the force sank their boats and destroyed supplies that they could not carry with them. They began their homeward march by a new land route north of the Tennessee River. These were the first troops that had seen the richest lands of the present Hamilton, Rhea, Knox, and the north part of Jefferson counties. After their return home, a new and increasing current of emigration was turned to this beautiful country.

This well-timed expedition against the Chickamaugas, combined with the removal of Governor Hamilton and his associates to Virginia, not only prevented the proposed meeting of northern and southern Indians and their British allies, but also completely disorganized the major movements of the enemy in the west.

Furthermore, the Montgomery-Shelby campaign against the Chickamauga towns was an important demonstration in using the water route to the Ohio and Cumberland rivers in preference to the more dangerous and difficult land route. A few months later, Colonel John Donelson and other leaders carried settlers to the Great

*Indians fleeing an attack
on their village,
taken from an old engraving.*

Salt Lick on the Cumberland River by the same water route.

About this time John Stuart, the British Superintendent of Indian Affairs, died in Florida. This interrupted the flow of British goods and propaganda which was constantly inciting the southern tribes to rise against the Americans.

THE BRITISH ADVANCE

The year of 1780 was a serious one in both the east and west. At war for five years and still unable to subdue the rebellious colonies, the British decided to attempt another attack on the coast of South Carolina. Sir Henry Clinton and Lord Cornwallis, with a fleet commanded by Admiral Arbuthnot, were ordered to take Charleston. They left Sandy Hook the day after Christmas, 1779, but it was not until March 30 that the actual attack began. On May 16, they finally succeeded in taking the city.

Awaiting supplies from the conquered port of Charleston, Lord Cornwallis ex-pected to make a rapid conquest of North Carolina, pass through Virginia with little opposition, and to continue into Maryland and Pennsylvania.

Soon British units had overrun South Carolina and Georgia and were approaching the western frontier of North Carolina. One group, under the command of Colonel Patrick Ferguson, was particularly troublesome. He had established his headquarters at Gilbert Town, and from here was sending out raiding parties. Colonel Ferguson also dispatched a message to Colonel Shelby and the Wataugans. His messenger was one of Shelby's troopers, Samuel Phillips, who had been taken prisoner and released on parole on condition that he carry the message across the mountains. The insolent message declared that Ferguson would soon cross the mountains, burn the settlements, and hang all the leaders. Phillips fulfilled the pledge to Ferguson by delivering the message, but offset this unpleasant duty by giving to Shelby much valuable information concerning the strength and location of the British.

Immediately after his talk with Phillips, Shelby mounted his fastest horse and rode forty miles to confer with John Sevier. They discussed the situation for two days and completed plans for raising every available rifleman and making a surprise attack on Ferguson. They were to meet at Sycamore Shoals on the Watauga on September 25.

In the meantime, Lord Cornwallis had advised Ferguson of an unsuccessful attack on Augusta by the Americans and had ordered him to intercept the retreating troops and refugees. While attempting to carry out this order, Ferguson approached the scene of his last battle.

Beyond the mountains, men who had been trained in Indian warfare and in frontier shooting matches and hunts had learned some spectacular tricks of their own. They cleaned their Deckard rifles, filled their powder horns and shot pouches, and made ready to march against Ferguson. The chief trouble which confronted Sevier and Shelby now was finding horses for all of the volunteers and persuading a sufficient number of men to remain behind for the protection of the settlements.

The means of financing the expedition had raised some question. In attempting to borrow money on his own responsibility, Sevier found that the citizens in purchasing lands had placed practically all the cash of the community in the hands of the entry-taker, or John Adair, Esq.

Sevier and Shelby made personal pledges of responsibility for the fund and the matter of financing the campaign was quickly settled. Clothing for the troops was attended to quite as simply by the women of the settlements.

The force, ready to march, consisted of four hundred men from Virginia, under Colonel William Campbell; two hundred and forty from Washington County, under Colonel Sevier; two hundred and forty from Sullivan County, under Colonel Shelby; and refugees under Colonel McDowell. They kept their rendezvous at Sycamore Shoals on the appointed day.

Little attention had been paid to the matter of a commanding officer until the expedition was well on its way. Finally, on October fourth, after a conference of the colonels, it was agreed that steps should be taken to remedy the situation and Colonel McDowell was dispatched to General Gates, asking him to appoint such an officer.

Before Gates even had a chance to reply, however, Colonel William Campbell was chosen to be the chief in command. It was agreed that he would serve merely to execute the plans which would be decided upon daily by the colonels.

With this loose, yet extremely effective organization, the mountain men neared Gilbert Town, where Ferguson had recently encamped. Informed of their approach, he engaged in a series of movements designed to allow time for reinforcements to reach him and for Tory members of his force who had gone home to return to their commands. The backwoodsmen, seeking to contact him, found that he was retiring toward South Carolina in three separate forces—one attempting, still unsuccessfully, to intercept Colonel Clarke on his retreat from Augusta.

At daybreak, on October 6, after a night spent in picking the best men and horses, the chase began. In thirty-six hours, they halted only once—at Cowpens, where they were met by 400 men commanded by Colonel James Williams. Here, again, the swiftest horses and best marksmen were chosen, and the force dashed off after Ferguson.

Gathering of the Americans at Sycamore Shoals, before the Battle of King's Mountain.

THE BATTLE OF KING'S MOUNTAIN

In a short time, Shelby's party captured an advance post of Ferguson's army and it was soon found that he had established himself on King's Mountain. Actually, it was more of a large hill than a mountain, and it was nameless. Ferguson, however, christened it "King's Mountain," and boasted ". . . that if all the rebels out of hell should attack him, they would not drive him from it."

If the rebels had used bayonets instead of rifles, Ferguson might well have made good his boast. The battle was not to be fought according to the old rules, nor was its outcome to be determined either by the position of the contending armies or the type of weapon. The decisive element, in this case, was the new spirit which dominated the Americans. They did not move in masses, nor were they dependent upon the commands of a few officers.

"When we encounter the enemy," Shelby instructed his troops on the eve of battle, "don't wait for the word of command. Let each of you be his own officer . . ."

It appeared in the beginning that Ferguson's men had every advantage — a record of successful engagements, an apparently impregnable position, and the hope of early reinforcements. Many of them, armed with swords, bayonets, and new rapid-firing rifles of their commander's own design, had been drilled and trained by that master marksman himself.

While the British barricaded themselves behind their wagons and the great rock ledges, the westerners approached the mountain base, where they dismounted and hitched their horses, detailing a few men as guards. The rain which had fallen for hours let up about noon on October 7, giving each man an opportunity to prepare his rifle.

By early afternoon the American troops were in position. At three o'clock, Colonel Shelby's and Colonel Campbell's regiments began the attack, keeping the enemy under constant fire while the right and left wings were advancing to surround them. This was accomplished in about five minutes, and the fire became general all around.

Cleveland, Shelby, and Campbell advanced and poured deadly fire into Ferguson's ranks. The answer was a heavy bayonet charge which forced them to retreat in great disorder. They found shelter, however, reloaded their rifles and attacked again.

Throughout the battle, Ferguson lived up to his reputation as a brave and gallant officer. When it was first evident that the battle was lost, someone put up a white flag, but Ferguson cut it down. Soon another was raised and again Ferguson cut it down.

Finally realizing that there was no hope, Ferguson tried to escape through the enemy lines. But in a few moments, Ferguson received a fatal wound and the white flag of surrender was raised once again.

Having been deceived by the two earlier flags, the mountain men would not stop fighting until they were sure.

There was no time for assessing the value of their victory, particularly for Sevier and his men. They mounted and dashed homeward as fast as their horses could carry them, knowing that they had left only a weak force to defend their homes and that the Indians, again at British instigation, were ready to go on the warpath.

INDIAN WARS

On reaching Watauga, Sevier was met by two Indian traders sent from the Cherokee towns by Nancy Ward to warn the settlement that a large body of warriors was on the warpath. Pausing only long enough to replenish their supply of food, powder, and shot, Sevier and about a hundred men went to meet the invaders.

On the second night they made camp at Long Creek. From this position a few picked scouts went out to reconnoiter. As they came to the brow of a small hill, these men found themselves within forty yards of a large body of Indians. They fired from the saddle, whirled their horses about and rode madly back to camp to give the alarm. The Indians returned the fire, but without results.

Sevier immediately prepared to withstand a night attack, but none was forthcoming. The next morning, reinforced by an additional seventy men who had arrived during the night, he decided to attack the Indian camp. The party went forward, prepared for an ambush at any moment, but met no Indians. They did, however, find evidence of a large encampment.

Picking up the trail of the retreating enemy, they crossed the French Broad River at the Big Island and reached Boyd's Creek, where they encamped.

The next morning the advance party was fired on from ambush. According to plan, they retreated toward the main body. As anticipated, the Indians pursued them and were met with a devastating fire from

Sevier's line. Although many of the Indians escaped into nearby swamps, the victory was decisive.

This battle at Boyd's Creek was one of the most important and brilliantly fought engagements in the history of border warfare. But the Cherokees were not subdued by their defeat, nor were the British.

A number of unrelated events had an important bearing on the survival of the Cumberland settlements during the war years. The unprecedented cold of the winter of 1779-1780 made life difficult for the settlers, but worked an even greater hardship on the Indians who suffered both from the bitter cold and the scarcity of game. At the same time, smallpox ravaged the Indian nations, spreading death and terror in their towns.

When spring came in 1780 the Indians soon resumed their raids. The whole frontier from Pennsylvania to Georgia was attacked. The Shawnee tribe, which had once held the Cumberland Valley, tried to unite the northwestern tribes for a massive attack the next summer. In this plan they were aided by British agents at Detroit and on the Maumee.

The southern tribes were displeased with the building of Fort Jefferson in Chickasaw territory without their consent and prepared to drive out the invaders by force. The nearness of the Chickasaws to the Cumberland settlements was a cause of great alarm to the settlers. The first assault upon them, however, was not made by the Chickasaws, but by the Cherokees and Creeks.

These assaults were small but continuous raids on isolated parties and persons. They continued with such growing intensity that many families went to the more secure Kentucky or Illinois settlements; many talked of abandoning the entire Cumberland settlement. Only James Robertson and a few others were left to defend themselves and the settlements.

The ancient towns of the Cherokees, however, were growing weaker and weaker each year. About 1780, Attakullakulla died. A couple of years later, Oconostota died. As the power of the old towns waned, Dragging Canoe's villages grew strong.

During the remainder of 1780, there was further fighting in the Indian country. Christmas Day, 1780, found Sevier with some eight hundred troops quartered about the sacred village of Chota.

Finding that the Cherokee warriors had fled, the invaders destroyed the grain and cattle. Several villages, including the sacred village of Chota, were burned.

In South Carolina, General Nathaniel Greene was threatened by Cornwallis, who had now united the British forces and was attempting to redeem the defeats at King's Mountain and Cowpens. In answer to Greene's call for help, Sevier dispatched Major Charles Robertson with three small companies, not daring to send a larger force from the already weakened western settlements. Then with a command of approximately the same size, he undertook one of the most dangerous expeditions of his career.

Constant raids on the Nolichucky settlements made Sevier think that the guilty parties were from the Middle Towns of the Cherokees. These towns were located in areas so high up that they had rarely been visited by white men.

Despite their almost inaccessible position and the small force at his command, Sevier, in March, 1781 set out on an expedition against them. One hundred and thirty men accompanied him. His officers were Major Jonathan Tipton and Captains David Mc-

Nabb, James Stinson, and Valentine Sevier. They took Tuckasegee town and after that, destroyed fifteen other small towns.

FINAL VICTORY

Meanwhile, Major Charles Robertson's command, which fought with Greene in North Carolina in March of 1781, was defeated. Despite the victory, Cornwallis' army was greatly weakened. Fox, a British stateman of the period, declared: ". . . Another such victory would destroy the British Army!"

General Greene continued his calls for aid from the western riflemen. A small group joined Colonel Elizah Clarke at the siege of Augusta. When Augusta fell, there were far-reaching results, for the loss of British aid supplied by this post, was felt at once by the Cherokees. When they finally arrived at the Long Island for the promised treaty during the latter part of July, 1781, Old Tassel blamed the late British commandant for the deplorable condition of his people.

Finally, on October 19, 1781, Cornwallis surrendered to the Americans and French at Yorktown. The capture of this army was a death blow to the British and to all intents and purposes meant the end of the war.

Sevier and the mountain men had fought almost constantly since the outbreak of the Revolutionary War, but their battles were by no means over. Their eastern neighbors might look forward to a cessation of hostilities, but for them the year 1782 offered no hope of peace. Farther west, Robertson's little settlement on the Cumberland River had just barely survived the warfare of 1781.

In the fall of 1782, Sevier set out on an expedition against Dragging Canoe and the Chickamauga Indians. After this campaign, the Chickamaugas turned with greater frequency towards new settlements which were not yet strong enough to defend themselves. The Cumberland people also lived in danger of invasion by the Chickasaws.

Colonel John Donelson persuaded the Virginia authorities to finance a treaty with the Chickasaws and chose Nashville as the treaty site. John Donelson, Joseph Martin, and Isaac Shelby were commissioners to conduct the negotiations. Major John Reid of Virginia was sent out to make advance arrangements. This treaty, which was concluded in June, 1783 was later rendered null and void by the fact that Virginia did not have the right to negotiate. It is often overlooked by historians and omitted from lists of treaties through which the United States obtained Indian lands.

At that time, the most important treaty to all parties concerned was that between the United States and Great Britain, which was concluded at Paris in 1783. By it, the independence of the American republic was formally established.

From Territory to State

THE SEPARATE STATE MOVEMENT

At the close of the Revolutionary War, the impoverished national government looked for aid toward the states with extensive western lands. Virginia and North Carolina were at last prevailed upon to give up some of their rich western lands. The final cessions, however, were due quite as much to pressure from the western inhabitants, who favored separate states, as to that of the federal government.

The separate state movement which began in Kentucky in 1784, resulted in a decree of separation by Virginia in 1785. Prompt steps were then taken for the erection of a separate state and its admission to the Union. This arrangement was much better than that made for the cession of North Carolina's western lands.

North Carolina's plan, passed at the April, 1784 session of its General Assembly, provided that the land be ceded to the national government, but that a period of two years be allowed for its acceptance or refusal. During that time the North Carolina laws were to be in effect; but, significantly, the land office was to be closed.

This was the final blow. The western settlements could not strengthen themselves without emigrants, and emigrants would not come without lands. This situation resulted in open rebellion which was followed by immediate separation and creation of the independent State of Franklin.

The State of Franklin   The creation of the separate State of Franklin should not be considered as an isolated incident. It was the major example of the separatist movement in the west, and it grew from natural causes which were common to the entire section.

Vast distances, rugged terrain, and inadequate transportation removed any hope of profitable commercial relations between the east and the country beyond the mountains. At the same time, the opening of vast areas of cheap, fertile lands in the west threatened to depopulate the eastern states.

The first step in organizing the new state was taken when two men from each captain's company met in county conventions to choose representatives to meet in a general convention. These delegates met in August, 1784, and elected John Sevier, president and Landon Carter, secretary. They also called for a constitutional convention.

Meanwhile, Governor Martin of North Carolina wanted to know more about the situation in the west. He sent a letter addressed to Sevier by a special messenger. Since the Assembly was in session at this time, Sevier presented it to them for consideration. Their reply expressed in detail their grievances. Governor Martin answered the Franklin Assembly by saying that the cession act had been repealed and that North Carolina had created a new district, appointing an assistant judge and brigadier-general, in order to bring the Franklinites back to the mother state.

Sevier issued a proclamation, replying that Martin's manifesto sought to destroy the peace and tranquility of the ". . . new and happy country . . ."

The truth of the matter was that neither in her cession nor in its repeal did North Carolina consider the interests of the western country. The repeal was due largely to the uproar which cession of the western lands had caused in the eastern part of the state, although the prompt separation of the western counties was also a contributing factor.

At this time Governor Martin was succeeded by Governor Richard Caswell, a personal friend of John Sevier. Caswell pointed out to Sevier the difficulty in serving his state and his friends in the west at the same time.

Meanwhile, the State of Franklin flourished in spite of opposition from adherents of the old state. Lively and often bitter debates over the proposed constitution were common.

Early in 1786, Sevier organized an expedition to quiet the Cherokees. With one hundred and sixty horsemen, he destroyed three villages called the Valley Towns. About one thousand warriors led by John Watts made Sevier decide to retreat back to the settlements. The campaign was successful, however, in bringing a temporary quiet to the frontiers.

The new state continued to look forward hopefully to admission to the Union. While North Carolina continued to withhold her western lands and factions in Congress refused to hear its plea for admission, the State of Franklin continued in complete independence.

Within the State of Franklin, the year 1787 was characterized by dual governments, personal conflicts, Indian raids, and tense arguments between the adherents of the "Old State" and the Franklinites.

Now, fully aware that dissension had weakened the white settlements, the Cherokees increased their raids and attacks on isolated families. The settlers were driven into the forts, and Houston's Station, near the present site of Maryville, was built and garrisoned.

In danger, the frontiersmen once more turned to "Nolichucky Jack" Sevier. Sevier was no longer Governor of the State of Franklin, nor did he hold a military commission under either North Carolina or the now crumbling free state.

Sevier returned to the settlements, but there was no rest on the frontiers. Communications from Georgia advised of dangers of another Creek invasion and sought his aid in a joint expedition against them.

General Joseph Martin, putting aside his title as Indian agent, assumed his military duties and conducted a somewhat unsuccessful campaign against the Chickamaugas.

James Robertson, in the beleaguered Cumberland settlements, despairing of help from North Carolina, appealed to the Kentuckians and to Sevier for aid. Neither being in a position to help him, Robertson raised one hundred and thirty men and set out to follow the trail of a party which had lately invaded the Cumberland.

In the meantime, Caswell had been succeeded as governor of North Carolina by Samuel Johnston. On July 29, 1788, he issued a warrant for Sevier's arrest, accusing him of high treason, in levying troops to oppose the laws and government of North Carolina, and killing good citizens with an armed force.

When Sevier decided to leave town, he was pursued by John Tipton and a small body of eight or ten men. He was finally taken into custody like a common criminal.

Sevier's friends, however, were determined to rescue him. While he was in the courtroom, the rescue party brought Sevier his racehorse. Sevier ran from the courtroom, jumped in the saddle and made a dash for the mountains.

Although North Carolina had pardoned

Early print of a view of the Tennessee River and the surrounding country from Lookout Mountain. The rugged terrain made communication with the eastern states difficult.

all who had taken part in the Franklin revolt, Sevier was specifically excluded. Despite this fact, when elections for the General Assembly were held, the people of Greene County elected him to represent them as senator in the North Carolina General Assembly. On November 2, 1789, he presented himself at Fayetteville to assume this office.

After a few days, he was sworn in and seated, in spite of the fact that the act by which he was disqualified had not yet been repealed. He was also elected as a member of the Convention chosen to reconsider the ratification of the Federal Constitution, which North Carolina had failed to approve the previous year.

Soon he was to have another honor. North Carolina, in order to provide for its representation in the Congress of the United States apportioned itself into four districts —the westernmost of which included all of its territory beyond the mountains. This district promptly elected Sevier as its member of Congress, making him the first member of that body from the Mississippi Valley.

Congress formally accepted the cession of North Carolina's lands, forming it into the: "Territory of the United States of America, South of the River Ohio."

Later, President Washington appointed Sevier as brigadier-general of the territorial forces, thus making it clear that he and his friends were the acknowledged leaders of the new territory.

THE TERRITORY OF THE UNITED STATES OF AMERICA SOUTH OF THE RIVER OHIO

North Carolina's long-delayed cession of her western lands and the establishment of the new territory brought some stability to the west. It did not, unfortunately, bring peace with the Indians. It would be fifteen years before the last major Indian engagement was fought and more than twenty-five years before the rich territory now known as West Tennessee was acquired by treaty.

The First Territorial Governor During this time the westerners tried to form a permanent government and defend themselves against the Indians. Realizing the relationship between building a government and handling the Indian problems, President Washington chose William Blount of North Carolina as the governor for the new territory. Skilled in both fields, Blount became governor and superintendent of Indian affairs. Arriving in the west, Blount established official residence at William Cobb's home near Jonesborough. He began at once to familiarize himself with local matters, to make appointments, and to organize counties. His first official act was the laying out and organization of Washington County on October 22, 1790. The organization of Sullivan, Greene, Hawkins, Davidson, Sumner, and Tennessee counties followed in rapid succession. Military organizations and courts were established in each county and their governments were soon operating smoothly.

In 1790, Benjamin Hawkins, then the United States Senator from North Carolina, wrote to Daniel Smith, the territorial secretary, offering some sound advice:

"Your relative situation with the commercial part of the United States is such

William Blount, territorial governor.

that this is indispensible to your prosperity. You can raise fruit trees of all sorts, grapes for all sorts of wine . . . salt, iron, and clothing of cotton, flax, wool, and silk. You can never have much money, but you have facility in acquiring the necessaries and comforts of life from the richness of your soil and mildness of your climate unknown to any other country in my recollection . . ."

Governor Blount and other territorial leaders agreed that the development of agriculture and manufacturing should be prime objectives of the territorial government. But they also realized they must take steps to establish a satisfactory relationship with the Indians. One of Blount's first steps, therefore, was to arrange for the holding of a treaty.

The Treaty of the Holston Governor Blount made elaborate preparations to entertain and to negotiate with the ruling chiefs of the Cherokee nation near the fort which James White had built in 1786. These arrangements were designed to impress the Indians with the dignity and power of the young American republic. In this, Blount succeeded.

In 1791, the Treaty of the Holston was conducted in an impressive setting. Governor Blount appeared in full uniform, complete with sword, gold lace, and much gold braid. He chose as master of ceremonies, Trooper James Armstrong, who was well qualified to hold this important position. Each of the forty-one chiefs participating in the treaty was presented to Armstrong by an interpreter who was attired in Indian dress. Armstrong in turn, presented each of the chiefs to Governor Blount who had placed himself in an imposing seat of honor. Among the chiefs were Squollecuttah, Auquotaugue, Ninetooyah, Chuquelatague, and others with equally complicated names.

By signing the Treaty of the Holston, the Cherokees gave the settlers additional lands. In return, the Indians received an annual cash payment from the federal government.

Life at the Capital Governor Blount was pleased, not only with the success of the treaty negotiations, but with the site upon which it took place. It was here he decided to make his home and official residence.

Blount's choice of a name, Knoxville, for the territorial capital was a gesture of respect to Henry Knox, then Secretary of War. It was also to be the name for Knox County. By the latter part of 1792 and early 1793, Blount had built a two-story frame house—the first west of the Alleghenies—had furnished it, and brought his family west to make their home.

The influence of Governor Blount and his family on the social and educational life of the territory was important, but the governor made no effort to impose artificial standards on the society of the west.

An important member of the household was his daughter, Barbara Gray Blount, whose beauty and wit were famous. With at least three or four other ladies, she attended Blount College, now the University of Tennessee.

It is claimed that Barbara was the first woman in the United States to receive a degree from an institution of higher learning and that she and her friends were the first "co-eds." The hill upon which the University of Tennessee now stands was once called "Barbara Hill" in her honor, and many years later one of the girls' dormitories was named "Barbara Blount Hall."

Cultivated speech and civilized dress were not needed for entry to the governor's mansion. There, even the most humble Indians ate and were treated courteously.

PROTECTION OF THE FRONTIER

Despite the Treaty of the Holston, there was unceasing friction between the white men and the Indians. Men, women, and children were being killed constantly on

Rocky Mount, the home of William Cobb, near Johnson City. Here, Governor Blount established his first official residence and conducted the affairs of the territory.

Governor William Blount's mansion in Knoxville, the first frame house west of the Alleghenies.

both sides. Each year, thousands of dollars worth of property in horses, cattle, and household goods were stolen.

The federal government counseled moderation and patience. The frontiersmen demanded action in the form of swift retaliation, which John Sevier had found to be the only language the Indians could understand. The Indians, meanwhile, continued to wage a war against the settlements and the exposed frontiers.

Restrained by the government to a defensive warfare, frontiersmen could no longer go out to meet their enemy and fight him on his own lands. As much as this policy was detested, men such as Sevier and Robertson assisted Blount in carrying it out. All of them kept watchful eyes upon the frontiers and, in cases of extreme danger, they took the courses they thought necessary, explaining to the government afterward.

Throughout the greater portion of the territorial period, William Blount was constantly criticized by the Secretary of War with regard to the protection of the western

frontiers. Blount's sympathies were with the settlers, but he and they both knew that the only real solution to their troubles was early statehood. This would give them a permanent form of self-government and would strengthen them by encouraging emigration. Without sacrificing the interests of the west, Blount and other territorial leaders tried to use tact and moderation. Many times, however, when neither was possible, William Blount did not hesitate to use a more aggressive policy.

Blount's correspondence with the federal government is filled with strong statements in defense of the west. One of the most interesting of these is a letter written in Knoxville, January 14, 1793. It not only sets forth Blount's own attitude in regard to the frontier situation, but also gives important information on both the Cumberland (or Mero) and the Holston settlements.

"The protection of that district (Mero), the most difficult to protect in the Union, of its size, as well as every other part of the territory south of the Ohio, was confided to me by the President. This placed me between the Government and the people of the territory, answerable to the Government that I did not incur too great an expense in giving protection to the frontier inhabitants, nor yet suffer them to be killed or robbed of their property; and to the people themselves, who looked to me, from the nature of my appointment, that I should not suffer them to be murdered and robbed . . ."

DESTRUCTION OF NICKAJACK

Conditions in Mero district kept going from bad to worse. Congress, failing to authorize an expedition against the hostile Chickamauga towns, left the people at the mercy of marauding parties and in danger of an immediate large-scale invasion.

Fortunately for the Mero district, James Robertson, its brigadier-general, did not wait for Congress to take action. He assembled a body which finally reached a total of 550 men. The troops were eager to reach the Indian towns, for many of them had relatives who had been killed or carried into captivity. They were also convinced that

their frontiers could never be made safe until the lower towns were subdued. Major Ore was placed in command and was ordered by General Robertson to destroy the towns.

On September 7, the troops began their march to the town of Nickajack and the famous Tecallassee, or Nickajack Cave, where the Creek and Cherokee banditti had a retreat.

One of the leaders of this expedition was Joseph Brown. As a boy, Brown had been held captive in their Lower Towns. In returning to destroy these towns, he fulfilled the prophecy of an old squaw who declared, when his captors had spared his life, that he was old enough to remember the murders of his father and brothers and that some day he would return with an army and ". . . cut them all off . . ."

When the towns of Nickajack and Running Water were taken on September 12, 1794, Brown was recognized by some of the Indian women who remembered the old squaw's prophecy. They realized that he had come in revenge for the sufferings of his family.

The expedition resulted in the last major

Nickajack Cave near Chattanooga. Its location was a closely kept secret among the Indians.

engagement against the Indians within the boundaries of the present state of Tennessee. James Robertson, gratified by its success, willingly accepted the blame for violating the orders of the federal government. He did not have the dashing bravery of John Sevier, nor the cultured diplomacy of William Blount, but he was not inferior to either of them. His strong hands, his deep unfailing wisdom, and his quiet courage, had an important part in building all three grand divisions of the state.

CONSTITUTIONAL CONVENTION

On November 28, 1795, Governor Blount called for a convention, the initial step toward admission to the Union. Twenty-seven days after the convention opened, on February 6, 1796, the first Constitution of Tennessee was completed.

William Blount, William Cocke, John McNairy, Andrew Jackson, James Robertson, and John Sevier came to Tennessee's Constitutional Convention and together worked out a system of government which Thomas Jefferson described as ". . . the least imperfect and most republican . . ." yet adopted by an American state.

Governor Blount, elected president of the Constitutional Convention was instructed to send a copy of the constitution to the Secretary of State. He was also authorized to call an election for state officers and members of Congress. This he did promptly, without awaiting the sanction of the federal government. This soon caused friction between federal officials and the impatient citizens of the newest commonwealth. Consequently, the state election held in March of 1796 was repudiated by the federal government.

THE BILL OF RIGHTS

Self-government, in those days, was a new and vital subject. That it was considered carefully by the men who framed the Tennessee Constitution was evident from the deep interest which they showed in establishing for themselves and their posterity the fundamentals of freedom.

The bill of rights in the Tennessee Constitution begins by stating that ". . . all power is inherent in the people, and all free governments are founded on their authority, and instituted for their peace, safety and happiness. For the advancement of those ends, they have at all times an inalienable right to alter, reform, or abolish the government in such manner as they may think proper . . ."

Continuing, it describes in detail such basic rights as the freedom of the press, freedom of assembly, freedom of religion, trial by jury, and other matters pertaining, in general, to human freedom. Then, having taken care of these basic freedoms, the authors of the constitution looked to local rights and specified that ". . . the people residing south of French Broad River and Holston, tween the rivers Tennessee and Big Pigeon, are entitled to the right of preemption and occupancy in that tract . . ."

Furthermore, they declared that ". . . an equal participation in the free navigation of the Mississippi is one of the inherent rights of the citizens of this State; it cannot, therefore, be ceded to any prince, potentate, power, person or persons whatever . . ."

These provisions, as well as the premature setting up of the State government were resented by Congress and resulted in debates between the federal government and representatives of the new state. The fact that at the time the Tennessee constitution was be-

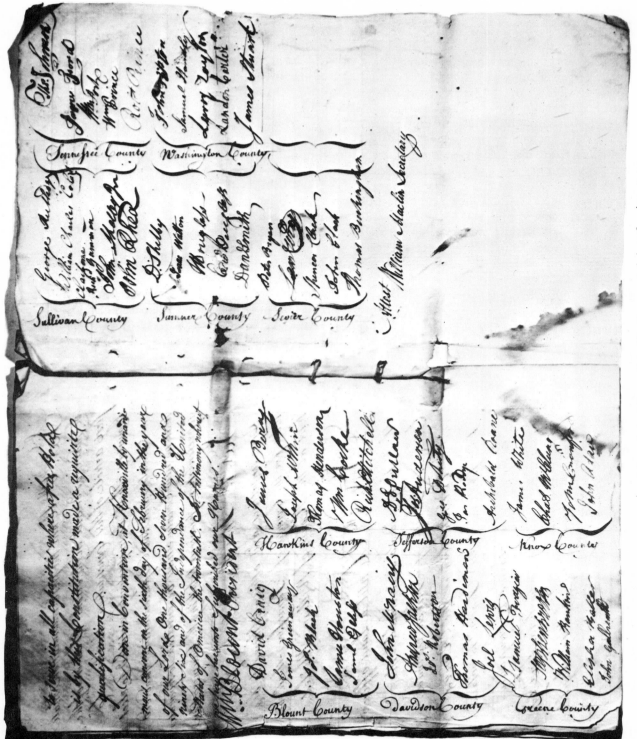

The last two pages of the original State Constitution, containing the signatures of the famous men who together founded Tennessee.

ing written the United States was on the verge of bartering to Spain the navigation rights of the Mississippi River for a period of twenty-five years, probably caused more hard feelings than any other one subject. On several occasions, the people on the western waters had become so aroused on the subject that they threatened to march down and take not only the river, but the ports at its mouth.

Since 1796, Tennessee has had four constitutional conventions—in 1834, 1870, 1953, and 1960. The basic principles upon which the state was founded have not been changed, however, and the alterations made in the original document have been related mostly to matters of contemporary interest.

THE SIXTEENTH STATE

After framing their constitution, Tennesseans lost no time in setting up their state government and assuming what they believed to be their rightful place among the sisterhood of states.

John Sevier was elected governor and soon after, the legislature elected William Blount, the retiring territorial governor, and William Cocke to represent the new state in the Senate of the United States. These two men, among the most popular in the west, were also among the most cultured gentlemen in the nation's capital.

Blount and Cocke, arriving in Philadelphia during the first week of May, 1796, promptly presented their credentials to the Senate. Instead of being welcomed as representatives of a new, rich addition to the national Union, the door was literally slammed in their faces.

Although credentials of the Tennessee senators had been presented early in May,

no definite action on the seating of the senators was taken until May 23, when the following motion was passed:

"That Mr. Blount and Mr. Cocke, who claim to be Senators of the United States, be received as spectators, and that chairs be provided for that purpose until the final decision of the Senate shall be given on the bill proposing to admit the Southwestern Territory into the Union."

It began to appear that debates in both houses would continue until it would be too late to secure Tennessee's admission before adjournment. That, most of all, was feared by impatient Tennesseans.

While there was little danger of Tennessee's failure to gain admission to the Union, there was a serious threat that it might have been delayed for a long while, quite possibly until the Territory had been divided and admitted as two or more states. Each of these divisions would need a minimum of 60,000 inhabitants, which could have continued the territorial status for a period of years. Had this happened, there is no doubt that the steady stream of emigrants then pouring into Tennessee would have slowed down. This was what many eastern politicians, fearing the growth of political power in the west, wanted.

Samuel Sitgreaves of Pennsylvania was one who argued that both natural barriers and political considerations made it absurd to connect the Holston and Mero districts under one government. Others, however, spoke forcefully and courageously for Tennessee's early admission into the Union. Among them were such men as James Madison and Robert Rutherford, of Virginia; Thomas Blount of North Carolina; Albert Gallatin of Pennsylvania, and many others.

While representatives argued in the House,

the Senate was also engaged in lively debates on the subject. Finally, on May 26, the bill laying out into one State the territory ceded by the State of North Carolina to the United States and providing for the enumeration of inhabitants thereof, was read for the third time. Several amendments were introduced, debated, and some incorporated into the bill, the most important of which being the amendment providing that as soon as ". . . it shall appear to the President of the United States that the territory by this act laid out, and formed into a state, doth contain sixty thousand free inhabitants, then it shall be lawful for the President, by his Proclamation, to declare the same . . . And, until an enumeration shall be made, under the authority of Congress, for the purpose of apportioning Representatives, the said State of Tennessee shall be entitled to choose one Representative . . ."

On May 31, the Senate approved the admission of Tennessee to the Union, making it the first state to be created from a territory.

President Washington signed the bill on June 1, 1796, and Tennessee thus became the sixteenth state to enter the Union.

As a final gesture, on Wednesday evening, at 5 o'clock, June 1, the Senate resolved, ". . . that the Honorable William Blount and William Cocke, Esquires, who have produced credentials of being duly elected Senators for the State of Tennessee, be admitted to take the oath necessary for their qualification, and their seats accordingly."

Early Statehood

FIRST PROBLEMS

Admission to the Union was an important step toward the eventual solution of many of Tennessee's most serious troubles. The fact that the two major settlements, Knoxville, on the Tennessee River in East Tennessee, and Nashville, on the Cumberland River in Middle Tennessee, were separated from each other by two hundred miles of wilderness still held by the Indians, represented one of the greatest difficulties. It was also true that these two settlements had wide differences of opinion on many subjects. Both settlements, not trusting the weak federal government during the period of the Confederation, had received representatives of the Spanish government in the lower south. The Cumberland settlements had gone so far as to acknowledge the Spanish governor, Don Estevan Miro, by naming their district Miro in his honor.

Another serious matter, which Governor Sevier promptly took to the first General Assembly for consideration, was the unfortunate condition in which settlers south of the French Broad River found themselves. The Dumplin Treaty, negotiated by the State of Franklin, was ignored, leaving these people, in the eyes of the federal government, as trespassers on Indian lands.

In his April 11, 1796, message to the General Assembly, Governor Sevier called attention to the fact that Tennessee's senators were about to depart for Philadelphia and suggested that, before leaving, they be instructed to present the plight of these settlers to the Congress.

". . . In my humble opinion," Governor Sevier declared, "it is a matter of great public importance, and particularly interesting to the state and to individuals, to either have the Indian claims extinguished, or the adventurers compensated for those lands . . ."

The Assembly acted promptly to carry out the Governor's suggestion. But as its members, the two senators and the governor soon learned, none of their acts and none of the persons elected by the premature legislature of the State of Tennessee were considered by the federal government to have any legal standing. It became necessary, after Tennessee was admitted to the Union, to hold new elections and to re-enact certain measures already passed by the first General Assembly. At this time, Andrew Jackson was elected as a member of the House of Representatives, under provisions of the section of the bill admitting Tennessee to the Union.

It was to be many years before titles to the lands which the Indians held within the boundaries of the present State of Tennessee were extinguished. For the settlers south of the French Broad River, many inconveniences and much suffering were yet to be endured. For a quarter of a century, much of the business of the chief executive and members of the General Assembly, as well as representatives of the federal government, had to do with negotiations with the Indians, surveying new acquisitions of land, and providing for the settlement of thousands of emigrants who were pouring into Tennessee. By the end of Governor Joseph McMinn's third administration in 1821, the

John Sevier, leader in the fight for statehood.

"... Inasmuch as 'the line of experiment' run by the United States Commissioners had proved to be quite objectionable to Tennessee citizens and officials, for the reasons set out in their remonstrance, it will be noted that the way out for the President of the United States (John Adams) was to call for another treaty with the Cherokee Indians. In the meanwhile, Tennessee citizens were forcibly removed from their homes by Colonel Butler's military detachment, and passports from the Governor were necessary for citizens to be permitted to return to their former homes in order to gather their crops or attend to business matters ..."

THE FIRST CHIEF EXECUTIVE

Governor Sevier, who had been elected chief executive of the state in 1796, 1797, and 1799, could not under the constitution serve another consecutive term. During his six years in office, he had, however, set the new commonwealth well on the way to success and his popularity had increased rather than diminished.

Many important events, entirely out of his jurisdiction as governor, had taken place during this period. One of the most unfortunate was the expulsion of William Blount from the United States Senate on the charge of treason and provisions for his impeachment trial. He was the first man to be expelled but, instead of going home in disgrace, he returned to Tennessee to receive a royal welcome by its citizens.

A letter said to have been written by Blount to James Carey, made it appear that he was attempting to engage in a conspiracy with England to bring about an armed invasion of Florida and Louisiana; that he attempted to discredit the President of the

lands of present West Tennessee had been acquired and settlement of that rich important section of the state was well on the way.

After its first setback, due to the fact that the new State of Tennessee had set up a complete organization and had begun operations *before* it had been admitted to the Union, the government began to function smoothly. During the called sessions of the General Assembly, which convened on July 30, 1796, steps were taken to harmonize the state's legislation with that of the federal government and to send elected senators and its one member of the House of Representatives to the Congress of the United States. Having attended to these matters, Governor Sevier turned his attention to two subjects of local interest, the plight of the settlers south of the French Broad River and the building of roads.

The problem of the settlers south of the French Broad was of intense interest at the time. Dr. Robert H. White, State Historian, explains the situation:

United States and his agents among the Indians; and that he was attempting to swindle the Indians themselves. It was never proved that he had written the letter or that if he had, he had actually committed any of the offenses with which the Senate charged him.

Soon after Blount's return to Tennessee, however, the sergeant-at-arms of the United States Senate, James Matthers, appeared in Knoxville to arrest him and take him back to Philadelphia for trial. Matthers was received politely, permitted to serve papers on Blount, and was entertained with apparently sincere hospitality for several days.

When he decided it was time to leave with his prisoner, a body of horsemen appeared and told him pleasantly that they would ride out with him to start him on his way, but that he could not take William Blount from Tennessee soil. They did just that and the rest of his return journey Matthers made alone. Eventually, for many legal reasons, the impeachment was dismissed.

This refusal to surrender Blount to federal authorities was but one example of the confidence which his fellow Tennesseans felt in him. James White, who was at that time speaker of the State Senate, promptly resigned not only this position, but also his membership in the Senate, leaving both positions vacant. Blount was immediately elected without opposition and, at a called session of the State Legislature, was, on December 3, 1797, made speaker of the Senate.

Many other important matters took place during the first six-year period Sevier served as governor of Tennessee. Among them were the creation of Robertson County, named for James Robertson, and Montgomery County, named for Colonel John Montgomery, from

State parks help to keep the land much as it looked when the country was first settled.

Tennessee County, which had surrendered its name to the new state. Tennessee's three electoral votes were cast for Thomas Jefferson and Aaron Burr, showing that John Adams' feeling that the backwoodsmen would not support him was well founded.

VISITORS IN THE SETTLEMENTS

During the years immediately following Tennessee's admission to the Union, curiosity about this new part of the country led many visitors, as well as prospective settlers, to make tours of the major settlements. Among the most important were Louis

Philippe, later to claim the throne of France, and his two brothers, sons of the Duke of Orleans, who began their visit to Tennessee in the spring of 1797.

They first traveled in East Tennessee, visiting Governor Sevier and other leading citizens, and spending some time among the nearby Indians. Among both the Indians and the pioneer citizens they were introduced to such native foods as wild turkey and bear meat, as well as to the crowded and often quite crude sleeping conditions at the taverns they found on their way.

From Knoxville they came to Nashville, crossing the Cumberland Mountains, sometimes swimming their horses across rivers and enduring the everyday hardships of such travel. Enroute to Nashville, they passed through Dixon Springs, Bledsoe's Lick, and other places of interest in present Middle Tennessee.

Another Frenchman, M. Genet, minister of Republican France to the United States, created a sensation in the West during the years of 1792-1794. Genet visited Tennessee and Kentucky with the idea of alienating several of the leading men from the United States and bringing them into an alliance with France, the object being a military expedition against the Spanish along the Gulf Coast.

". . . It is known that many of the best patriots on the frontier," Ramsey states, "contiguous to the possessions claimed by Spain, yielded for a time to the seductive influence of these feelings and prejudices. And it required all the vigilance and decision of Washington to arrest the expedition, and restrain the impulsive western soldiery from an invasion of Louisiana, alliance with France, and a possible separation from and dismemberment of the Union."

ARCHIBALD ROANE

Sevier's successor as governor of Tennessee was Archibald Roane, a scholarly, dignified gentleman, brilliantly educated in law, who had served well in that capacity from the time he arrived in the Tennessee country in 1788. Although his administration deserves recognition for other things, it is often remembered chiefly for the fact that during it legislation was passed for the formal adoption of an official seal for the State of Tennessee. While his one administration was not noted for any spectacular change or accomplishment in government, it was a well-ordered and productive period.

In his final message to the legislature, September 20, 1803, Roane was able to report:

"Since the last session we experienced some embarrassment in trade, by an unjustifiable denial of the right of deposit at New Orleans as stipulated by treaty. But the prompt, firm, and prudent measures adopted by the national government, have been effectual. Those embarrassments are removed, and we are secured against any danger which might hereafter arise from the same cause.

Archibald Roane, Tennessee's second governor.

It is understood that a treaty has been concluded, by which New Orleans and its dependencies and the extensive and fertile province of Louisiana will be possessed by the United States. As this treaty was signed on the 30th of April last, to be ratified in six months from that date, the President has by proclamation, required the members of congress to convene on the 17th of October next. The business is important to the United States, particularly to the Western Country, and we ought to be fully represented. It will therefore be necessary to elect a Senator at an early period of the session; as the time of service of one of our Senators has expired."

At last, the problem of access to southern ports was solved in this purchase by Thomas Jefferson, the friend of the western people.

This legislative message was delivered by Governor Roane as he relinquished his office to John Sevier. Having vacated the governor's chair for one term, Sevier was qualified under the constitution, for reelection.

JOHN SEVIER

The whole structure of government was also undergoing change. Governor Sevier, in the first legislative message of his fourth term, October 7, 1803, emphasized the need of reframing the laws under which the State of Tennessee was then operating, instead of continuing to adhere to the laws of Great Britain.

"The different states within the United States have framed their constitutions and forms of government upon republican principles, and reason will suggest, that the common law of England, or any other European nation, are not suitable for republican states to adopt. As also the impropriety of decisions in matters of higher concern, affecting

Tennessee's roads have progressed from rough paths to modern superhighways.

the lives and properties of the citizens, in conformity to the laws of foreign nations, which in my opinion we are not bound to support or be governed thereby, I therefore flatter myself you will discover the great necessity of passing laws amply competent for our own internal regulations, and no longer be subservient to laws which few can know any thing about or become acquainted with . . ."

Many matters had become almost routine problems by the end of John Sevier's sixth term as governor in 1809. He and the legislatures which served during these years were faced with the need of extinguishing Indian titles to the wide expanse of wilderness which still separated the Holston and the Cumberland settlements. The plight of the settlers south of the French Broad River was still serious, and the growing need of "waggon" roads which would connect Tennessee with the Atlantic seaboard and the Gulf of Mexico, became a perennial problem. Roads from South West Point to Nashville, and from Tennessee to Georgia were also subjects of legislation during this period.

Serious rumblings of the War of 1812 were already being heard when Governor

Sevier delivered his September 24, 1807, legislative message:

"You have heard," he told the General Assembly, "of the late unprovoked attack made upon the United States Frigate *Chespeake*, by the British ship of war, the *Leopard*; of the murder of our fellow-citizens, and the degradation of the American flag, together with other insults and outrages committed on board the said frigate. It would be useless to take up your time in further detailing the particulars of the unprecedented and unprovoked outrage, in consequence of which, the President of the United States has necessarily requested the state's quota of militia. The necessary instructions have long since been issued, and I inform you with great pleasure of the promptitude and alacrity with which the citizens of the state are tendering their services in defence of their injured and insulted country. It does them great honor, and entitles them to the respect and confidence of their fellow-citizens of their neighbouring states . . ."

Once more Tennesseans, as they had done since Dunmore's War of 1774, offered their services as volunteers. They would not, however, be called into battle until several years later.

GOVERNOR WILLIE BLOUNT

By 1809, when Willie Blount, half-brother of the territorial governor, William Blount, succeeded John Sevier as governor of Tennessee, much progress had been made. There were titles to Indian lands still within the boundaries of the state to be extinguished, roads to be built, an educational system to be supported and expanded, and many other things related to the needs of a rapidly growing population to be considered.

Governor Willie Blount.

During the first years of his three terms as governor of Tennessee, Willie Blount went about the business of his office in a thorough and efficient way, but the full measure of his abilities was not evident until the actual outbreak of the War of 1812. His state papers of this period were filled with eloquent appeals to the patriotism of his fellow Tennesseans, but more than that, they were backed up by a willingness to use not only public resources, but private fortunes as well to promote the war effort.

But, the War of 1812 was to be Andrew Jackson's war, a war which would make him not only a national hero, but also, eventually, elevate him to the presidency of the United States. Jackson could not have subdued the Creek Indians; pushed on to Pensacola; and finally, passed on to his smashing victory over the British at New Orleans, had he not received the constant support and material backing given him by Willie Blount.

Andrew Jackson and the War of 1812

*Andrew Jackson, seventh president
of the United States. His inauguration was
a turning point in national affairs.*

JACKSON'S EARLY YEARS

During the last part of Sevier's third administration and in the election of his successor, Archibald Roane, a new figure was appearing with increasing prominence on the state political scene. It was Andrew Jackson, the red-headed, fiery-tempered, young lawyer, who with John McNairy and others arrived in Jonesborough in 1788 and, very soon thereafter traveled to Nashville, then the farthest outpost on the western frontier.

Jackson was born March 15, 1767, in the Waxhaws settlement, in the home of his mother's relatives near the then poorly-defined line between the states of North and South Carolina.

The circumstances of his birth and of his early years were tragic. His father died a few weeks before his third son, who was named for him, was born. His mother with two other sons, Hugh and Robert, had sought shelter in the homes of her sisters. They, with the Jacksons and a number of other relatives and friends, had left Ireland a few years earlier to seek their fortunes in America. At the time of Andrew's birth, the Jacksons were prospering, but like people of the other colonies, were already resentful of British oppression.

In these friendly homes of his mother's relatives, Jackson spent his infancy and early boyhood. His physical needs were met, his education was begun, but his childish eyes looked upon tragedy and his heart was touched by sorrow. War, bitterness, and cruelty, he knew when he was a child.

Finally, there was open rebellion among the settlers along the western borders of the Carolinas and Virginia. Soon the Revolutionary War broke out and young Andrew, before he was twelve years old, and his brothers, who were but little older, were engaged in active warfare.

Hugh died as a result of his participation in the engagement with the British at Stono Ferry. Later Robert and Andrew took part in the fighting, were captured, and held as prisoners by the British. They suffered from unattended wounds and from smallpox to such a degree that Robert died shortly after his release. Andrew recovered, but for the rest of his life he bore scars of wounds he received from the sword of a British officer whose boots he had refused to black. Bitter memories of those years of suffering gave him an undying hatred for the British.

Soon he knew more sorrow. His mother, who had gone on a mission of mercy for her nephews and other American prisoners held by the British at Charleston, became ill, died, and was buried in a grave which her son was never able to locate. The lonely boy grew to manhood in the homes of his mother's sisters. With their help and that of their husbands, Andrew received a fair education. About the time he reached his majority, he received a small inheritance from his father's estate. He read law in Salisbury and eventually was licensed to practice law.

In 1788, having reached his twenty-first birthday, Andrew put a few law books, some clothing, and other personal belongings into his saddle bags and riding one fine horse and leading another, set out for the new country beyond the mountains. He stayed for a short time in Jonesborough, but by the early autumn of 1788, he had appeared in the Cumberland settlements where he was destined to make his home and carve out his spectacular career.

During these early years, Jackson spent much time traveling back and forth between the Holston and Cumberland settlements. In both places he participated fully in the rough life of the frontier. He took part in the Indian fighting, cock fights, brawls, and quarrels which, in accordance with the customs of the day, often resulted in duels. He also took part in the more elegant social life of the period, for he had been trained well in manners and social graces.

Every issue of the Knoxville *Gazette*, Tennessee's first newspaper, for the greater part of 1792, 1793, and 1794, carried stories of the slaughter of men, women, and children along the frontiers and voiced pleas to Congress and the east for intelligent consideration of the situation.

"It is shocking to describe the bloody scenes that have taken place in this district," one gentleman in the Miro district wrote to the *Gazette*. "The Indians have killed and scalped a great number of persons, among them Colonel Isaac Bledsoe, who was massacred within a hundred and fifty yards of his house . . ."

During these times, Andrew Jackson and his friend John Overton traveled back and forth through the Indian-infested country to wilderness courts which gave, in their own way, some semblance of law and order to the frontiers. No one was secure, no fort was strong enough to defend itself successfully against the organized attacks of large bodies of Indians, and no frontiersman, however brave, was safe from the enemy.

RACHEL ROBARDS

During his early years in the Cumberland settlements, Andrew Jackson lived at the home of the widow of John Donelson. Also boarding at the widow Donelson's was John Overton, who had lived at Mrs. Donelson's home in Kentucky a short time before she and most of her children returned to their lands in the Cumberland settlements. It was in Kentucky that John Overton first knew Rachel, the youngest daughter of the family who in 1785 had married Lewis Robards. The Robards family was respected and well known in Kentucky, but Lewis unfortunately had a jealous nature. Overton knew both families well and was fully aware of the fact

Rachel Robards, whose marriage to Jackson raised a storm of political controversy.

that Robards' unreasonable jealousies were making his young wife extremely unhappy. She, however, stayed in Kentucky after her mother and the remainder of her family had returned to the Cumberland.

When Overton arrived in Nashville, he took up lodgings again at the home of Mrs. Donelson and soon persuaded Andrew Jackson with whom he had become friends, to board there with him. After a short time, Rachel, no longer able to endure her husband's jealousy and harsh treatment, sent word begging her mother to send someone to bring her home. Mrs. Donelson sent her son Samuel on the errand and Rachel was returned to her mother's care. Here, Andrew Jackson first met her.

It was not long until Robards came to Nashville to attempt a reconciliation and even bought some lands, apparently meaning to make it their home. Soon, however, he became insanely jealous again. This time he accused Andrew Jackson. Instead of set-

tling down in the Cumberland, he vowed publicly that he would return to Kentucky and force his wife to go with him. Rachel, determined not to go back, sought refuge with a Colonel Stark and his family, friends of the Donelsons who were on their way to Natchez, Mississippi. Both the Donelsons and the Starks had friends in Natchez and Rachel planned to stay with them.

Since Colonel Stark was an old man and there were few men in the party, Andrew Jackson was asked to accompany the party to help protect it from the Indians. This he agreed to do, but after seeing the party to its destination safely, he returned to Nashville promptly and was present for the April term of court in 1791.

After some time, word came to the Cumberland that Robards had been granted a divorce by the Virginia Legislature. Andrew Jackson returned to Natchez in the late summer of 1791 and he and Rachel were married.

Strangely enough, no evidence has been found to prove that Andrew Jackson and Rachel Donelson Robards were married in the neighborhood of Natchez, Mississippi. Determined and continuous search for such evidence has been made since William B. Lewis spent several weeks in Mississippi in 1827 and returned to Tennessee only to remain silent on the subject. No word of the details of the Natchez marriage, other than the bare statement that it took place, appears in the documents of the Nashville Committee which were prepared in 1827 to contradict the vicious publications of Jackson's political opponents.

Even the most bitter attacks made during the presidential campaigns of 1824 and 1828 did not bring from either of the Jacksons one word concerning this marriage, nor from their friend, John Overton, who must have known the full details concerning the story.

Although the circumstances of the Natchez marriage gave Jackson's enemies cause for unjust gossip, it was nothing in comparison with the blow which fell in late 1793 when it was learned that a divorce had not been granted. Virginia had merely given Robards the right to sue for divorce in the courts of Kentucky. This he did, making the most slanderous of charges. After the divorce was finally granted, the Jacksons were remarried. The marriage bond made in Davidson County, dated January 7, 1794, was signed by Andrew Jackson, Robert Hays, and John Overton. Another ceremony followed, but the unfortunate affair did not injure the social standing of the Jacksons among the leading people of Nashville. In fact, not too much was made of it, except by Jackson's political enemies who were increasing in number.

JACKSON'S VIOLENT NATURE

It was inevitable that there should be disagreement between Jackson and John Se-

vier. As early as 1797 Jackson criticized an official act of Sevier who retaliated by calling him ". . . a poor pettyfogging lawyer . . ." This was settled however, and in 1798, Sevier appointed Jackson as judge of the Superior Court of Law and Equity.

A new source of friction arose in 1801, when both were being considered for the position of major-general. Sevier, then out of office, was by experience and personal popularity, well qualified for it. His strength was chiefly in the eastern part of the State, while Jackson's lay in the Miro District. Field officers met on February 5, 1802, to elect an officer to fill this vacancy, with the result that Sevier and Jackson tied with 17 votes each. The tie was broken when Governor Roane cast a deciding vote in favor of Andrew Jackson.

When Roane ran for re-election, Jackson actively supported him, thereby widening the breach between him and Sevier. A violent quarrel followed between Jackson and Sevier, who had defeated Roane and was again governor of Tennessee. Sevier had been charged with land frauds in regard to certain grants made by North Carolina.

Andrew Jackson's violent temper often endangered his political career. This print illustrates his duel with Charles Dickinson which almost cost Jackson his life.

These charges were not upheld. The quarrel continued, however, even after Sevier had been inaugurated for his fourth term as governor, with Jackson persistently challenging him to a duel and Sevier constantly refusing.

The quarrel finally ended in a chance encounter. Jackson, still trying to taunt the governor into a duel, had gone to South West Point, where he had offered to meet him. After some time Sevier did not appear, and Jackson left. They met each other unexpectedly, and both dismounted. At this point Sevier's horse bolted. Because his pistols were in his saddle holsters he was left without any weapons. Jackson could not shoot an unarmed man, so he chased him about a bit with his cane until friends separated them and patched up the quarrel as well as was possible.

Jackson's aggressiveness was one of his great faults, and it was not until it led him into more serious trouble a few years later that he finally stopped dueling. It is said, however, that his violent anger at Sevier was due chiefly to the fact that Sevier was reported to have made a disparaging remark about Mrs. Jackson and the Robards affair. This, to Jackson, was the one unforgivable offense. Frontiersmen, however, were now becoming civilized and finding more dignified ways of settling disputes.

THE APPROACHING WAR

On the national scene, war seemed to be approaching in 1809 when James Madison succeeded Thomas Jefferson as president of the United States. Tennessee watched the developments in the Creek nation with as much concern as they did the growing quarrel with England. Tennesseans were convinced that

An early lithograph of Tecumseh.

the resumption of Indian hostilities was the result of British influence and that there would be no peace until the British were stopped.

Under the protection of the federal government and with the aid of eastern organizations, the Creeks had made much progress toward the adoption of a more civilized way of life. But this peaceful state of affairs was upset in 1812 when Tecumseh, brother of the Shawnee medicine man, The Prophet, came into the Creek nation. Tecumseh encouraged the Creeks and other southern tribes to war against the Americans and to throw off the "American" habits which they acquired.

After arousing the Creeks to a religious frenzy and a rage against the Americans,

Tecumseh ordained a chief prophet to carry on his work among them. Then, with several Creek warriors, he returned to his own nation. Here he established a line of communication with the Creeks and other southern tribes, organizing them into a dangerous conspiracy against the whole southwestern frontier.

WAR IS DECLARED

On June 18, 1812, the War Hawks in Congress had their way and the United States declared war against England. The news reached Nashville nine days later. The entire town erupted in celebration of this longed-for event. Tennessee had its arms and ammunition ready, a military leader in command, and a volunteer soldiery anxious to fight not only the Indians, but also the British, should they attempt their threatened naval invasion of the far south.

When Jackson organized the force at Nashville, he had over 2,000 volunteers, approximately 700 infantrymen, and 1,400 cavalrymen. The cavalry, under General John Coffee's command, was dispatched by way of the Natchez Trace to the lower Mississippi. On January 7, 1813, General Jackson and the infantry embarked on flatboats for the slow, dangerous voyage to Natchez. They reached Natchez on February 19, and General Coffee's command arrived a few days later. Camp was set up, men drilled, and everything made ready for action. After a month, it became apparent that the British threat against the Louisiana coast had not materialized. Soon General Jackson received an order from John Armstrong, Secretary of War, confirming this and ordering him to turn over his military stores to General James Wilkinson, commander of the Seventh Military District, who was stationed nearby.

General Jackson flatly refused to abandon his men so far from home and began at once to make arrangements for the difficult return trip by way of the Natchez Trace.

Hearing Jackson's plans, General Wilkinson threatened grave consequences for Jackson's disobedience. Recruiting officers were sent to Jackson's lines, attempting to enlist his men. But Jackson went on with his preparations. The quartermaster who was to provide wagons for the sick and for excess baggage on the return journey, pretended to carry out his order. The day before the camp was to be broken up however, he countermanded the order. Jackson promptly seized the wagons still within his lines, and forced them to proceed with the transportation of the sick.

"OLD HICKORY"

It was a long, hungry march back to Nashville. Andrew Jackson trudged along on foot with the men who were able to walk, giving his horses and theirs to the sick. At that time of year, the roads were extremely bad and the swamps through which they had to pass were deep and full from the early spring rains.

"He's tough!" the men whispered to each other as they plodded along with him.

"Yeah," was the answer, "as tough as hickory."

Before the weary march had come to an end in Tennessee, Jackson was affectionately called "Old Hickory," a nickname which he would always carry from that time on.

It was nearly April as the tired men approached Tennessee, and with each mile

The Creek Indians attack Fort Mims. This bloody massacre provoked the state government into action and Andrew Jackson was sent to subdue the Indians.

their spirits rose. On April 20 they reached Columbia where General Jackson discharged those living in that neighborhood. The remainder marched to Nashville where they were discharged.

THE CREEK WAR

On August 30, 1813, the Creek Indians, led by their chief, Red Eagle (who was largely of white blood and better known by his English name, William Weatherford), fell upon Fort Mims, near Mobile. The entire frontier was stunned by news of the attack, for the garrison was overrun and some five hundred men, women, and children were massacred. In Nashville, Governor Blount responded by asking the legislature for 3,500 volunteers to be added to General Jackson's force.

By January of 1814, General Jackson had enough men and supplies to undertake a limited expedition into the Creek country. Before he could attack towns on the Coosa and Tallapoosa rivers, his troops were discovered by the Creeks. A ferocious battle followed in which there were many casualties.

In a letter to his wife, Jackson wrote that Major Alexander Donelson, her brother, had been killed. General Coffee, always a hero, was wounded again. Carroll, Captain Gordon's spies, and others were conspicuous for their bravery.

With his weakened force, Jackson did not attempt to burn the town. Because his number of wounded were increasing, his horses were starving, and his men " . . . in some degrees . . . panic-struck . . .", it became necessary to turn back to Fort Strother.

As he prepared for the journey, it became clear that the Indians were planning another attack. Jackson began the march and had succeeded in getting the last wounded man across the creek before the second battle, Enotachopco, began.

The battle was a fierce one. At a critical moment, many soldiers attempted to flee, but Jackson stopped them by riding into their midst.

Only the force of his command and the examples of his officers spared Jackson the actual use of his sword.

Returning to Fort Strother, Jackson began preparations for the final push into the Creek country. In Tennessee, Governor Blount and other prominent citizens were leading in the recruiting. Even Judge Hugh Lawson White of the Tennessee Supreme Court, joined in the effort.

Soon, about 5,000 men marched to join Jackson, 2,000 under General John Cocke; 2,500 raised for a three month term of enlistment by Governor Blount; and the remainder under Colonel John Williams of the 39th Regiment, United States Army.

THE BATTLE OF HORSESHOE BEND

With these men, Jackson started out once more, this time to assure a final victory over Weatherford and his warriors. It took him eleven days to march his army through the 55 miles of swamps, cane, and forests stretching between Fort Strother and the enemy's strongly fortified position in the bend between the source and the mouth of the Tallapoosa River. Meanwhile Weatherford and his warriors, inspired by Tecumseh's encouragement, awaited the approach of the Americans.

On the night of March 26, General Jackson camped about six miles from the Bend. Early the next morning, he detailed General

Although Indian casualties were heavy, only 51 of Jackson's 3,000 men were killed in the Battle of Horseshoe Bend. Today, this cannon marks the site of the battlefield.

Coffee, with almost his whole force, to cross the river at a ford about three miles away and surround the bend so that there could be no escape by crossing the river.

With his artillery planted at some height, Jackson opened a brisk fire whenever the enemy showed themselves. Meanwhile, Captain Russell's company of spies, a force led by Colonel Richard Brown, and Colonel Morgan crossed to the end of the peninsula in canoes and set fire to a few buildings there. They advanced towards the breastworks and began firing upon the enemy lying behind it.

Neither cannonballs nor rifle bullets did great damage, however, for the enemy was protected by logs and earth used to construct the fort's walls. Finding that the Indians could not be dislodged without changing his tactics, General Jackson decided to take the breastworks by storm.

After some time, the American troops succeeded in gaining possession of the opposite side of the works. Although the enemy fought bravely, many fighting even after they were wounded, they were finally defeated. As Jackson described it, "The whole margin of the river which surrounded the peninsula was strewed with the slain . . ."

Of the many heroes of the Battle of Horseshoe Bend, two who were to become important in the future history of the nation stand out—Sam Houston and Davy Crockett.

A PEACE TREATY

After the victory at Tohopeka, Jackson pushed deeper into the Creek country. His progress was hindered by high waters, however, allowing many remaining warriors to escape before he reached them. When he came near to the junction of the Coosa and Tallapoosa rivers, he stopped to erect a fort which his men named Fort Jackson, in his honor. From here he sent word to the Creeks that Weatherford must be delivered to him.

Weatherford soon appeared at Jackson's tent, alone and unarmed. Surprised that he had not been brought in as a prisoner, Jackson admitted him. There are countless versions of this meeting. A reliable one is that written by Jackson's aide, Major John Reid:

" 'I had directed,' continued Jackson, 'that you should be brought to me confined; and had you appeared in this way, I should have known how to have treated you.' Weatherford replied, 'I am in your power, do with me as you please. I am a soldier. I have done the white people all the harm I could. I have fought them bravely. If I had an army I would yet fight and contend to the last. But, I have none. My people are all gone. I can now do no more than weep over the misfortunes of my nation.'

Pleased at his firm and high-toned manner, Jackson informed him that he did not ask him to lay down his arms or to become peaceable. 'The terms on which your nation can be saved, and peace restored have already been disclosed. In this way, and none other, can you obtain safety.' "

General Jackson continued, explaining to Weatherford how peace might be brought to his shattered nation, to which Weatherford replied sadly:

". . . There was a time when I had a choice, and could have answered you. I have none now, even hope has ended. Once I could animate my warriors to battle, but I cannot animate the dead. My warriors can no longer hear my voice. Their bones are at Talladega, Tallushatchee, Emuckfa, and Tohopeka. I have not surrendered myself thoughtlessly. Whilst there were chances of success, I have never left my post, nor supplicated for peace. But my people are gone, and I now ask it for my nation, and for myself. On the miseries and misfortunes brought upon my country, I look back with deepest sorrow, and wish to avert still greater calamities..."

VICTORIOUS RETURN

News of Jackson's victory at Horseshoe Bend had reached Nashville and the cannons roared in celebration. The victorious Tennesseans were met on their return from the Creek country by citizens of Huntsville, Alabama. Crossing the Tennessee line, marching through Fayetteville and the smaller settlements and farms, they were met by hundreds of enthusiastic citizens. In Nashville, Governor Blount and other officials took part in a great celebration. After this victory, Jackson ceased his military activities briefly and returned to his Hermitage to enjoy for a few weeks the comforts of home.

During this period, he wrote Secretary of War Armstrong concerning terms of indemnity for the war. On June 8 he acknowledged the receipt of the Secretary's letter naming Jackson to fill the office of Major General, having just been vacated by Major General Harrison.

One of Jackson's first duties would be to go into the Creek country again for peace negotiations. Jackson set out from Nashville for Fort Jackson and arrived there on July 10. Calling the proud but starving Creek chiefs together, Jackson succeeded in closing the negotiations on August 9, 1814.

The treaty with the Creeks following their defeat at the Horseshoe was defined as a *capitulation* or surrender to be conducted on strictly military terms.

Immediately after the Creeks signed the treaty, General Jackson wrote ". . . the whole of Alabama and the valuable part of Coosa and Cahaba, in all containing about 22 Mills (millions) of Acres are contained in this cession . . ."

This vast empire went to the young American republic. In addition, Jackson had deliberately divided the Creek nation and separated it from contact with Pensacola by running a strip of the ceded lands through their nation. Once this was completed, however, Jackson turned his attention to the desperate condition of the Creeks.

". . . The whole Creek nation is in a most wretched state," he wrote Secretary Armstrong, "and I must repeat that they *must* be *fed* and *clothed* or necessity will compel them to embrace the proffered friendship of the British. You will find, from the information contained in the letters from Pensacola, that the British officers are clothing the Indians in their best scarlet . . ."

THE BURNING OF WASHINGTON

While Jackson was still negotiating the capitulation of the Creeks, dangerous tensions were increasing in the East. With a growing number of patriots, President Madison was struggling to save the nation. But disagreement and disorganization existed.

Napoleon's descent from the French throne had made it possible for England to reduce her forces in Europe. Now England could send the Duke of Wellington's troops to support naval forces already at the shoreline of the United States. Not only would land forces be sent to invade the chief cities along the Atlantic seaboard, but ships would carry troops to invade the more vulnerable coast along the Gulf of Mexico.

Until this time, England had been satisfied to blockade American seaports and to fight a largely naval war. But now they were able to invade the coastline cities, placing the national capital itself in danger.

Cochrane, the British admiral, had reached Bermuda with an 80-gun-ship and 3,000 troops commanded by General Ross. Sailing into the Chesapeake, he joined Rear Admiral Cockburn. They landed and proceeded to Bladensburg, where General Stansbury was stationed with the Baltimore militia.

The Americans were tragically unprepared. Their military leaders, as well as government officials, were hopelessly impotent. The battle, therefore, resulted in chaos and defeat.

With his cabinet, President Madison had galloped over to Bladensburg to see the battle. They galloped back quite as rapidly when the action began. Fortunately, the enemy had no cavalry to pursue them and take them as prisoners.

On August 24, 1814, with only a small bodyguard, Cockburn and Ross rode into Washington. The only resistance offered to this invasion of the Capital was the firing of one shot killing General Ross' horse. After the commanding officers entered, the British troops marched in.

One of the first places entered was the House of Representatives, where chairs, desks, and every available combustible material were piled high and set afire. The library, in which the nation took such pride, and many invaluable documents were quickly consumed in flames. Leaping from the windows and reaching the roof, the flames illuminated the entire building, transforming it into a torch which terrified the countryside.

Dolly Madison remained at the presidential mansion as long as possible. A carriage loaded with important government papers, silver, jewels, and other valuables waited for her at the door. But in spite of pleas from friends, she refused to leave until she received a message from her husband advising her where to join him.

At last the penciled note arrived, but delaying the departure even further, Dolly sought to take the Stuart portrait of George Washington with her. Finding it would take too long to remove it from the wall, she slashed it from the frame, rolled the canvas carefully, and carried it out.

THE BATTLE OF NEW ORLEANS

On October 7, Jackson wrote a letter to Governor Blount in which he begged for the recruitment of Tennesseans to meet the national emergency. Three days later, he wrote to Secretary Monroe telling him of the presence of the British and Indians in Pensacola. He also reported that he had placed his entire disposable force at Fort Bower, at the entrance to Mobile Bay, and reminded the Secretary of the necessity of taking Pensacola.

By October 26, General Jackson made up his mind to march against Pensacola without waiting for authorization from the government. He entered Pensacola, drove the British out, subdued the Indians, and withdrew.

At such a distance from the Capital, by the time orders reached Jackson, the whole Lower South would have fallen to the enemy. Although he desperately lacked the men and supplies for a decisive battle with the British, Jackson decided to take matters into his own hands. He sent urgent

Andrew Jackson leads his troops to victory at the Battle of New Orleans. Although a peace treaty had been negotiated, the war would have continued if the Americans had not won this battle.

pleas for aid to the national government, to Tennessee, Kentucky, and Georgia. Finally he went ahead, using whatever manpower and materials were available.

Military organizations and the citizens of Louisiana were asked for their support. Jean Lafitte and his band of Baratarian pirates generously offered their aid. In addition, Jackson also called upon the "free men of colour" to join their white countrymen in the defense of the city.

By December 1, 1814, Jackson had arrived in New Orleans. Major General William Carroll landed with the West Tennessee militia at Natchez on December 14. Brigadier General John Coffee was now in position and ready to join in the defense of city. Meanwhile, 2,300 Kentuckians commanded by John Thomas were on their way.

Although the people of New Orleans were shocked at the rough appearance of these westerners, they soon looked at them with genuine respect. For their part, the backwoodsmen were completely unawed by the stylish dress and stilted manners of the city dwellers they had come to defend.

Efforts to prepare the city for an early attack by the British continued day and night. In less than a month after he reached New Orleans, General Jackson fought his first battle. The defense of New Orleans consisted of three battles with the British: the first, on the night of December 23, 1814; the second, on the morning of January 1, 1815; and the third, on the morning of January 8, 1815.

In the battle of December 23, Jackson surprised the British in a night attack shortly after they landed their forces. This move led the British to believe that the American forces were greater than they actually were. After the battle, Jackson retired to the city, realizing that he was not strong enough to push the advantage gained in the battle. The next few days were spent strengthening his defense and preparing to repulse the British when they renewed their attack on the city. One preparation which was to prove effective in later battles, was the widening of the Roderigues Canal.

The second attack began about ten o'clock on the morning of New Year's Day, 1815. Firing stopped around noon that day, with Jackson still secure in his position. Then both camps continued to prepare for the inevitable showdown.

On January 4, after traveling for nearly a month, Major General Thomas and his Kentuckians arrived to join Jackson's forces. Many of them had no weapons, but every effort was made to equip them for the coming battle. Meanwhile, the British were also receiving reinforcements.

On January 8 all was ready. The British batteries, which had been demolished on the first of the month, had been re-established during the preceding night. Showers of bombs and cannonballs poured upon the American troops. Then some 8,000 British troops, under the command of Sir Edward Packenham, began to advance in close formation. Major General John Reid describes the defense: "A thick fog . . . enabled them to approach within a short distance of our entrenchment, before they were discovered. They were perceived advancing, with firm, quick, and steady pace, in column, with a front of sixty to seventy deep. Our troops, who had for some time been in readiness . . . , gave three cheers. . . . A burst of artillery

and small arms, pouring with destructive aim, mowed down their front, and arrested their advance. In our musketry there was not a moment's intermission; as one party discharged pieces, another succeeded: alternately loading and appearing, no pause could be perceived—it was one continuous volley . . ." British losses have been estimated at 2,600, of which seven hundred, including Packenham, were killed. Only seven Americans were killed and six wounded.

The American officers and men were not professional soldiers. They were inferior in both numbers and equipment to the British Army. Their only military training was learned from fighting Indians. The victory at the Battle of New Orleans, however, had won them and their commanding officer fame. Because of the victory, Jackson and many of his men were to achieve positions of political power which would dominate the nation for at least half a century and would have a lasting influence on the country.

A HERO'S WELCOME

In May of 1815, General Jackson reached Nashville where he was welcomed as the conquering hero. He and his family soon settled at their simple log Hermitage, for such a life was his wife's greatest wish. But fame had already claimed Jackson.

The same day he reached home, Jackson found two important letters. One from Alexander J. Dallas, Secretary of War, offered him appointment to one of the two positions as major-general in the United States Army. The other demanded an explanation of Jackson's order to continue martial law in New Orleans after the danger of a British invasion had passed, and his consequent argument with Judge Hall of the United States Dis-

The Hermitage was originally a rustic cabin. To please his wife, Andrew Jackson built this large comfortable house but retained the name.

trict Court which resulted in the general being fined for contempt of court.

As to the latter, Dallas charged: ". . . the Judge himself was arrested by your order . . . and conducted under a strong guard to the barracks . . . Mr. Dick, the Attorney of the United States was arrested by your order, and lodged in the barracks . . . Judge Hall was released . . . but escorted to a place outside the city . . . with orders not to return until peace was officially announced . . ."

All of this was quite true. General Jackson had considered that for a time martial law was necessary and that it should temporarily supersede civil authority. The Judge had fined him one thousand dollars for contempt of court and he had paid it, but with a dignified reprimand to the court.

Later, the citizens of New Orleans raised an amount to reimburse General Jackson for the fine. Refusing it politely, he asked that it be given to widows and orphans of men who had died defending the city.

In the autumn of 1815, General and Mrs. Jackson went to Washington. On their way, every town and village they passed honored them. Washington outdid itself in entertaining the hero and his family, and the State of Tennessee also shared in the glory, for Jackson was one of its heroes.

The parlor in the Hermitage. A portrait of Rachel hangs beside the fireplace.

THE GREAT CHICKASAW CESSION

Willie Blount's third term as governor of Tennessee was coming to an end when the triumphant Tennesseans returned from New Orleans. It was his privilege to enjoy their victory for a few months. In September, 1815, he delivered his last message to the Legislature, giving a review of Tennessee's participation in the war.

Succeeding Blount was Joseph McMinn who had been a member of the Constitutional Convention of 1796. Dr. Robert H. White, State Historian, gave the following estimate of McMinn's accomplishments as governor:

". . . McMinn served as governor through years that witnessed a nation-wide panic as the aftermath of the War of 1812. He conceived the idea of establishing a state operated Loan office for the alleviation of hard times, with the result that his "paper institution" accelerated rather than abated the financial crises confronting his people. He rendered a much greater service to his state by negotiating treaties with the resident Indians whereby large cessions of land were yielded to Tennessee. In fact, the Great Chickasaw Cession of 1818 occurred during his administration whereby a treaty entered into with the United States Commissioners, Andrew Jackson and Isaac Shelby, that transferred to Tennessee the largest single cession of land ever to take place in the entire history of Tennessee."

The large acquisitions of land were just the beginnings of a great period of expansion and development for Tennessee. If at that time one stood on the highest mountaintop of the eastern borders of Tennessee, and gazed towards the Mississippi River, its western border, one never could have imagined the changes which would come to the state and its people within fifty years.

Years of Growth

PRESIDENT JACKSON

Between the victory at New Orleans in 1815 and the presidential election in 1824, Andrew Jackson was constantly busy. His duties as treaty maker occupied much of his time. Late in 1817, when the Seminole Indians of Florida became troublesome, he was ordered to subdue them. Once again, Pensacola became the center of trouble and once again on his own responsibility, Jackson seized it.

The ethics of Jackson's action became the subject of long disputes between Washington and Spain. After many arguments over the transfer of Florida from Spanish to American rule, a treaty was finally negotiated by which the southern territory became a United States possession.

With this accomplished, General Jackson was appointed Governor of Florida. Neither Jackson nor his wife had wanted the governorship; both were eager to get back to their new brick Hermitage. Nevertheless, Jackson went to Florida to assure the United States possession of the territory. He and Mrs. Jackson remained only long enough to establish the government and get it into operation. By November, 1821, they had returned to Nashville.

In 1822, the Tennessee Legislature passed a resolution supporting Jackson as the presidential candidate for the elections of 1824. Thinking it important to have their candidate on the national scene, members of the General Assembly of Tennessee elected Jackson to the United States Senate in 1823.

In 1824, the presidential campaign had so many candidates that the final vote in the electoral college was divided among Jackson, John Quincy Adams, William H. Crawford, and Henry Clay. Jackson received the most votes, but was still short of the number necessary to win the presidency. The election was thrown into the House of Representatives. Here, Clay turned his influential following over to John Quincy Adams and thus gave him the victory.

The next presidential campaign had its official beginning in October, 1825, when the Legislature of Tennessee again submitted Jackson's name to the American people as

The third state capitol (from 1812-1815) at Nashville, Tennessee.

a candidate for the presidency. Leaders assembled at the Hermitage to outline plans for the campaign. This time their efforts were not in vain. In 1828 Jackson was elected President of the United States.

Jackson's victory was paid for by much personal suffering. Never in the history of American political campaigns has a presidential candidate and his family been more viciously and unscrupulously attacked.

On December 22, 1828, shortly after Jackson's victory, Rachel died suddenly. Although heartbroken and lonely, Jackson remained dedicated to his country. Among the things he accomplished during his term in office were payment of the national debt, collection of the overdue debt from France, prevention of nullification by South Carolina, and proving that by their vote, the people could choose their leaders and have a hand in government.

Always a loyal supporter of the Union, Jackson also believed in the rights of states. "In proportion, therefore as the general government encroaches upon the rights of the states, in the same proportion does it impair its own power and detract from its ability to fulfill the purposes of its creation."

GOVERNORS HOUSTON, HALL, AND CARROLL

In 1827 Sam Houston was elected governor. Six months before the end of his term he suddenly resigned when he and his recent bride separated. Houston then went to live among the Cherokees, with whom he had spent three years as a youth.

After the resignation of Sam Houston, William Hall, speaker of the State Senate, became governor. Hall occupied this position for five and a half months, when William

Sam Houston, governor of Tennessee and president of the Republic of Texas.

Carroll was again elected chief executive. During his short administration, Hall found time to consider the matter of public education and the safeguarding of public funds for that purpose.

Governor Carroll favored the establishment of public schools and expressed this position in many of his papers. In his legislative message of September 17, 1827, Carroll dwelt upon the importance of education, connecting it with argriculture, the main occupation of Tennessee citizens at that time.

After the failure of a plan to finance public education by sale of public lands, Carroll and others realized that an adequate system could be obtained only by provisions for and protection of a common school fund. This was one of the many important accomplishments of the Constitutional Convention of 1834. It appears in Article XI, Section 10 of that Constitution and reads:

"... it shall be the duty of the General Assembly, in all future periods of this Government, to cherish literature and science. And the fund called the 'common school fund,' and all the lands and proceeds thereof, shall remain a perpetual fund, the principal of which shall never be diminished by legislative appropriation."

While retaining the basic democratic principles in the 1796 Constitution, the Constitution of 1834 made important changes in regard to taxation, the judicial system, property qualifications for office holders, elections of various officials, and other matters relating to contemporary needs.

A POWERFUL WHIG VOTE

In 1835, William Carroll decided to run for re-election. This would make his fourth consecutive term. Carroll based his eligibility for office on the theory that the constitution of 1834 had completely abolished the constitution of 1796 and with it, the provision making it unconstitutional for a man to serve more than three consecutive terms.

Newton Cannon, Carroll's Whig opponent, contended that "... we have no new constitution, but ... the same good old constitution revised and amended ..."

At the same time, Hugh Lawson White, the great Whig leader of Tennessee, was a candidate for the presidency of the United States. White was running in opposition to Vice-President Martin Van Buren, whom the Democrats chose as Andrew Jackson's successor. Under the strong Whig influence in Tennessee White carried the state against Van Buren even in Andrew Jackson's Hermitage district. Cannon was elected by a majority of 11,800 votes over Carroll. Andrew Jackson was shocked and humiliated.

A painting of the sheepshearing at which Hugh Lawson White met his wife. White retired from the political scene after being defeated for the presidency.

Even though Tennessee had temporarily moved away from the Democratic party, Van Buren was elected to the presidency by a majority. Newton Cannon, in spite of Jackson's opposition, was re-elected for a second term. During Cannon's second administration, the final chapter of the history of the Cherokee nation east of the Mississippi River was completed.

THE TRAIL OF TEARS

In 1828 when gold was discovered there, Georgia annexed the Dahlenega District. This portion of Cherokee territory was then distributed to white citizens. The Cherokees, meanwhile, had set up an independent state within the boundaries of Georgia rather than submit to the laws of that state as citizens. A long and bitter fight over these and other subjects developed; for the Cherokees, it was a losing one. The nation itself was divided between the factions led by the powerful chiefs, John Ross and Major John Ridge.

John Ross, a chief of the Cherokee Nation, bitterly opposed moving the tribe west.

Finally, the Treaty of New Echota was made in 1835. The Cherokees agreed to surrender all of their territory east of the Mississippi River and move to the West. The faction responsible for signing the treaty was led by Major John Ridge; Ridge had become convinced that the only hope for his nation was acceptance of the treaty.

Among other things, the treaty provided payment of five million dollars, a joint interest in the territory occupied by Cherokees that had moved west earlier, payment for the cost of removal, and improvements.

Jackson, who was president when the Treaty of New Echota was signed, had negotiated an earlier treaty with the Cherokees in 1817. This treaty had begun the movement of Cherokees to the West. Jackson believed that relocating the Indian tribes in better hunting grounds of the west was the only solution to the problem.

Jackson's political enemies, Daniel Webster, Henry Clay, Edward Everett, David Crockett, and others, took sides against him and painted him as a brutal Indian fighter and an Indian hater—a picture which has been handed down through the years.

General Winfield Scott of the United States Army, with a command of about seven thousand men, was in charge of the removal of the Indians who refused to leave their homes. Women, children, and those too sick or old to make the trip by land were sent by the longer water route.

The last organized land party had scarcely begun its journey, when the winter of 1838 approached. Organized at Charleston, Tennessee, the party traveled south of Pikeville, through McMinnville, to Nashville, and then to Hopkinsville, Kentucky. Crossing the Ohio River near the mouth of the Cumberland River, they continued, finally reaching their destination in March of 1839. The journey, during the bitter winter, was one of such hardship and sorrow that it is still referred to as "The Trail of Tears."

When the Indian Territory was finally reached, the controversy between the Ross and Ridge factions was still raging. Not until Major Ridge had been killed was it possible to obtain some measure of agreement.

According to the roll kept by John Ross, the total number of Cherokees who moved to the west was 13,149. Nearly a thousand hid in the Smoky Mountains where they escaped capture. Later they were allowed to draw benefits from the United States Government. The Qualla Reservation, where many of their descendants still live, was formed along the borders of North Carolina and Tennessee.

As Tennessee's frontier pushed westward and well-organized counties and towns began to spring up in the wilderness, hunters, trappers, and explorers began to move into the Texas country. Following them were the land-hungry settlers seeking profitable investments. But the frontier opened between 1820 and 1830 was under question as far as land titles, relations with Mexico, and Indian claims were concerned.

When Sam Houston resigned as governor of Tennessee, it was to his Cherokee friends in Texas that he fled. The war for Texan independence finally offered Houston an opportunity for a complete "comeback." As he had written Andrew Jackson, ". . . it is hard . . . for an old Trooper to forget the note of the Bugle!"

REMEMBER THE ALAMO!

In 1835 General Santa Anna, the dictator of Mexico, began a military campaign to conquer the rebellious Texans, who had recently declared their independence from Mexico. Unable to meet Santa Anna's army without reinforcements and supplies, General Sam Houston ordered a retreat. However, the Texans at the Alamo remained behind.

Meanwhile, Santa Anna crossed the Rio Grande with seven thousand men. He reached the town of Bexar on February 21, 1836 and made a surprise attack on the little Texas garrison in the Alamo. During the siege, the Texans were reinforced by thirty-two men from Gonzales, making a total number of one hundred and fifty men.

For ten days, Santa Anna's men fired into the fortress, only to be shot down by the return fire of the Texans, many of whom had acquired their marksmanship on the frontiers of Tennessee and Kentucky. During the prolonged attack, the Americans suffered few casualties, but they were literally starving. Each day they became weaker, but they

Major John Ridge, the Cherokee chief who persuaded his people to give up their lands.

did not permit their condition to interfere with their devastating fire.

Finally, on the night of March fifth, in spite of his terrific losses, Santa Anna ordered scaling ladders to the walls of the fort. Soon the Mexicans were piling into the fort, in such numbers that the men in the garrison were hopelessly outnumbered. Not one was left to tell the story.

Davy Crockett, veteran of the Battle of New Orleans and idol of the frontiers, was there at the Alamo. He had come to Texas after he was defeated for re-election to Congress in 1835. As hunter, Indian fighter, and statesman in Tennessee, he had already become known to the American people. But his death at the Alamo made him one of America's most beloved heroes.

After retreating and reorganizing, General Houston now turned against his foe. The Mexicans, marching in three divisions, with the center commanded by Santa Anna himself, were pushing forward in full force, con-

Davy Crockett, hero of the Alamo.

fident that they would easily destroy Houston's little army.

Houston selected Santa Anna's division as his target and made a forced march against it. Houston was victorious, and Santa Anna was captured. On May 14, 1836 Santa Anna signed a treaty acknowledging the independence of Texas, and the Rio Grande became the western boundary of the new republic.

Texas Joins the Union As president of the Republic of Texas, Houston's story was to be the story of Texas, and in a way, the story of Tennessee. Two Tennessee presidents of the United States and many other Tennesseans came to Texas to join Houston in building the republic. James K. Polk was president when the final war was fought for the possession of Texas and the entire Pacific coast of the United States. Andrew Jackson, at the end of his second term, returned to the Hermitage and continued his fight for the annexation of Texas.

After much discussion and negotiation, it was finally agreed that the "Lone Star" Republic of Texas should be annexed to the United States. In March, 1845, Congress passed a resolution annexing the territory. President John Tyler signed the document. In July, 1845, Texas ratified it and became a part of the United States.

JAMES K. POLK

But the final chapters of the story were yet to be written for Mexico did not willingly abide by the treaty. President James K. Polk succeeded Tyler and accepted the responsibility for bringing Texas into the Union as a full-fledged state.

President Polk's life greatly contrasted with the lives of colorful characters like Jackson and Houston. His private life lacked dramatic interest; it was free of sensationalism or scandal.

Early Years James Knox Polk was born in Mecklenburg County, N. C., on November 2, 1795. His father was Major Samuel Polk, son of Colonel Ezekiel Polk who had been important in the Mecklenberg declaration of independence. His mother, Jane Knox, was the daughter of James Knox, a captain in the Revolutionary Army.

About 1806, the Polks established themselves in the fertile Maury County section of Middle Tennessee. They immediately began to take an important part in the development of the area.

Major Samuel Polk first lived about six miles from Columbia, where he had extensive land holdings. There his home was built of logs as was the custom in those early days. Later he built a brick house in Columbia. It is now preserved as the ancestral home of his son who was to become president of the United States.

As a boy, James K. Polk was frail and his education was somewhat delayed because of it. Little more than thirty years passed between the completion of Polk's education and his death. Of this, twenty-four years were spent in the public service. Polk was graduated from the University of North Carolina in 1818, taking the highest honors in his class. In 1819, he began studying law at the office of Felix Grundy, one of Tennessee's most noted lawyers. In 1822, he became the chief clerk of the State House of Representatives and in 1823, was elected to membership in the State Legislature. In

President James K. Polk.

1825, he became a member of the United States House of Representatives which he served for fourteen years. He was chosen Speaker of the House in 1835 and in 1837 was re-elected to that position.

Governor   In 1839, leading Tennessee Democrats and Andrew Jackson, Polk's friend and political ally, urged Polk to come home to run for governor. The Whig sentiment was strong in Tennessee. In 1836, Hugh Lawson White, the Whig candidate for president of the United States had carried Tennessee by about ten thousand votes over Martin Van Buren, Jackson's choice as his successor. And now, the powerful Whig, Newton Cannon, was expected to run and be elected for his third consecutive term. It seemed impossible. that with the strong Whig support, the popular Cannon could be defeated. Yet James K. Polk, faithful to the Democratic party and his friend Jackson, came home to Tennessee to run against Cannon.

In his campaign against Cannon, Polk adopted a technique which contrasted with his scholarly and sedate personality. He employed the custom known as "stump speaking." Use of this term began when a politican would stand on a stump where trees had been cut down and deliver speeches to crowds too large for the small public buildings of the time. Even today, a candidate who goes from place to place making speeches, regardless of the size of the auditorium in which he appears, often is said to be "stumping" the state. Adapting his speeches to his surroundings, Polk engaged in verbal battles with Governor Cannon. He ridiculed him, mocked him, and literally laughed him off the "stump."

In the end, Polk won the election and became governor. At the time, the state, the nation, and the powerful nations of the world were in the midst of a severe financial crisis. During his two years as chief executive, Polk was involved in complicated banking and financial problems. Long experience in the House of Representatives and excellent legal training prepared Polk for handling these problems.

WHIGS AND DEMOCRATS

In 1841, when Polk ran for re-election, he was defeated by a younger man—James Chamberlain (Lean Jimmy) Jones. Born in Wilson County in 1809 Jones was the first native-born governor of Tennessee. He was tall, thin, and probably had the greatest gift of mimicry which had ever been used in Tennessee politics. As a public entertainer and an astute politician, he had no equal. The Whigs thoroughly enjoyed Jones' clever way of turning Polk's own weapons against him.

The race had been so bitter, however, that the General Assembly was hopelessly split during Governor Jones' first term, 1841-43. The Whigs had a small majority in the House of Representatives. In the Senate, there were twelve Whigs and thirteen Democrats. The great clash between the two parties came when the Whigs attempted to elect United States senators. The thirteen Democrats in the Senate, knowing that in a combined ballot of the two houses the Whigs would have a small majority, refused to meet in joint session. This group, "The Immortal Thirteen," led by Andrew Johnson and Samuel H. Laughlin, was successful in preventing the election of senators. Since Governor Jones did not fill the vacancies by appointment, Tennessee was not represented in the United States Senate for two years.

Other actions of this state legislature were the passage of a resolution favoring the annexation of Texas and the enactment of legislation which fixed the permanent state capital at Nashville. Governor Jones and the legislature immediately took steps to have a suitable statehouse built. William Strickland, an architect from Philadelphia, was chosen to design the building. The building took twelve years to complete and was considered by Strickland to be his masterpiece. At his own request, he was buried in the vault which he had built for that purpose in its walls.

After his defeat in 1841, James K. Polk returned to his private law practice in Columbia, Tennessee. But Polk had not retired from the national scene. He was already being considered as a candidate for the vice-presidency in the election of 1844.

A "DARK HORSE" PRESIDENT

When the Baltimore convention met, Polk was not chosen as candidate for the vice-presidency, but for the presidency itself. Thus Polk became the first "dark horse" in the history of American politics. The nomination had been brought about by the campaigning of his friends and the Jackson support in such states as Pennsylvania. Emphasizing his close connection with Andrew Jackson, Polk was immediately dubbed: "Young Hickory." George M. Dallas was nominated for the vice-presidency.

A major issue of the presidential campaign was the admission of Texas to the Union. Polk strongly favored the admission and was bitterly attacked by the abolitionists and anti-slavery groups of the north and

The home of James K. Polk,
built by his father in Columbia, Tennessee.

the east. When he was elected, the state was admitted as a member of the Union.

On March 3, 1845, Congress passed a joint resolution approving the annexation of Texas. On the same day, President John Tyler, whom Polk succeeded, signed the document. Mexico, however, still claimed Texas as one of its provinces.

In his first message, President Polk urged that by an immediate act of Congress, Texas be admitted to the Union with the same rights and privileges as the other states. He then sent an army commanded by General Zachary Taylor into Texas to hold the country. In a short time, the Mexican War broke out. On May 26, 1847, Governor Aaron V.

Brown called for 2,800 volunteers from Tennessee. Thirty thousand responded!

As the war continued, other calls for troops were made and men from Tennessee continued to volunteer in numbers surpassing each call. Many Tennesseans served as distinguished officers and many more served with conspicuous bravery in the ranks. When the war ended and Texas was finally won, "The Volunteer State" had covered itself with glory.

On the day of his inauguration, Polk had outlined to Bancroft, the historian, four measures he hoped to accomplish during his administration: reduction of the tariff; an independent treasury; settlement of the Oregon question; and acquisition of California. In all four he was successful. Before he completed his one term as President of the United States, he had answered the question thrown at his supporters in the Baltimore Convention: "Who is James K. Polk?"

By his policies and negotiations, Polk added a territory to the United States exceeded in size only by Jefferson's Louisiana Purchase. President Polk did not seek re-election for a second term. He was never robust and the burdens of government had rested heavily upon him. Preparing for retirement, he purchased the residence of Felix Grundy in Nashville. To this home, later known as "Polk Place," he came after his administration. Polk was arranging his library and preparing for retirement when he contacted cholera during the epidemic of 1849 and died at the age of fifty-four.

DEMOCRAT AND WHIG GOVERNORS

Between 1845 and 1853, Tennessee had been alternating between the Democrats and the Whigs. After Democrat Aaron

V. Brown was elected in 1845, Neill S. Brown, a Whig, was elected in 1847, and General William Trousdale, a Democrat, succeeded him.

Governor Trousdale's administration saw the completion of the movement to mark the place where Meriwether Lewis died on October 11, 1809. This movement had begun with the appropriation of $500 for that purpose during the administration of Governor Neill Brown. Lewis, commander of the famous Lewis and Clark expedition to Oregon, 1803-1806, had won national fame. For many years Lewis' grave lay unmarked, but a committee of competent historians verified the location and directed the placement of the monument. Years later, the federal government recognized the importance of the site and made it a national park.

In 1851, General William B. Campbell, a Whig, was elected after a lively race against Governor Trousdale, who sought to succeed himself. Both men had splendid military records and both were popular. Trousdale, known as the "War Horse of Sumner County," had served in the War of 1812, the Florida War, and the Mexican War. Campbell had commanded the "Bloody First" regiment in the Mexican War and was also ranked high among the state's heroes. Their race for governor was undoubtedly one of the most courteous ever known to Tennessee history. Although the Whigs won by a small majority, Campbell was to be the last Whig governor.

ANDREW JOHNSON

Governor Campbell, refusing nomination for re-election, retired to private life. Determined to hold power in Tennessee, the Whigs nominated Gustavus A. Henry, the "Eagle Orator," to oppose Andrew Johnson who had been chosen as the Democratic candidate. This was a ruthless, hard-fought campaign.

Andrew Johnson was a powerful orator. He had been a member of the U.S. House of Representatives for ten years. Determined to defeat him, a Whig legislature had redistricted the state in a way which made his re-election highly improbable. In Congress, he had already made a record for himself as champion of the "common man" and for his "Homestead Act," through which vast government lands in the west were opened to families which could not afford to purchase them.

Eventually, Johnson's campaign convinced enough people to assure his election as governor of Tennessee. However, he was still a controversial figure and among an increasing number of people, becoming a very unpopular one. Still he continued his blunt, forceful interpretation of democratic government. He shocked the inaugural committee by refusing to take his place with the outgoing governor in the carriage which was to head the elaborate inaugural parade. Instead, he walked from his hotel on the Nashville public square to the Capitol.

By defeating Henry, Johnson had brought an end to the Whigs in Tennessee. But his chances for re-election at the end of his first term were slim. He was to campaign against Meredith P. Gentry, the candidate of the newly-organized "Know Nothing" party. Never in the history of Tennessee politics has there been a more bitter battle than that fought during the Gentry-Johnson race.

Even before this campaign, the Know Nothings had aroused Johnson's anger. This was a secret organization with secret signs, grips, passwords, and midnight meetings. It

Andrew Johnson, seventeenth president.

was based on intolerant attitudes towards the Irish, the Masons, the Catholics, and foreigners in general. During debates, Johnson expressed his vehement opposition to such attitudes. Johnson certainly did not make this stand in the hope of winning votes. He made it for only one reason — his hatred of injustice and his determination to uphold the guarantees of the Constitution of the United States.

The Gentry-Johnson debates continued for almost three months, gathering momentum and bitterness each day. Andrew Johnson's life was threatened many times; finally, men attending came armed.

The intensity and violence of these debates can be attributed quite as much to the times as to the two men who engaged in

them. The question of slavery, the fight to determine whether new states admitted to the Union would be slave or free, and the writings and speeches of abolitionists and religious fanatics, were exciting both sections of the country to dangerous extremes.

Johnson was accused of being an abolitionist—which he was not. Johnson believed that the ownership of property in slaves was sanctioned by the federal Constitution and until it was changed, the institution must be respected. He was also accused of not being a southern man. In some respects that was true, for Johnson had often voted with those whom the South considered its enemies. He strongly opposed the secessionist sentiment which was already sweeping the South, and certainly did not share the aversion to Abraham Lincoln which most southerners felt.

While campaigning in Memphis, where there were thousands of secessionists, the great question of the day was asked:

"What will you do if Lincoln is elected?"

"As for myself," he answered, "I shall stay inside the Union and there fight for southern rights. I advise all others to do the same."

But the opposition was strong. Whatever his intention may or may not have been, Johnson was winning the hatred of a large portion of Tennessee, as well as the other southern states. Nevertheless, he defeated Gentry and again became governor. At the end of this term, he would run for the United States Senate, and in spite of the mounting opposition, would be elected to serve in that office during one of the most critical times in the nation's history.

A House Divided

THE SOUTH SECEDES

Slavery was the main issue of the presidential election of 1860. Abraham Lincoln, the Republican candidate, declared he would not interfere with slavery where it already existed, but he opposed allowing slavery in the newly formed territories. The Democratic party was divided. The Southern Democrats nominated John C. Breckinridge, who wholly supported the existence and the spread of slavery. The Northern Democrats supported Stephen A. Douglas, who held that the question of slavery should be determined by the popular vote of the people. A fourth candidate, nominated by the Constitutional Union party, was John Bell of Tennessee. He recommended that the solution be sought within the methods set up by the federal Constitution.

Although he won less than half the popular vote, Abraham Lincoln was elected President of the United States. Upon receiving this news, South Carolina seceded from the Union. Mississippi, Florida, Alabama, Georgia, Louisiana, and Texas soon followed South Carolina. On February 4, 1861, these seven states met and formed a new union — The Confederate States of America.

The southern states believed in states' rights. They held that they had freely joined the Union, and therefore they could withdraw from it at will. The northern states disagreed. They considered the secession of the South an act of open rebellion. Lincoln considered the coming conflict not a war against slavery, but rather a war to preserve the Union.

In the beginning of 1861, in a special election, Tennessee voted to stay in the Union. But on April 12, 1861 when the first battle was fought between Confederate and Federal forces at Fort Sumter, popular opinion shifted. Like the other border states, Virginia, North Carolina, and Arkansas, Tennessee could not openly fight her southern cousins.

A special session of the Tennessee legislature was held. The state declared itself on the side of the Confederacy, seceded from the Union, and began to raise troops, arms, and money. This action was ratified by the people, and on June 24, 1861 Governor Harris declared Tennessee's independence and joined the Confederacy.

By the end of 1861, the Confederates in Tennessee had made splendid progress in their war effort. Their factories were producing, the harvest had been completed, thousands of men were in the field, and the people were contributing to the cause.

TENNESSEE'S FIRST BATTLE

The new year had hardly begun when the Confederates suffered their first major blow. On January 19, 1862, at the Battle of Fishing Creek, near Somerset, Kentucky, General Felix K. Zollicoffer, a brilliant and popular man, was killed. Under a flag of truce, granted by General George H. Thomas, the Confederate general's body was brought back to Nashville for burial.

This battle, though fought beyond its borders, soon made Tennessee the battle-

A soldier's sketch of Union forces crossing Fishing Creek. The defeat of the Confederates here left Forts Donelson and Henry open to attack.

ground of the West. Two important forts, Fort Henry on the Tennessee River and Fort Donelson on the Cumberland River, were attacked by the Union Army. Fort Henry, attacked first, was commanded by Brigadier-General Lloyd Tighlman, with a force of 2,610 men.

General Ulysses S. Grant, yet unknown but later to become commander-in-chief of the Union armies, began shelling Fort Henry on February 4, 1862. He was supported by seven gunboats, commanded by Flag Officer A. H. Foote. Holding out until February 6, General Tighlman ordered Colonel Heiman to lead the greater part of the command to Fort Donelson. Tighlman and a group of sixty-six men held out for two hours, during which they damaged two of the Union gun-

boats. Seven of the fort's eleven guns had been put out of commission, and Tighlman surrendered after the main body of his men had had time to move to Fort Donelson. This was the first battle fought on Tennessee soil.

Next in line for attack was Fort Donelson. On the morning of February 12, General Grant, with an army estimated at between thirty and fifty thousand men, marched across the narrow neck of land which separated the two forts and began the attack. Grant also had six Federal gunboats, but these were soon disabled and out of the battle. The Confederate force, estimated at between twelve and twenty thousand men, was commanded by Generals Pillow, Buckner, Johnson and Floyd.

On February 13, the attack on General Johnson's left wing was repulsed. The next day the Union gunboats were forced out of the battle by Confederate fire. On February 15, when it seemed that the Confederates were winning, a misunderstanding arose between the generals with the result that Generals Floyd and Pillow turned the command over to General Buckner and left. Meanwhile, General Albert Sidney Johnston had telegraphed, "If you lose the fort, bring your troops to Nashville, if possible."

General Buckner decided to surrender. But Lieutenant Colonel Nathan Bedford Forrest disagreed and led his cavalry in an escape. Meeting no Federal opposition, they made their way to Nashville.

On February 16, General Grant, part of whose forces were already in retreat, accepted with some surprise the surrender of Fort Donelson and about 15,000 Confederate troops. Now the way to Nashville lay undefended.

THE FALL OF NASHVILLE

Nashville, capital of Tennessee, was, the prize target in the West and it was here,

within a few days that Grant would probably make another attack. Knowing this, and shocked by Buckner's surrender, Governor Harris and General Albert Sidney Johnston, with the aid of civil and military leaders, prepared to evacuate the city and remove all possible military stores.

When Forrest arrived in Nashville on the morning of February 18, the city was in the hands of a mob which respected neither public nor private property. Wagon loads of food and other goods from the stores were being carried away for private use. Valuable military goods were abandoned instead of being carried to safety beyond the city limits. Forrest was put in command of the military supplies and soon brought about enough order to begin moving them beyond the reach of the invading army, expected at any moment. Food and other materials which could not be moved were given to the citizens.

General Buell, in command of the Union forces, had arrived in Edgefield, and the Union gunboats were on the river. Forrest calmly going about his work, did not make any move to leave until Buell was actually entering the city. He then followed General

Union gunboats operating on the Mississippi River.

Albert Sidney Johnston in his forced retreat, covering the army's rear.

Meanwhile, Buell had made terms for the surrender of Nashville with public officials. On February 24, Federal troops occupied the city without firing a shot. The Confederate flag was lowered and the Stars and Stripes were hoisted over the Capital. Confederate government in Tennessee was at an end.

THE BATTLE OF SHILOH

Leaving Nashville to the enemy, Johnston retreated to Corinth, Mississippi. All of Middle Tennessee was now open to the invading Union Army. Ordered to follow Johnston, Grant moved a force of some 40,000 men to Pittsburgh Landing, Tennessee, about thirty miles north of Corinth.

Generals Johnston and Beauregard, knowing that Buell would soon join Grant with more men, decided to attack at once. The two armies met on April 6, 1862, in what has become known as the Battle of Shiloh (for a church on the battlefield). On the first day Grant barely managed to hold his line in the face of a furious Confederate assault which cost General Johnston his life. The following day, with additional troops from Buell, Grant forced Beauregard to retreat back to Corinth.

After Shiloh, the war gained momentum. Island Number 10 in the Mississippi River was captured by Union troops on April 8, and on May 13 Corinth fell, leaving Memphis defenseless. On June 6, after a spectacular naval battle with the Confederate fleet, Memphis fell and was occupied by Union troops. Control of the Mississippi River was fast passing into the hands of the Union, for less than a month before, on April 24, a Union fleet commanded by a Tennessean, Admiral David G. Farragut, attacking from the south, captured New Orleans.

ANDREW JOHNSON, MILITARY GOVERNOR

In March, 1862, following the fall of Nashville, President Lincoln appointed Andrew Johnson, a member of the United States Senate although his state had seceded, as military governor of Tennessee. Even then, Lincoln was thinking of "reconstructing" the seceded states and bringing them back into the Union. In Tennessee, he saw an opportunity to make a model for restoration of the Union. It seemed fortunate that Johnson, a loyal Union man, was available for this experiment. He was also an East Tennessean, and both he and President Lincoln expected that part of the state to take an important part in the work of bringing the state back into the Union.

In spite of his political power and support of the Union armies, Andrew Johnson was powerless to establish a legitimate state government. The Union sympathizers themselves were divided. Most of them were southern men and, despite loyalty for the Union, were in sympathy with the southern way of life. Others, like Brownlow, were extreme Radicals. Conservative Unionists disapproved of secession, although many of them were slaveholders. It was for this reason that President Lincoln, in his Emancipation Proclamation, exempted Tennessee—by simply omitting its name. Other sections of the south occupied by Union troops were also omitted, but all, or most, of them were designated by name.

After the Emancipation Proclamation was issued on January 1, 1863, Abraham Lincoln wrote his military governor a very frank

At Shiloh, the Union Army barely withstood the initial Confederate attack. On the second day, however, the reinforced Union troops forced the Confederates to retreat.

letter, expressing, among other things, his doubts about his own re-election: "Hon. Andrew Johnson: All Tennessee is now clear of insurrectionists. You need not be reminded that it is the nick of time for reinaugurating a loyal State government. Not a moment should be lost. You and your co-operating friends can better judge of the ways and means than can be judged by any here . . . It is something on the question of time to remember that it cannot be known who is next to occupy the position I now hold, nor what he will do. I see that you have declared in favor of emancipation in Tennessee, for which may God bless you. Get emancipation into your new State government constitution and there will be no such word as fail for your case. The raising of colored troops, I think, will greatly help every way. Yours, very truly, A. LINCOLN."

Another reason for Johnson's failure to organize a state government was the presence of Southern cavalry units commanded by men such as Nathan Bedford Forrest, John Morgan, Joe Wheeler, "Red" W. H. Jackson, and others.

THE BATTLE OF MURFREESBORO

The day after Christmas, 1862, General W. S. Rosecrans left Nashville with over 40,000 Federal troops to attack Bragg and his Confederate Army of Tennessee at Murfreesboro. Rosecrans was put to a great disadvantage, however, by General Wheeler's cavalry raid on his forces on December 29. Wheeler skirting Rosecrans' army, destroyed most of the four wagon trains which carried Union supplies for the forthcoming siege. Completing this action successfully, Wheeler reached Bragg in time to take part in the opening day's battle on December 31.

Both armies, during the three-day battle suffered terrific losses, but the fighting was not a complete victory for either side. Robert Selph Henry, in his book, *The Story*

This battlefield monument stands in tribute to the brave men who fought at Shiloh.

of the Confederacy, says: "The next day, January third, both armies remained in position, watching and wondering who had won the battle. During the night of January third, Bragg settled the question. He withdrew from the field and took up winter quarters in Tullahoma. . . ."

THE BATTLE OF CHICKAMAUGA

In the fall of 1863, Rosecrans moved against Chattanooga and Bragg's army. When Bragg retreated, Rosecrans, not realizing that he was badly outnumbered, set off in hot pursuit. Bragg turned, and on September 19 crossed the Chickamauga, opening what was to be one of the bloodiest battles of the war. For two days the battle raged, at great cost of lives to both sides.

After heavy fighting during the first day, darkness brought a lull. The next day's fighting was even worse, for the situation of the Union forces grew more desperate hour by hour. Only General George H. Thomas, of the Union Army, held his line. From his staunch resistance he earned his nickname: "The Rock of Chickamauga." Rosecrans, with his shattered army, retired to the little city of Chattanooga—to starve. Bragg's forces occupied Lookout Mountain, Missionary Ridge, and other high ground south of the city, completely cutting off the Union forces from their supply base.

THE BATTLE OF CHATTANOOGA

The Union Army took immediate steps to relieve the troops cut off in Chattanooga. Sherman was ordered up from Vicksburg and Hooker down from Virginia. Grant, now in complete command, replaced Rosecrans with Thomas.

The strongly reinforced Union troops were assembling for battle, but General Bragg, had foolishly divided his forces after the Chickamauga victory. Longstreet had been

The Battle of Chickamauga (above) ended in a defeat for the Union Army. One of the bloodiest battles of the war, this victory cost the Confederates some 17,000 men. The quiet and serenity of Chickamauga today (below), now a National Military Park, tells little of the intensity of the battle that raged here in 1863.

sent to fight Burnside at Knoxville and Wheeler, who was desperately needed at Chattanooga, was sent with him. A number of his leading officers had already protested this action, but his force faced the enemy in a seriously weakened condition.

On November 23, General Thomas moved from his position across the valley from Bragg to the foot of Missionary Ridge. Sherman crossed the Tennessee during the night and, by the morning of November 24, was in position for action.

The weather, however, contributed nothing to their prospects for the day. It was one of those cold, gloomy November days — cloudy, with mist and fog obscuring the landscape to such an extent that the mountaintops were scarcely visible. Hooker and his command managed to scale the cliffs of Lookout Mountain, drag themselves to the top, and take this strategic point from the Confederates defending it.

Weather improved on the next day—the skies were clear and the sun shone brightly. The situation of the Confederates who were fighting bravely against heavy odds had not improved. They courageously contested every step of the enemy's advance, and even Sherman's command was endangered. More than once Union troops went forward without orders from their officers. The most remarkable of these advances was at the foot of Missionary Ridge, when the men who had been ordered by Thomas to take certain Confederate rifle pits took them—and simply kept on going until they had routed the enemy and had taken the Ridge.

Bragg retired to Ringgold, Georgia. In his report he placed responsibility for the disastrous defeat upon his men—but they and the southern people placed the blame upon Bragg himself, who had so foolishly divided his forces in the face of the enemy.

After the first day's battle, Longstreet had been ordered back from Knoxville to join Bragg. Before he could obey, the battle was over and Grant had sent Sherman to the aid of Burnside at Knoxville. Sherman, being then between Bragg and Longstreet, prevented any possibility of their joining forces. There was nothing for Longstreet to do but to move up the valley above Knoxville, where he remained until the spring of 1864, holding the last section of Confederate territory in the State. His presence there did not greatly affect the military situation, though it was annoying to the politicians who besieged Lincoln to free East Tennessee from the invader.

NATHAN BEDFORD FORREST, CAVALRY HERO

During the spring and summer of 1863, there were cavalry raids in Middle Tennessee. Some of them ranged from around Nashville to the northern borders of Tennessee, northern Mississippi, Alabama and Georgia, where Nathan Bedford Forrest was fighting. Most spectacular of these was Forrest's famous Streight's raid. General Rosecrans, during the latter part of April, had ordered Colonel Abel D. Streight, of Indiana, with two thousand cavalry, to move up the Tennessee River to North Alabama, where General Grenville M. Dodge, of Grant's command, was stationed. From there, Streight was to cross North Alabama and Georgia until he reached the railroad from Atlanta to Chattanooga, where he was ordered to destroy it, thereby cutting off General Bragg's supplies.

Streight, leaving the area of Dodge's command on April 26, headed toward Rome, Georgia. Ninety miles away, Nathan Bedford Forrest, ordered into northern Alabama to oppose Dodge's eastward advance, heard

The relentless Nathan Bedford Forrest leads his troops through the snow.

of Streight's movements and, with a handful of his cavalry, started out in hot pursuit. Reaching the top of Sand Mountain on April 20, he found Streight and attacked at once, starting a three-day running battle. Streight, with his larger group, commandeered all fresh horses in the countryside, leaving his sore-footed ones behind. Forrest had no such advantage, but his men and his horses kept close on the heels of the enemy.

Streight, crossing the Big Black Creek, burned the bridge behind him, and rode on feeling confident that the pursuit would be delayed or stopped. Had it not been for a courageous southern girl this might have been true. Stopping at the house of Widow Sanson, near Gadsden, Alabama, Forrest inquired about a crossing. One of her daughters, Emma, said that she knew of an almost

forgotten ford and would show it to them. She was placed on Forrest's horse behind him and raced with him to the ford. On the other side, Union sharp-shooters began to fire. Forrest, helping her down, got her to safety, but not before her wide skirts had been riddled by bullets. He then began crossing his men as fast as possible and continued the wild pursuit.

Near Rome, Georgia, on Sunday, May 3, Streight surrendered with his whole command.

Throughout 1864, Forrest had been in northern Mississippi repelling repeated expeditions sent from Memphis to open the way to the Gulf of Mexico and take Mobile, the only Southern port not in the hands of the enemy. General Sherman had ordered that Forrest be taken, demanding that his generals bring him in "dead or alive." But each time they were driven back to Memphis in defeat and disgrace.

In midsummer, 1864, General A. J. Smith, on his second expedition, nearly succeeded. Forrest, badly beaten in an earlier fight with Smith, had retreated before him to the town of Oxford, Mississippi, where Smith stood before him with a superior force. Since he could not meet Smith in battle with any hope of success, Forrest decided upon another plan. He left General Chalmers with half of his men, and with the other half, slipped out at dusk on August 18, and headed for Memphis. Memphis, one hundred miles away, was strongly fortified, and in that city General Hurlbut and General Washburn, felt secure.

Forrest made his way through mud, rain, and swollen rivers and creeks, stopping sometimes to direct his men and join with them in building bridges. At dawn on Sunday, August 21, Forrest and his men rushed into Memphis in one of the wildest and most incredible attacks known to military history. On the way to Memphis his force had been reduced by eliminating men and horses which had become exhausted. The attack had been well-planned and, in the heavy fog, the attackers had slipped in without arousing Union pickets. However, with the first encounter, Gaus, the veteran bugler, sounded the charge. With wild Rebel yells, the men dashed into the heart of the city, each group having its previously assigned objective—for Forrest and many of his men knew Memphis well.

Colonel Bill Forrest, brother of the General, with his men galloped wildly to the Gayosa House and rode into the lobby, where they left their horses in charge of orderlies. They searched the rooms, looking for General Hurlbut, who had a room there, but on that night had stayed elsewhere.

Another group, sent to capture General Washburn, also had bad luck. The general managed to escape before the Confederates arrived at his quarters, but in his haste, the general fled in his night clothes to avoid capture. Others were not so fortunate. A number of Washburn's officers were captured and carried out of the city in their night clothes. Rich hauls of military supplies, horses and food were made.

Smith, in disgrace, was recalled from Oxford, and Forrest, hailed as the savior of Mississippi, was called by General Dabney H. Maury, to come to Mobile. Finding that at that moment, Mobile, was not in danger, Forrest was ordered back to Tennessee.

In the latter part of October and early November, Forrest and his men went into West Tennessee on their last and most remarkable, raid. At Johnsonville, on the Tennessee River, there were large stores of Union property and, to guard it, a number of gunboats patrolled the river. Forrest conceived the idea of attacking these great warehouses and, by skillful maneuvering, made a land attack on the Yankee Navy in which he destroyed the town, burning three gunboats, eleven steamers and fifteen barges, and also burned most of the stores on the landings and in the warehouses.

THE FINAL CAMPAIGN

Meanwhile, after the battle of Missionary Ridge, both General Grant and General Sherman had returned to Nashville, where they conferred frequently over the spring campaign of 1864. In March, President Lincoln made General Grant, who was at that time in Nashville, commander-in-chief of the Union armies. Grant had a three-pronged offensive in mind. General Meade would move against General Lee in northern Virginia and take Richmond; General Sherman would proceed from Chattanooga, advance into Georgia, and capture Atlanta; General Banks would strike from New Orleans at Montgomery, Alabama, and then link up with Sherman. Grant himself, would accompany Meade and the Army of the Potomac.

Nashville, overcrowded with Union troops and the materiel of war, could barely handle the stores of supplies and animals Sherman was assembling for his campaign. Railway cars which carried shipments to Nashville from Louisville were commandeered and sent to Chattanooga loaded with guns, ammunition, and other supplies. Men and animals were also sent on foot. The redheaded, high-tempered general who had declared that "war is hell," prepared to give Georgia a taste of it at its worst.

Reaching Chattanooga at the appointed time, Sherman and Grant began their marches simultaneously early in May. Both were stubbornly resisted. Meanwhile, Banks, had been so badly defeated by General Richard Taylor at the Battle of Pleasant Hill on April 9 that he was no longer an effective force in Grant's strategy.

The Fall of Atlanta

As Sherman neared Atlanta, after a series of hit-and-run encounters with Confederate forces, President Davis, displeased with the way General Johnston was conducting the resistance, gave the Confederate command to General Hood. Hood failed to stop the Union forces, and on September 2, 1864, Sherman marched into Atlanta.

Hood now elected to invade Tennessee, confident that if Sherman would follow he could defeat him in mountainous terrain. Sherman however, ordered General Thomas to undertake the defense of Tennessee and gave him General John Schofield and some 30,000 troops for this purpose. Then he began his famous "March to the Sea."

The Battle of Franklin

Crossing the Tennessee River on November 16, Hood pushed northward and by November 29 was at Spring Hill, Tennessee. Here, by some freak of fortune, the Union forces, under Schofield, marched by unnoticed during the night and made their way to Franklin. The next day just before dark, Hood's army reached Franklin and fought one of the bloodiest battles of the war.

Much of the fierce battle centered around the Carter House, where some of the worst fighting occurred. The Confederates lost about 4,500 killed, wounded, and captured; the Federals some 2,300.

The Battle of Nashville

The victory, however, went to neither side, for Schofield immediately fell back toward Nashville. On December 1, Hood followed and for two weeks stood before Nashville waiting to engage General Thomas in battle.

The main cause for Thomas' delay was a terrible siege of winter weather—the cold rains had turned into sleet and ice which covered the ground. Finally, on December 15, the ice had melted and Thomas came out to make the attack.

Furious fighting broke out along a crescent-shaped line which extended from the Cumberland river, on the east side of the city, to Charlotte Pike on the west. The greatest concentration was in the neighborhood of Franklin Pike, where Confederate General Stephen D. Lee's line crossed the pike at Thompson Lane.

At the end of the first day the Confederate line fell back southward toward Brentwood Hills, where the line of the second day's battle formed. It, too, resulted in defeat for Hood's army—but not in its capture. Covered by Forrest's cavalry, Hood retreated into Mississippi.

THE CONFEDERACY SURRENDERS

General Johnston was restored to command, and with his men went into the Carolinas to try to halt Sherman in his drive north from Savannah to join Grant. But it was too late. On Sunday, April 9, 1865, at Appomattox Court House in Virginia, General Robert E. Lee surrendered to General Ulysses S. Grant. When this news reached North Carolina, General Johnston surrendered to General Sherman.

Sherman, who had declared that "war is hell," and had done all in his power to make it so, exhibited amazing consideration and generosity in his terms of surrender.

On April 26, the formal surrender of Johnston's army took place—on the same terms as those on which General Grant had accepted General Lee's surrender. On May 4, General Richard Taylor made terms with General Canby for the surrender of all the troops in the far South—which included General Forrest's command. These troops were the last to surrender east of the Mississippi River.

General Forrest, knowing that surrender was inevitable, struggled for several days to decide upon his future course. He wanted to march to Texas or to Mexico with those of his men who wanted to go. Finally, he decided to yield to the wishes of those who preferred to remain at home and help rebuild the country. In his farewell address to his men he told them:

". . . The cause for which you have braved dangers, endured privations and sufferings, and made so many sacrifices, is today hopeless. The government which we sought to establish and perpetuate is at an end. Reason dictates and humanity demands that no more blood be shed . . . It is your duty and mine to lay down our arms, submit to 'the powers that be,' and to aid in restoring peace and establishing law and order throughout the land . . ."

Amid these promising proceedings, the news of the assassination of President Abraham Lincoln on April 14, 1865, came like a thunderbolt. Sherman and Johnston alike were stunned by it. On April 18, in a dispatch to General H. W. Halleck, Chief of Staff, General Sherman described its effect:

". . . The news of Mr. Lincoln's death produced a most intense effect on our troops. At first I feared it would lead to excesses, but now it has softened down and can easily be guided. None evinced more feeling than General Johnston, who admitted that the act was calculated to strain his cause with a dark hue, and he contended that the loss was most serious to the people of the South, who had begun to realize that Mr. Lincoln was the best friend the South had . . ."

In radical Northern circles, however, Sherman's generosity brought a storm of criticism, new terms for the treaty with Johnston were demanded, and Sherman was ordered to resume hostilities. Sherman, however, held stubbornly to his course, though he was powerless to control the acts of radical politicians.

"I believe this assassination of Mr. Lincoln will do the cause of the South more harm than any event of the war, both at home and abroad, and I doubt if the Confederate military authorities had any more complicity with it than I did . . ."

Johnston surrenders to Sherman after the news of Lee's surrender to Grant at Appomattox.

The War's Aftermath

TENNESSEE RETURNS TO THE UNION

When the government of the Confederacy collapsed, all civil government and administration in the South disappeared. No money was available for the support of the state governments and there was no authority to collect taxes. Union troops were brought in to preserve order and many cities, such as Chattanooga, Nashville, Memphis and Knoxville were under military occupation.

In areas where federal troops were not available, roving bands of maurauders looted and terrorized citizens. Farms were ravaged, machinery broken, and the great transportation systems built before the war were useless. Andrew Johnson tried to take advantage of every opening, but he was unable to set up a civil government during the politically eventful year of 1864. He did, however, win second place on the presidential ticket. In the fall of 1864 he was elected Vice-President of the United States. It was not until the early part of 1865, that he was able to set up a government which seemed sufficient to gain Tennessee's re-admission to the Union. The convention that he called for this purpose granted Tennessee slaves their freedom, set up machinery for a state government, and manipulated the election of "Parson" William G. Brownlow as Governor of Tennessee.

President Lincoln had outlined a plan under which seceded states could be returned to the Union. If 10% of the people who voted in the next election and take a loyalty oath in support of the Union, a new state government could be formed and recognized. It was his position and Johnson's that the States had never been out of the Union, and, when the rebellion was quelled, they could return to the Union and enjoy their former rights and privileges. The so-called Convention authorized Governor Johnson to issue a proclamation for an election to be held on February 22—an election

A soldier surveys the twisted wreckage of a railroad line. When the war was over, much of the South was in ruins. Many of the railroads that had played such a large part in the prosperity of Tennessee were destroyed.

The home of Andrew Johnson. Johnson tried to carry out his plan for Reconstruction but eventually failed.

in which only unconditional Union men could vote.

Having arranged these things, Andrew Johnson went to Washington where he and Abraham Lincoln were inaugurated on March 4th. From that moment, Johnson was to be the subject of scathing abuse, for he was undoubtedly under the influence of intoxicants and made a spectacle of himself during the inaugural ceremonies. The enemy press made it sound much worse than it was, but it was bad enough at best. The incident was never forgotten, although it in no way affected Johnson's future usefulness. He was in no sense then, before or afterward, a drunkard.

The election was held and, the total vote —26,865 to 67—was large enough to amount to ten per cent of the vote cast for President in 1860, which Abraham Lincoln had demanded for reinstatement. The final step in Tennessee's re-admission to the Union came in 1866 with the ratification of the fourteenth amendment to the Constitution ensuring Negroes the right to vote.

It was boasted then, and has been through the years that Tennessee was last to leave the Union and the first to return. The state-

ment is true, although the State was taken into the Union on the basis of acts by an illegally constituted convention in January, 1865; an illegal election in February, 1865; and the fraudulently reported ratification of the 14th Amendment to the Constitution of the United States, during the special session of the State Legislature in July 1866. By a joint resolution approved July 24, 1866, Tennessee was readmitted to the Union, the first of the seceding States to return.

THE BROWNLOW REGIME

William G. Brownlow took office on April 5, 1865. Under his Radical Unionist regime the Tennesseans who had fought under Forrest, Johnston, and others did not come home to peace and an opportunity to rebuild their war-torn states. They came home to a new kind of war—a political war in which they were denied even the weapons to protect themselves. They were denied the right to vote, to serve in public office, or to participate in making laws by which they were governed. Obstacles were created for those who attempted to establish themselves in business or the professions. Titles to lands which they owned were endangered by Radicals in Brownlow's legislature who sought to confiscate property of all those who had served in the Confederate Army or who had aided the Confederate cause. The Radicals felt that all Confederate supporters were guilty of treason and should be punished harshly.

One of the first acts of Governor Brownlow's legislature was the passing of the Franchise Act which took away the right to vote from anyone who had willingly supported the Confederacy. No one was allowed to vote unless he could show proof that he had never been against the Union. A certificate signed by a commissioner and supported by the testimony of two well-known Union men was required at the polls.

Brownlow also accused ex-Governor Isham G. Harris, who had announced Tennessee's secession, of treason and offered a five-thousand-dollar reward for his capture. Because of this, Harris was forced into exile in Mexico, and, for a year, in England, where he established a commercial business. In his message of July 1, 1867, however, Governor Brownlow advised the repeal of the offer of this reward.

Many other harsh laws were passed. Men recently discharged from the Union Army could carry fire-arms while ex-Confederates could not. Criticism of the Brownlow administration or the Federal Government was forbidden.

In 1867, the Congress empowered Brownlow to call up a state militia, but with the provision that the "Tennessee State Guards shall be composed of loyal men," men who would swear their allegiance and had never been disloyal to the Union. This excluded all ex-Confederates and Confederate sup-

porters. Oppression was fast becoming intolerable.

Carpet-baggers descended upon the state. The term "carpet-bagger" applied to the northerner who had come South, carrying all his possessions—said to have been nothing more than a dirty shirt and a worn pair of socks—in a carpet-bag who had invaded Tennessee to prosper on its misfortunes and seek public office.

The term "carpet-bagger" was never applied to the northerners who came South to invest labor or capital in the great effort to rebuild the South. Their aid was eagerly sought by the best class of southern business and professional men. And, when it was obtained, the newcomers were received, made to feel at home, and soon actually became Tennesseans.

This effort to bring new capital and new labor to Tennessee had begun when the first men returned home from the battlefields. It had been hampered, to a great extent, by the unsettled political condition of the State and the disturbances which followed Brownlow's drastic policies.

In spite of these difficulties the real work of reconstruction, the actual rebuilding of the state, was going on. Northern soldiers who chose to remain in the state, immigrants who came to seek their fortunes and, especially, a band of conservative Unionists of Tennessee, worked with the disfranchised Confederates until the battle was won.

The important fact—and, the one that mattered most to the disfranchised Confederates, was that federal and state relations were restored and that many Union men opposing the radical Brownlow regime could participate in and, perhaps influence the federal government. Such men—even in his own hand-picked legislature—had gone far toward opposing Brownlow in his course of persecution and misuse of the powers of government, but the time had not yet come for ending his disastrous regime. In time, Tennessee, other Southern states, and the nation were restored by the labor of the best and most reasonable men on both sides.

Again, Nathan Bedford Forrest was a great leader. General Forrest, with a $2,000,000 fortune at the beginning of the war, now had nothing but his lands. He brought several Union officers home with him and helped get them established; he tried his hand at railroad building, operated his plantation, ignored as much as possible the radical politicians, and exerted his influence which even disfranchisement could not curtail.

Loyal Leagues The Loyal Leagues were branches of the Union League of America, a Northern organization that had tried to control Negro votes. The Loyal Leagues promised to meet the economic and social demands of the Negro, and many Negroes, coping with the problems which faced them as they enjoyed their new freedom, had joined these organizations.

Since the South had always been Democratic in political sentiment, Republicans like Governor Brownlow, cooperated with the organizers of the Loyal Leagues, the carpetbaggers, because their Republican government depended on the Negro vote. These local Republicans were referred to as "scalawags" and were much hated.

The attempt by the Brownlow regime to organize the enfranchised ex-slaves caused much bitterness in the ex-Confederates who were still unable to vote. Resentment toward the discrimination against Confederate supporters grew. There was no approach to the carpetbag and scalawag governments which

had been established in every county and city by Brownlow.

The state of affairs had become so desperate that even the most levelheaded men began to realize that drastic action would have to be taken.

The Ku Klux Klan In Pulaski, Tennessee, a group of young ex-soldiers had formed, largely for their own entertainment, a sort of social club which they called the Ku Klux Klan. The group was at first no different than any other fraternal organization. The group was bound to secrecy and, dressed as ghosts, adopted the habit of nightly visits to scare people. They pretended that they were the ghosts of ex-Confederate soldiers. The Negroes were very superstitious and the Klan found them very easy to frighten.

At first, the Klan did no more than this. But soon the mysterious organization began to make its appearance at meetings of the Loyal Leagues with the intention of breaking them up. Often, some of the Klansmen would ride into the crowds, shouting "Hurrah for Jeff Davis" and shooting into the air. If this did not break up the meeting, more drastic measures were taken. Gradually the Klansmen succeeded in discouraging the organizers of the Loyal Leagues and reduced the attendance at the meetings.

Other ex-Confederates saw in the Klan the chance to protect themselves from the scalawag Brownlow regime, and the carpetbaggers. They knew it would lead to more persecution to defy the Radicals openly, but through the Klan they had the opportunity to work in secret. Many ex-Confederates joined the various branches of the Klan that had sprung up throughout the South. Nathan Bedford Forrest became its Imperial Wizard. The Klan's declared purpose

Ku Klux Klan members preparing to burn a wheatfield.

was to maintain "all that is chivalric in conduct, noble in sentiment, generous in manhood, and patriotic in purpose."

Soon a rougher element joined the organization, floggings and murders were committed, and the Radical Republican element in the government and the Negroes were being persecuted. Governor Brownlow denounced the Klan, and anti-Ku Klux Klan legislation was passed making membership in the organization punishable by fine and imprisonment.

In March, 1870, only a few weeks after Brownlow's resignation, the Grand Wizard of the Ku Klux Klan issued an order for the disbanding of that organization. In his message he declared that the objects for which it had been formed had been accomplished, and that the Klansmen had come to the time when their services were no longer needed. Members were ordered to burn their uniforms and other evidences of their existence and to disband quietly and permanently. This was the end of the original Ku Klux Klan. Loyal Leagues also disappeared, for the times were no longer conducive to their well-being.

Unfortunately, however, activities somewhat similar to those of the Ku Klux Klan continued and, in many instances, resulted in atrocities which would never have been committed by the original Klan. This and similar organizations were active within the Southern states, most of which were still under strict military rule and carpetbag legislatures.

The present organization has no connection whatever with the original one, which was created and allowed to continue to protect the helpless women and children when no other means were possible; and to protect the lives of former Confederate soldiers. As soon as a semblance of law and order was restored, the original Ku Klux Klan was abandoned forever.

During the Brownlow administration the State Legislature was in session almost constantly. To keep himself and his political machine in power, the Governor found it necessary to have enacted more and more stringent legislation. Re-elected for a second term in 1867, Brownlow had seemed confident that he at last had the state under his control. But the rise of the Ku Klux Klan, counteracted the efforts of the Loyal League to stir up strife, and at the same time, gave to disenfranchised ex-Confederates some hope of defending themselves and their families against the lawlessness and brutality of Brownlow's militia. His heavy-handed tactics also lost him the support of the Democratic moderates and Conservatives within his administration who had wanted order restored as soon as possible.

Brownlow, after having wreaked vengeance upon a disarmed, disfranchised people, and having split his own party, was elected by the legislature to serve in the United States Senate to succeed David T. Patterson, son-in-law of President Johnson. He resigned the office of Governor on February 25, 1869 and was succeeded by the Speaker of the State Senate, DeWitt Clinton Senter, of Grainger County, Tennessee.

DEWITT C. SENTER

Governor Senter was a conservative Union man. He was born in Grainger County, Tennessee, March 26, 1830, the son of William Tandy Senter, a farmer, and Methodist preacher, who had served one term in Congress. Senter had studied law and, like many lawyers, was also a farmer. He had served in the State Legislature both before the War and during the Brownlow regime. However, his accession to the Governor's chair was hailed by the disfranchised men of Tennessee, for he was known to be a man of high principles.

The State Legislature, in 1867, had given the franchise to Negro voters, but had done nothing to ease the restrictions on disfranchised white men. By the time Senter became governor it had become evident that action should be taken on this and other important questions. Senter, with only a few months of Brownlow's term to serve, had to be elected governor before he could take any real action.

On assuming the governor's chair, he had promptly announced his candidacy. The Radical Republicans, determined to regain power, called a State Convention, which met in Nashville on May 20, 1869. On the first day, there was an effort to seat a friend of Governor Senter as presiding officer, which ended such disorder that the convention broke up. The second day was even worse, and the convention adjourned in great confusion, the delegates for Governor Senter and those for Col. William B. Stokes, his opponent, meeting in separate places to make their own nominations.

A joint debate between the two candidates began in Nashville on the fifth of June and continued until the election on August 5, 1869. The elective franchise and the necessity of holding a State Constitutional Convention to consider it were the chief subjects of debate.

Colonel Stokes, on this question, declared: "When the killing of Union men ceases and the hellish organization of the Ku Klux Klan is abandoned, then I am willing to entertain a proposition to amend the State Constitution so far as to allow the disfranchised to come in gradually, providing that the Legislature may by a two-thirds vote remove the disabilities of those who petition, and come well recommended by their loyal neighbors."

But Colonel Stokes was to have no voice in the matter. Disfranchised ex-Confederates promised Senter that they would vote for him if given a chance, so he, exercising the same laws which Brownlow's Radical followers had provided for him, removed a large percentage of Radical Republican election officials and filled the vacancies with conservative Republicans. Senter won by a majority of over 65,000 votes.

Under Senter's administration, the State Legislature which met October 4, 1869, was Democratic for the first time since 1861, and the Confederate element, under the leadership of General John C. Brown, had gained control of the State. An act submitting the question of holding a constitutional convention was submitted to the state and was passed with the provision that ". . . every male person not convicted and rendered infamous for crime, of the age of twenty-one years, being a citizen of the United States, and a citizen of the county where he may offer his vote six months next preceding the day of election, is hereby authorized to assemble on the third Saturday in December, 1869 . . . and vote for or against calling a convention . . . and no certificate or other qualifications than the foregoing, shall be required . . ."

There was a 40,000 majority in favor of holding the convention, which assembled on January 10, 1870. It has been generally called one of the most intelligent assemblies which ever convened in Tennessee.

This convention made no major change in the Constitution which had served the State since 1834, although new conditions brought about by the war might have justified minor ones. Concentrating on removing the political disabilities of a large part of its population, the leaders avoided anything which might cause controversy and centered its efforts on the elective franchise. The final provisions gave suffrage to Negroes as well as to disfranchised whites, and left to them the details of restoring the state to its former prestige and prosperity.

GOVERNORS AFTER SENTER

John C. Brown John C. Brown, a democrat, followed Senter as governor in 1871. Governor Brown, when he assumed office, was confronted with problems which would have overwhelmed him, had not the recent victory given to him and to the true leaders of the State a new hope and new confidence that they could solve these problems. But, when Governor Brown made his inaugural address—in fact until 1877—Federal troops were still stationed in Nashville.

When Governor Brown took office, Tennessee was in ruins. Its people were impoverished; its treasury burdened by a staggering debt; state penal, charitable, and educational institutions in shambles; many railroads bankrupt; a public school system almost non-existent; and roads made practically impassable by the passage of heavy military vehicles. The three governors who succeeded him—James D. Porter, 1875-79; Albert S. Marks 1879-81; and Alvin Hawkins, 1881-83; faced identical problems. Both Porter and Marks had served with distinction and honor as Confederate Officers. Governor Hawkins, a strong Union man, was elected when the Democratic party had split and put two candidates in the field, allowing him to win by a small margin. He also was a man of ability and devoted to the state, but could do little more than progress, slowly toward the time when growing material prosperity would help solve many problems.

William B. Bate The chief problems facing General Bate when he became Governor in 1883 were those of refunding the state debt and finding enough sources of taxation to support state government and rebuild institutions, roads and schools without placing too heavy a burden on the people.

GEOGRAPHY

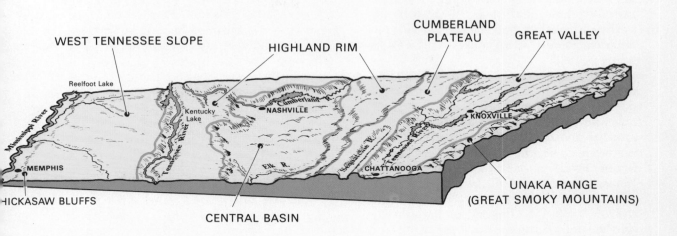

WEST TENNESSEE SLOPE

HIGHLAND RIM

CUMBERLAND PLATEAU

GREAT VALLEY

Reelfoot Lake

Mississippi River

Kentucky Lake

NASHVILLE

Cumberland R.

KNOXVILLE

MEMPHIS

Elk R.

CHATTANOOGA

HICKASAW BLUFFS

CENTRAL BASIN

UNAKA RANGE
(GREAT SMOKY MOUNTAINS)

HISTORY

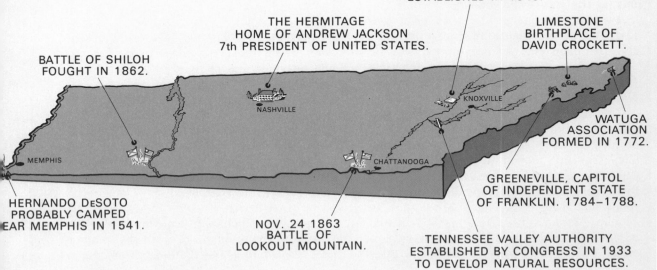

OAK RIDGE PROJECT
TO DEVELOP ATOMIC BOMBS
ESTABLISHED IN 1943.

THE HERMITAGE
HOME OF ANDREW JACKSON
7th PRESIDENT OF UNITED STATES.

LIMESTONE
BIRTHPLACE OF
DAVID CROCKETT.

BATTLE OF SHILOH
FOUGHT IN 1862.

NASHVILLE

KNOXVILLE

WATUGA
ASSOCIATION
FORMED IN 1772.

MEMPHIS

CHATTANOOGA

HERNANDO DeSOTO
PROBABLY CAMPED
NEAR MEMPHIS IN 1541.

GREENEVILLE, CAPITOL
OF INDEPENDENT STATE
OF FRANKLIN. 1784–1788.

NOV. 24 1863
BATTLE OF
LOOKOUT MOUNTAIN.

TENNESSEE VALLEY AUTHORITY
ESTABLISHED BY CONGRESS IN 1933
TO DEVELOP NATURAL RESOURCES.

Governor Bate and the Legislature, faced with the necessity of taxing foreign corporations doing business in Tennessee—railroads and manufacturing industries, were harassed by lobbyists. In an effort to be fair to the corporations and the people, the Governor commented in an address to the Legislature in 1883:

"While corporations should have all just rights maintained, and proper encouragement to make their work useful and profitable, yet as they grow mighty in their strength and strain for unjust power, as they are prone to do, they should be checked for lines of legal limit, and told in unmistakable terms, 'thus far and no farther shalt thou go.' "

From 1883 until the end of the century, problems of taxation were of major interest to the governors and the legislative bodies of Tennessee. Scientific discoveries and inventions were being applied to everyday life, and were opening new sources of taxation as well as new problems for regulation. Life was being revolutionized, not only for Tennessee, but for the rest of the country.

Tennessee was never slow in adopting new ideas and developments. It eagerly accepted the steamboat and put it into operation. It undertook to build railroads from the time the earliest ones were put to use in the United States.

The telegraph, whose first message was sent from Baltimore to Washington, D.C., on May 24, 1844, was in wide use during the Civil War and, played an important part in the movements of both armies. Nathan Bedford Forrest kept telegraph lines and railroads operating from North Mississippi to Mobile, Alabama, until late in 1864. Knoxville, Chattanooga, and Nashville were generally in contact with Washington after those major cities were captured by Union troops early in the war.

However, these men knew the full value of the railroads. As soon as they returned from the war, Nathan Bedford Forrest and others went into the business of rebuilding them. The governors of this period found both telegraph lines and railroads suitable subjects for proposed taxation. Before the century was over, the telephone was to be added to the list.

Another great development during the last half of the nineteenth century was the invention of turbines and generators which made possible the development of hydroelectric power in Tennessee. This was accomplished only after years of patient experimentation. By 1900 hydroelectric power had become a commonplace reality though, not as widespread as today.

During this eventful period several able governors served Tennessee. Governor Bate was succeeded by Robert Love Taylor, 1887-1891; John F. Buchanan, 1891-1893; Peter Turney, 1893-1897; and, Governor Taylor again, 1897-1899.

Buchanan and Turney Governor Buchanan served during a troubled period and did not reconcile the contending political and economic groups.

However, he was president of the controversial Farmers Alliance, organized to defend farmers against the decline of prosperity in the South by cooperative buying and selling of farm products. When these efforts failed, the Alliance entered politics, and by 1890 practically controlled the Democratic party in the South.

Democrat Buchanan gave intelligent attention to the problems of state government and, considering the circumstances, made a very good record. When only sixteen years old, he had shouldered a musket and joined the Confederate Army.

Governor Peter Turney, also a Confederate veteran, suffered to the end of his life from injuries received on the battlefield. Well trained in the legal profession he served many years as a judge. His two administrations were beset with political feuds and controversies, which were characteristic of the period.

ROBERT LOVE TAYLOR

For more than a decade Robert Love Taylor's colorful personality dominated the political scene in Tennessee and was not without influence far beyond the borders of the state. He was an able governor, who understood the complex problems connected with the state debt, and had a keen interest in the public schools, in the charitable, and penal institutions. He was also interested in cleaning and repairing the handsome, but somewhat dilapidated State Capitol, and managed efficiently the many problems—great and small—which came to his office.

But the drama, color, humor, and excitement which hailed his coming into office, his eloquent oratory, his sense of humor, his fiddling, and his personality made it difficult for the public to remember prosaic things as routine responsibilities and understanding the intricate details of running a State. They loved Bob Taylor for himself and they wanted to see and to hear him.

For several years he had been growing in popularity and, by 1886, he was urged to become a candidate for governor. He held the job of Pension Agent at Knoxville, a job which paid a salary equal to that of Governor and did not necessitate the heavy ex-

Robert Love Taylor.

penses of the Governor's office. He was still considering the nomination when the Republican Party nominated his brother Alf for Governor, thinking that they had blocked Bob's acceptance of the Democratic nomination. But it did not and soon the two brothers took the stump against each other. Early in the campaign Bob had declared that he and his competitor were "two roses from the same garden—he, the white rose of York and his brother Alf, the red rose of Lancaster."

The "War of the Roses" was on in earnest. Never had there been such a campaign. As it gathered momentum, the delighted people of Tennessee thronged to hear the brothers argue and poke fun at each other on every major issue of the times—and a good many of the minor ones. They debated the protective tariff and other national questions, as well as state and local subjects.

After serving two terms as governor, 1887-1891, Bob Taylor returned to private law practice, which was not as profitable as he had hoped, so he returned to the lecture platform. His series of lectures, called "The Fiddle and the Bow" soon became a nation-wide success and was followed by another series "Yankee Doodle and Dixie," in which he was joined by his brother Alf. This series of debates patterned after those of "The War of the Roses" enjoyed a great national popularity and was extremely successful from a financial standpoint.

After he had enjoyed such national triumphs it was natural that Tennessee planning to celebrate the one hundredth anniversary of its statehood, should turn to Bob Taylor as the ideal man to serve as governor during this eventful period. On the last day of the ninety-ninth year following Tennessee's admission to the Union a Nashville paper carried a tribute to him and congratulated the state on its good fortune in having such a man at such a time.

". . . The new century hails Robert Love Taylor as a man worthy of a new epoch and fitted to lead in the line of march toward a bigger and grander achievement in all avenues of development and endeavor, and peculiarly suited in the purity of his life and beauty of his character to reform government so that it shall get back to its original purpose, the conservation of human happiness."

TENNESSEE'S CENTENNIAL, 1897

Tennessee, like other Southern States, had been slowly and painfully emerging from the disastrous period of the Civil War and the more than a decade of reconstruction which followed it. Devastated fields were once more yielding harvests, improved methods of agriculture had been inaugurated, immigration had been encouraged, the wheels of industries were humming, and education, the arts, and sciences were beginning to flourish again.

Since there had been some difficulty at first in securing the public support necessary to provide a suitable celebration, the centennial exposition was a year late. The Exposition was an ambitious and successful display of the State's progress. Among the attractions were many handsome buildings, but most beautiful of them all was the exact replica of the Athenian Parthenon. There were great art exhibits, not only of the work of Tennessee artists, but of the world's great artists, including Zolnay, the sculptor; George de Forest Brush, an American artist born in Shelbyville, Tennessee; Victor Herert, gave concerts and wrote at least a part of one of his great operettas while in Nashville. Great scientists and statesmen from all parts of the country lectured and participated in the numerous social activities.

With all splendor, Tennessee's best barnyard fowls cackled or crowed in their part of the Exposition grounds, cotton and tobacco fields which had been planted and carefully cultivated, flourished. Flowers in the landscaped gardens and in the horticultural building perfumed the air. Most spectacular of all was a tower, 100 feet tall, crowned with multicolored electric lights that flashed proudly: "Tennessee Centennial."

THE SPANISH-AMERICAN WAR

The great Centennial year had hardly closed, when a more serious matter, the Spanish-American War, demanded the at-

The Grand Military and Industrial Procession at Nashville's Centennial Celebration in 1880.

tention of Governor Taylor and the people of the State.

This war was brought on primarily by strained relations between the United States and Spain, caused by Spain's long years of oppression and mistreatment of the people of Cuba. In 1895, Cuban uprising cruelly suppressed by Spain, aroused great public sympathy in the United States. During the early part of President McKinley's administration, Congress appropriated a sum of $50,000 for use by the suffering victims. At last, on February 15, 1898, the U. S. Battleship, *Maine*, was blown up in the harbor of Havana. This was followed by declarations of war by both countries.

The first shot in the war was fired from the Gunboat *Nashville*, by its commanding officer, Commander Washburn Maynard. The war spread also to the Philippines, where Admiral George Dewey took Manila on May 1, 1898. It was concluded at the Treaty of Paris, December 10, 1898, under the terms that Spain agree to withdraw from Cuba, to cede Puerto Rico and Guam, and, for the sum of $20,000,000 sell the Philippines to the United States.

Tennessee, as usual, lived up to her name, "The Volunteer State," and furnished her full quota of troops. Among them was Cordell Hull, who had just begun his career in state politics. Another Tennessean destined to achieve fame was Lieutenant Commander (later Admiral) Albert Gleaves.

The Twentieth Century

BENTON McMILLIN, THE CENTURY'S FIRST GOVERNOR

Tennessee's governor at the beginning of the twentieth century was Benton McMillin. Elected in 1898, he succeeded Bob Taylor and, in 1901, had been re-elected for another term. An important and popular political figure in Tennessee, McMillin finished a twenty year term as a member of the United States House of Representatives when he was elected governor.

At the beginning of the twentieth century, the "Confederate Brigadiers," who had been fighting the South's battles on the floors of Congress for two decades, were fading away. William B. Bate, former governor, was serving as senior senator. Junior senator was Thomas B. Turley, of Memphis, who was appointed to serve out the unexpired term of Senator Isham G. Harris.

The chief interest now was the building of a prosperous, progressive economic system. Prime objectives were the encouragement of immigration; establishment of new industries; improvement of agriculture, marketing and transportation; provision for better schools; a uniform textbook law; and teacher training. The first step to obtain these and many other things was the re-establishment of the state's credit, a subject which had already received considerable attention.

Many of the problems which confronted McMillin when he took the governor's chair in 1901 originated during the war and reconstruction periods. He, and the legislatures which sat during his administration, were able to see the results of their actions and also those of earlier administrations.

Governor Benton McMillin encouraged education and succeeded in reducing Tennessee's debt.

These had struggled since 1869 to restore the state's war-torn economy and to emerge from the staggering debt incurred by carpetbag legislatures and the failures of railroads.

McMillin was successful in paying off one million dollars of the state's sixteen-million-dollar debt, which had been adjusted during the administration of Governor Bate, and to pay the $850,000 floating state debt. Public education received encouragement. Small increases were made in appropriations for teachers' institutes and first steps were taken toward standardization of textbooks and regulation of their prices.

OTHER GOVERNORS

The Democratic candidate for governor in 1902 was James B. Frazier of Chattanooga. His Republican opponent was Judge Henry T. Campbell of Carter County—a man whose personal accomplishments and family background made him a formidable opponent. Frazier was elected and, assuming office in January, 1903, continued the measures designed to reduce the state debt.

Governor Frazier resigned early in his second term to become United States Senator, succeeding the veteran soldier and statesman, William B. Bate, whose death occurred March 5, 1905. Succeeding Frazier as governor was John I. Cox, speaker of the State Senate.

Governor Cox, because of his position as speaker of the State Senate, was familiar with the Frazier legislative program and, followed for the most part, the major policies of his predecessor. He exercised unusual ability in guiding measures through the legislature and in administering affairs of state during the remainder of the term. During his administration $1,874,200 was paid on the state's debt; a liberal appropriation was made for public schools; the compulsory education bill was passed, and progressive work was done along many educational lines under the direction of S. A. Mynders, state superintendent of schools. It was also during Cox's administration that a state flag was adopted.

Cox was not accorded the usual courtesy of nomination for a second term. Malcom R. Patterson, an able and forceful man, who had served three terms in Congress as the representative of Tennessee's tenth district, waged a vigorous campaign for the Democratic nomination. A newspaper, the *Tennessee Lancet*, was established in Nashville by Patterson's supporters and waged a bitter campaign against Cox.

This fight, carried into the 1906 Democratic state convention, was one of the most dramatic in Tennessee. Personal encounters, fistfights, and verbal battles rose to such a pitch that it approached a riot state and passed completely beyond the control of the presiding officer, W. K. Abernathy.

At this moment, a tall broad-shouldered young man made his way to the speaker's stand, snatched the gavel from the presiding officer and, through a commanding presence and sheer force of personality, began to bring order out of the chaos. The young giant was Luke Lea, twenty-seven-year-old son of a wealthy and socially prominent Nashville family which, from pioneer days, had played an important part in the state's history.

When the riot had subsided, Lea maintained his leadership and on the following day, the convention nominated Patterson as its candidate for governor. For something like a quarter of a century, the young man who had quelled the riot was destined to have not only an important part in selecting governors and other public officials, but also to serve as United States Senator in 1911.

Patterson's Republican opponent in the 1906 general election was the Honorable H. Clay Evans. Evans, well-qualified for the office, had an integrity and popularity which helped him to win a much larger number of votes than is customary for the minority party in Tennessee. Patterson received 117,053 votes and Evans 92,809.

The race for the United States Senate increased animosities which had been aroused by the gubernatorial contest. Edward Ward Carmack, elected by the State Legislature to succeed Senator Turley, had served one term and was not a candidate to succeed himself. Robert Love Taylor, former governor and congressman, whose personal popularity was probably without precedent in Tennessee political history, was now put forward to oppose Carmack. Thus, two of the greatest orators Tennessee has ever produced were competing against each other.

Taylor, confident of his influence with the people, sought and obtained from the Democratic State Executive Committee, permission for a primary election in 1908. As anticipated by his large following, he defeated Carmack.

PROHIBITION AND POLITICAL PROBLEMS

This defeat, leaving Carmack free to seek other offices, led him to oppose Governor Patterson who, in 1908, was a candidate for reelection. The race for nomination in the Democratic primary resolved into a statewide joint debate which opened in Chattanooga on April 16, 1908. The burning issue of the period was prohibition. Carmack carrying the banner of the prohibitionists and Patterson representing the "wets," the faction that wanted to adopt local option. Local option was the right of individual cities and counties to vote on whether they wanted liquor within their boundaries. George H. Armistead, editor and political writer, managed Carmack's campaign and Austin Peay, later governor of Tennessee, was Patterson's manager. Although they had not voted as yet, women participated actively in the campaign through the Women's Christian Temperance Union and local temperance groups. Members of these temperance organizations were admirers of Carmack.

Patterson was victorious, but, so intensive had been the campaign of the "drys," that a majority favoring statewide prohibition was elected to the State Legislature. When the prohibition law was passed, Patterson vetoed it—deploring in his veto message that women had become involved in this bitter, hard-fought political battle. The bill was immediately passed over his veto.

In spite of the storm scenes which accompanied the passage of the statewide prohibition bill, the Fifty-sixth General Assembly passed such important legislation as the General Education Bill of 1909; appropriation of $250,000 for the George Peabody College for Teachers; and other progressive legislation.

There was no prospect of peace, however, during the Patterson administration. There was much resentment toward him for his neglect of prohibition laws and his liberal attitude in pardoning criminals. In 1910, when three Supreme Court and two Court of Appeals judges repudiated a Patterson-controlled primary and accepted the nomination of a mass meeting held in Nashville, the Democratic party was completely divided. Forming a coalition with the Republicans, the independents elected their judicial candidates by a majority of more than forty thousand votes.

Now fully confident of their power the independents, at a convention held September 14, 1910, pledged their support to the Republican nominee for governor, Ben W. Hooper. Governor Patterson was a candidate for reelection for a third term, but, in the face of strong opposition from within the "regular" Democratic ranks, withdrew in an effort to obtain harmony. A new state Democratic committee persuaded United States Senator Bob Taylor to run for governor, but even his popularity could not bring the party together. Hooper defeated Taylor by only a small margin.

Scenes during the early part of the Fifty-seventh General Assembly, which convened January 2, 1911, were tempestuous beyond description. Efforts were made to repeal the statewide prohibition law; elections of members were so bitterly contested that legislative proceedings were impossible, and controversies on all fronts reflected the disturbed political scene in Tennessee.

Hooper, in spite of political difficulties and the prohibition problem which had continually plagued him, made a good governor and, in 1912, was a candidate to succeed himself. Benton McMillan opposed him and was defeated by the coalition of independent Democrats and Republicans. Governor Hooper was reelected by a majority of some twelve thousand over the former governor and congressman. As Bob Taylor had failed to reunite the Democrats in 1910, Benton McMillin failed in 1912. Forces which had split the party were still too strong to be put down by an individual, however popular. Even the national Democratic victory and election of Woodrow Wilson did not bring the warring Tennessee factions together.

When the General Assembly convened on January 6, 1913, it appeared for a time as if some degree of harmony might prevail. The coalition of independent Democrats and Republicans which had elected Hooper was still in power and reinforced by the powerful Shelby County delegation. Prohibition was the most important issue. Both wets and drys were eager to promote legislation favorable to their causes, but, knowing the explosive action which would greet the first move on either side, they refrained temporarily from breaking the calm.

The unstable majority created by the Republican–Independent Democrat coalition and the Shelby delegation was upset, largely as a result of the passage of Senator William Robert Webb's bill prohibiting the shipment of liquor from wet states into dry states. His speech and the success of his bill led Tennessee prohibition forces to seek further legislation to increase its effectiveness. The Shelby delegation, which had refrained from seeking to change the state's prohibition and election laws, now went over to the wets—thereby endangering the whole prohibition movement in Tennessee.

To avoid possible repeal or serious alteration of the liquor law, the Republican-Democratic coalition in the House of Representatives "bolted" and crossed the state line into Middlesboro, Kentucky. Because the legislators were not in the state, only an occasional constitutional quorum was obtained during the long, stormy session which, after 202 days, adjourned on August 23, 1913. Two extra sessions were called that year by Governor Hooper—for the purpose of making necessary appropriations and attend to other business which had not been considered during the stormy regular session.

Two years of a national Democratic administration, however, along with the healing influence of time, began to reunite the warring factions. Tennessee, being largely Democratic in sentiment, soon chose to reconcile differences between factions of its major party and return its vote to the Democratic column by 1914.

WORLD WAR I

When Governor Tom C. Rye was elected in 1914, rumblings of war in Europe were already being heard, but so remotely that no one realized that in a short while the whole civilized world would be drawn into it. The immediate cause of the war was the assassination of Archduke Franz Ferdinand, heir apparent to the Hapsburg throne, by a Serb, at Sarajevo, capital of Bosnia, on June 14, 1914. Austria sent an ultimatum to Serbia. Germany sent an ultimatum to Russia and to France. And, in a short time, England and Italy were involved. Germany invaded Belgium on August 4, 1914, soon overran it, and passed into France. The launching of Germany's unrestricted U-boat warfare, which, by 1917, had become intolerable, was the major reason for the declaration of war against Germany by the United States, April 6, 1917.

By 1916, when Governor Rye was re-elected for a second term, the rumblings of war had become more ominous and Tennessee, as well as the rest of the nation, had become aware of the fact that the United States itself was on the brink of war.

While there was a strong feeling that the increasingly ruthless submarine warfare used by Germany was on the verge of driving the United States into war, there was also a strong sentiment against such action. President Wilson, in his 1916 campaign for re-election, had pledged himself to keep the country out of war and, because of this, won the support of the enfranchised women of California, whose votes aided him greatly in being re-elected. Governor Rye, who had already been inaugurated for his second term, was ready, on April 6th, 1917, when war was declared, to throw the full strength of Tennessee into the war effort.

Living up to her past history, Tennessee furnished thousands of volunteers. In addition to men in the armed services, many women volunteered for duty in nurses' corps, ambulance units, the Red Cross, Y.W.C.A., and other organizations formed to aid servicemen in training and in the field, as well as their families at home. Many of these women volunteers served throughout the war in France and England.

TENNESSEE'S HEROES

One of Tennessee's outstanding heroes was Rear Admiral Albert Gleaves, who was placed in command of the transportation of American troops across the U-boat-infested Atlantic Ocean. During the first year of the war, under his command, ships carried nearly two million soldiers to the shores of France and back, with the loss of only three hundred lives. This was considered one of the greatest feats of the war.

The famous "Old Hickory," or Thirtieth Division, which, at the beginning of the war was composed largely of National Guard Troops from Tennessee, North Carolina and South Carolina, was famous for its brilliant action throughout the war, particularly for its part in breaking the famous "Hindenburg Line," the German line across France. The fifty-ninth Brigade, was commanded by General Lawrence D. Tyson, of Knoxville, who was with his command from the time it left Tennessee until the end of the war. General Tyson was awarded the Distinguished Service Medal by General John J. Pershing himself.

Colonel Cary F. Spence, also of Knoxville, was in command of the famous 117th Infantry, which was made up largely of Tennesseans. Not only was Colonel Spence cited by General Pershing, but 129 men of his command received crosses and medals. Some, who had fought with English and

French military units, received the coveted Victoria Cross and the French Croix de Guerre.

Two West Tennesseans who served with distinction during World War I were Gordon W. Browning, the Captain of Battery A, 114th Field Artillery; and Captain Clifton B. Cates, of Tiptonville. Captain Browning, who was born and reared on his father's cotton farm in Carroll County, was later a congressman and governor of Tennessee.

Captain Cates, who was awarded the Distinguished Service Cross during World War I, was later the commanding general of the U.S. Marine Corps and received also many medals and citations for his distinguished service during World War II.

A large number of men from Middle and West Tennessee served under Colonel Luke Lea, in some of the most gallant and spectacular actions of the war. Commanding the Fifty-Ninth Artillery Brigade, which later became the 114th Field Artillery, Colonel Lea led this outfit through the St. Mihiel and Meuse-Argonne campaigns and other operations.

ALVIN YORK

Hailed as the greatest hero of them all—indeed the greatest in the entire American Expeditionary Force—was a young man from the little village of Pall Mall, Fentress County, Tennessee, a beautiful, rugged, but then almost inaccessible section of the Cumberland Mountains. He was Sergeant Alvin York, soft-spoken and mild-mannered, in spite of his red hair; more than six feet tall, stalwart and wiry. He did not believe in war, but neither did he shirk his duty.

When all of the other officers of his detachment were killed or wounded, and it

Alvin York, a once-illiterate farm boy, was the outstanding hero of World War I. Not content to rest on past laurels, he returned home to fight for greater educational opportunities for the people of Tennessee.

appeared that the rest of the outfit would be wiped out by the fire of the enemy, he took command. Then, single-handed and armed only with his rifle and pistol, he set out to "quiet" the German machine guns on a nearby hill which were raining fire upon them. Before his one-man campaign was over he had captured a total of 132 German officers and men, had killed twenty-five and had captured the hill, which was fortified with thirty-five machine guns.

General John J. Pershing, commander-in-chief of the American Expeditionary Force, called him "the outstanding civilian soldier of the War."

Medals and praise were awarded him by other commanders of the Allied forces. When he came home in May, 1919, New York City staged in his honor the greatest celebration in its history. When he came back to Tennessee, he was welcomed with open arms and an overwhelming pride. When he returned to Tennessee, great companies offered him well-paying positions and business opportunities. Motion picture companies tried to exploit his fame, but in vain. His common sense and dignity led him to decline these offers. He went home to Pall Mall, married the girl who had been waiting for him, and settled down to a life which he tried to make useful to his own people. He wanted better educational advantages for the people of his own part of the state, who were, like him, mostly of English and Scotch-Irish descent. To these and other worthwhile things he devoted his whole life. Books and magazine articles were written about him—for some of which he received financial compensation. In his last years he was beset by business difficulties, but these he managed also. He died on September 2, 1964, at the close of a long life through which he had earned and received the love and respect of his own people, as well as the acclaim of the world.

POLITICS

In the Democratic primary of 1916, Kenneth D. McKellar, then representing the tenth district in the U.S. House of Representatives, defeated the incumbent, Luke Lea, and ex-Governor Malcolm R. Patterson for nomination as United States Senator. In the regular election, he defeated his Republican opponent, ex-Governor Hooper, and, on March 3, 1917, began his long career in the United States Senate.

Under Governor Rye's administration, the politically significant Compulsory Primary Law was passed in 1917. This provided that all party nominations be made through preferential primaries. Thus, the choice of gubernatorial nominees, as well as nominees for membership in the national Congress and General Assembly of Tennessee were removed from the party conventions. Rye was the last governor of Tennessee to be nominated by a party convention, as John K. Shields was the last United States Senator to serve a regular term to which he had been elected by the Tennessee Legislature.

These changes put nominations for public office on a more democratic basis and helped to relieve tensions which had often developed when nominees were chosen on the floors of conventions or the legislature and contesting factions faced each other.

Harmony, such as Tennessee had not known for many years, existed when the Sixtieth General Assembly met on January 1, 1917. In addition to compulsory primary legislation, the absentee voters' law was passed, county officers were put on salary instead of the fee system, constitutional revision was considered, and other measures were given attention.

While the year 1918 was devoted to measures for promotion of the war effort, there was also serious interest in the gubernatorial and senatorial contests.

Governor Albert H. Roberts, of Livingston, succeeded Rye as governor, having defeated Austin Peay, of Clarksville, in the Democratic primary and Judge H. B. Lindsay, Republican, in the general election.

Ex-Governor Rye opposed the incumbent, U.S. Senator John K. Shields, in the Democratic primary, but was defeated. It was understood in political circles that President Wilson did not want to have Senator Shields returned to the Senate. Shields took a stand against the League of Nations, through which Wilson saw the hope of permanent world peace.

Later, many Tennessee Democrats who had supported Senator Shields deserted him because of his opposition to the League of Nations and his failure to support a Democratic president.

There was a large group which agreed with the senior senator, however, and Tennessee was split once more into bitter factions. The situation in East Tennessee was particularly difficult, where Charles T. Cate, former attorney-general, led the anti-Shields group. In the general election of 1918, Senator Shields was elected, having been unsuccessfully opposed by H. Clay Evans.

THE EMANCIPATION OF WOMEN

During World War I, many changes had taken place in Tennessee. Among the most important was the great increase in employment of women in work which they had not done previously. Many worked in factories, drove tractors and trucks on farms, learned to operate other types of machinery when necessary, and worked in offices. In many ways, women demonstrated their ability to work outside the home and outside the limited number of occupations which had previously been open to them.

Legislation of particular interest to women was sponsored by the Tennessee Federation of Women's Clubs and the various woman suffrage organizations from 1913 to 1920. The legislation proposed included such subjects as married women's property rights; laws making women eligible to serve on school boards and as notary public; municipal and presidential suffrage; the establishment of a Girls' Vocational School at Tullahoma; improvement of health and educational conditions; improvement of working conditions for women; child labor laws; as well as prohibition laws and temperance education, sponsored by the W.C.T.U. and similar groups.

These movements were carried to the legislature and state officials for approval by a powerful and active women's lobby. This feminine impact upon the Tennessee political scene was not without its entertaining and humorous side. The gentlemen were flabbergasted, but to their credit, they met the situation with the unfailing gallantry of the old-school Southern gentleman.

Governor Rye was not only receptive to the pleas of Tennessee women for enactment of such legislation, but he was an earnest and faithful co-worker in the movement which the ladies sponsored during his administrations. In 1914, women's property rights legislation was passed. The House Joint Resolution proposing a woman suffrage amendment to the State Constitution, passed on May 14, 1915, was signed by Governor Rye on the same day. But women's suffrage was still not assured. The nineteenth amendment to the United States Constitution was yet to be ratified by the Tennessee legislature.

Governor Roberts, who succeeded Governor Rye, also supported the cause of women's rights. He called a special session of the state's sixty-first General Assembly to consider the question.

In his message to the special session, Governor Roberts not only explained legal aspects of the woman suffrage amendment and stated the favorable action on it by both major political parties, but also made a strong personal plea for its ratification.

Governor Roberts' active support did not secure immediate unopposed ratification of the amendment. The session was a stormy one, rich in drama as well as humor. The anti-suffrage lobby, representatives of the country's greatest news agencies, and politicians from many parts of the nation, as well as woman suffrage leaders and their strong lobby, converged on Nashville. At one time, the legislature "bolted." Even when a quorum could be had, the battle was fought night and day, on the floor of both houses of the legislature, in the halls of the capitol, in hotels, at social functions, and on the streets.

During this momentous and stormy session, Andrew L. Todd, of Rutherford County, was Speaker of the Senate. Seth Walker, of Nashville was Speaker of the House of Representatives. After a long, hard-fought battle, the suffrage amendment was finally ratified and several other bills, including the eighteenth amendment to the Constitution in favor of prohibition, were passed.

Earlier in the year, Tennessee women were given equal representation in the Democratic Party and, for the first time in history, were official delegates to the State Democratic Convention. This convention, held in Nashville in June, 1920, did not have the nominating powers of past conventions, although policies were formed and various party officials and delegates were chosen. Conventions, now held in presidential election years, are chiefly for the purpose of electing delegates, discussing policies, and hearing keynote speeches.

In spite of his service to the cause of woman suffrage, Governor Roberts was not rewarded with re-election by the women he had helped enfranchise. The suffragettes, who actually constituted a very small proportion of the state's population, were organized for crusading, not for practical politics. Had they been skilled politicians, it is doubtful that they could have withheld the Republican landslide which swept Warren G. Harding into the presidency in 1920 and made Alfred H. Taylor governor of Tennessee.

During Governor Roberts' administration, provisions were made for erecting a memorial to Tennesseans who had fought in World War I, workmen's compensation, creation of a highway commission and a state highway department, a comprehensive survey of the state school system, granting municipal and presidential suffrage to women and other worthwhile legislation.

ALFRED TAYLOR

That Republican Alfred Taylor should become Governor of Tennessee at last was hailed as a bit of justice by most citizens of Tennessee. The "War of the Roses" was well remembered. The Democratic party, cha-

Alfred Taylor, governor from 1920-1922.

grined at its national and state defeats, was not happy over the situation.

There was no animosity toward Governor Taylor, however, and the subjects discussed by most Tennesseans who enjoyed his hospitality, more often than not, had to do with the fiddling and famous stories told by the Taylors in their various campaigns, not with politics.

The customary business and legislation were attended to, however, for the Taylors, in spite of their entertaining tales and engaging manners, were excellent statesmen. Governor Taylor's tact and winning personality were especially valuable during this period in reconciling labor difficulties. He was reasonable, fair, and trusted by all sides. However, the Democrats regained the governorship in 1922.

AUSTIN PEAY

For the governorship in 1922, Austin Peay contended in the primary against ex-Governor Benton McMillin, L. E. Gwinn, and Harvey Hannah, a brilliant orator, who had served as railroad commissioner and in other state positions. Peay won by a small majority.

During this period Dr. P. P. Claxton, who had served with distinction as United States Commissioner of Education for several years, was replaced by another Tennessean, Dr. John J. Tigert.

After an impressive inaugural ceremony on January 16, 1923, Governor Peay, with a cooperative legislature, undertook to reorganize the state's government and put it on a more efficient basis. With legislative assistance, he reduced the sixty-odd departments, commissions, committees, boards, and independent offices, to seven major units; the departments of finance, taxation, agriculture, institutions, public health, insurance and banking, and labor. Elected governor three times, Peay continued his policies and effected all possible economies and improvements. He was known particularly for his interest in road building, especially in East Tennessee, where mountainous terrain had not allowed the building of adequate highways. He was also interested in the improvements of schools, in agriculture, and in progressive methods of handling the state's business. Austin Peay was known as the "Maker of Modern Tennessee."

During Governor Peay's first term, the death of President Harding resulted in Calvin Coolidge's succession to the presidency. The following year, 1924, saw the defeat of Senator John K. Shields by General Lawrence D. Tyson, of Knoxville, who had served with distinction in World War I and was one of East Tennessee's most prominent citizens.

Governor Peay was reelected for a third term in the general election, November 2, 1926. This term was cut short, however, by his death, and he was succeeded by Henry H. Horton, Speaker of the State Senate. Horton, in the Democratic primary of 1928, was strongly opposed by Hill McAlister and Lewis Pope, but won by a narrow margin.

In 1928, Herbert Hoover was elected President of the United States, and Senator Kenneth D. McKellar was reelected to the United States Senate. General Tyson's death, August 24, 1929, left a vacancy in the United States Senate, which was filled by the appointment of W. E. Brock, of Chattanooga. In 1930, Brock was elected for the short term in the Senate. Cordell Hull, who had served in the House of Representatives, was elected for the long term.

Senator Hull, however, resigned on March 3, 1933, to begin his distinguished career as Secretary of State, to which he had been appointed by President Roosevelt. Nathan L. Bachman, of Chattanooga, was appointed to fill the vacancy left by Hull's resignation.

THE DEPRESSION YEARS

By this time, Tennessee and the rest of the nation had reached the depths of the Depression. This had begun with the crash of the New York Stock Market in the fall of 1929 and had struck with full force in more remote parts of the country the following year. The chaotic scene in Tennessee was a reflection of conditions existing elsewhere. War veterans marched on Washington and, camping there, demanded relief from President Hoover. Failure of banks, investment companies, industries, and the threat of foreclosures on homes and farms, drove men to ruin, and sometimes to suicide. Long lines of men, women, and children stood before soup kitchens, waiting for food.

It was a tragic period for which no men, or group of men, had been entirely responsible. After World War I, the country had enjoyed prosperity, but a prosperity which led to unsound methods of business and government. These were the conditions in Tennessee during the last part of Governor Henry Horton's term (1927-1933) and the conditions which faced Governor Hill McAlister, his successor, when he took office on January 17, 1933.

Tennessee was in the grip of the most severe financial depression the state had known during the critical days of the early 1930's. Despite the difficulties which confronted his administration, Governor McAlister set up one of the most comprehensive and effective studies ever made of the Tennessee educational system and aroused a vigorous interest in the improvement of the public school system. The Governor's previous experience in the office of State Treasurer had also prepared him for a full understanding of the state's financial difficulties and aided in working out the complicated problems which confronted him.

When President Franklin Delano Roosevelt was inaugurated on March 4, 1933, the desperate condition of the country demanded immediate action. Calling the effort to meet these needs "The New Deal," President Roosevelt and his staff began to set up an entirely new type of government.

TENNESSEE VALLEY AUTHORITY

The New Deal programs affected Tennessee much as they did the rest of the coun-

TRANSPORTATION

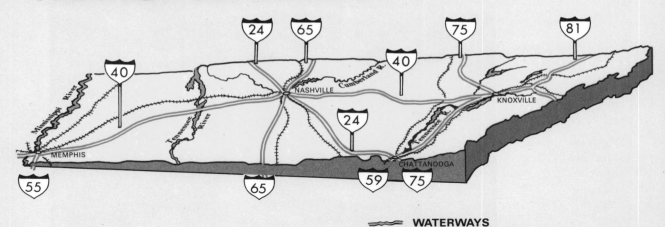

~~~~~ **WATERWAYS**
++++++ **MAJOR RAILROADS**
===== **INTERSTATE HIGHWAYS**
(Projected to completion)

ECONOMY

C	COAL	Z	ZINC
Cu	COPPER	P	PHOSPHATE ROCK
L	LEAD	I	IRON ORE

GENERAL FARMING

COTTON

TOBACCO & GENERAL FARMING

MOUNTAINS & FORESTS

BUSINESS AND INDUSTRY

MEMPHIS — Major cotton and lumber market. Paper, cotton and rubber manufacturing center.

NASHVILLE — State Capitol. Manufactures cellophane, rayon, shoes, metal products.

CHATTANOOGA — Woodworking, metalworking and textile industries.

KNOXVILLE — Manufactures stone products, textiles and food products

Norris Dam on the Clinch River controls floods and provides electric power for the Appalachian Ridge and Valley regions.

try, except that in the Tennessee Valley a great experimental project which was expected to have far-reaching effects was set up. It was called the "Tennessee Valley Authority," created by act of Congress in 1933, early in the Roosevelt administration. Its major purposes were to provide work for jobless men, and a long-range program for improvement of the Tennessee river system, as well as for flood control.

The major reason for the creation of the TVA was the government nitrate plant and Wilson Dam at Muscle Shoals. The plant and the dam were built under the National Defense Act of 1916 to manufacture nitrate during World War I, but the construction was not finished in time and the plant was then abandoned. The fact that this plant had remained idle for many years had been the subject of Congressional debate, especially when Henry Ford and other industrialists attempted to buy it from the government. The politician in Congress favoring continued government ownership of the Muscle Shoals plant was Senator George

Norris, of Nebraska, often called "The Father of TVA."

The TVA Act transferred control of the plant and the dam from the War Department to the newly created Tennessee Valley Authority. Here at last was a chance for Tennessee to renew her lands and forests which had been so ravaged by floods and improper farming methods over the years.

Dr. Arthur E. Morgan, David E. Lilienthal, and Dr. H. A. Morgan, later president of the University of Tennessee, were appointed as the first directors of the Tennessee Valley Authority—already called the TVA. These men, specialists in their own fields had different ideas of what TVA's major interests should be.

Dr. H. A. Morgan was noted throughout the South for his contributions to agricultural development from the time of the ravages of the Mexican boll-weevil which attacked the cotton crops in 1903. He also was one of the pioneers in important agricultural movements, including the farm and home demonstration clubs. These organizations taught farmers the value of diversified crops, improvement of breeds of cattle and seeds for farm crops, cooperative marketing, and other progressive features which, had already become highly successful.

Dr. Morgan's major activities in TVA, therefore, were directed along these lines and, especially, to the manufacture of cheap fertilizer at the converted World War I plant at Muscle Shoals.

Mr. Lilienthal, the administrator, was especially interested in the use of proposed dams to be built for the production of electric power and flood control. He was also considered a practical businessman and well-suited for administering these phases of the Authority.

The most important part of TVA in the early days was defined and discussed by Dr. A. E. Morgan, former president of Antioch College, who had been named chairman.

". . . the Authority's hope is to build a new kind of civilization in the Tennessee Valley under which the people will have work, plenty to eat, comfortable houses and recreation . . . It will be a merging of agriculture and industry into a harmonious pattern. . . .We are trying something that has never been tried before. We are trying to develop a system that will have order and planning. . . ."

As the creation of electric power became important, a controversy arose among private power interests in the Valley and also among interests in other parts of the country that feared further government control of their activities. Only a few years had passed before the diversified opinions of Dr. A. E. Morgan, Mr. Lilienthal, and Dr. H. A. Morgan caused an open breach—with Dr. "A. E." on one side and Mr. Lilienthal and Dr. "H. A." on the other. Finally, Dr. A. E. Morgan was removed from the directorship.

Other controversies connected with TVA arose: complaints against land condemnation policies and the legal eviction of people from their homes; flooding of rich, productive farmlands by the increasing number of TVA lakes. Yet, TVA grew and continued to erect new dams and acquire more territory until it was limited by law to its own area.

Each forward step of TVA was hailed with enthusiasm by those who had supported it. Their influence in Tennessee and in Congress

Utilizing the power of the Mississippi River, this electric plant generates power for the Memphis area.

assured greater appropriations from the government and gave TVA increased power through acts of Congress and state-enabling acts.

During Governor McAlister's administration a series of enabling acts, presented to the General Assembly of 1935, was passed by a majority large enough to assure the federal government that Tennessee was cooperating with its new agency. These acts were: a general TVA enabling act; a series of acts authorizing a Tennessee planning commission; a housing authority act; an act validating contracts among municipalities, counties, and TVA for operation of electric systems; a TVA navigation program; and removal from the State Railroad and Public Utilities Commission of all authority over TVA or TVA cooperatives and counties or municipalities.

The general TVA enabling act permitted any county, city, or town to acquire, operate, and maintain electric power plants or distribution systems and to issue bonds for financing such plants and systems. The TVA navigation bill authorized the state highway department to construct and operate landings, docks, and loading facilities.

The TVA venue bill provided for the trial of all cases involving transfer of power properties in the county where the majority of the property in question is situated.

As the demand for electric power increased it became apparent that the many dams built by TVA could not produce enough electricity to meet the needs of the area which it served. Many new powerful steam plants consuming millions and millions of tons of coal were built. Today, the TVA leads the nation in the amount of electric power produced and continues many varied activities.

Tennessee has made great progress since its first hydroelectric plants were built in the early part of the century. The story of these plants, built by private power companies, occurred during a period of pioneering and practical accomplishment. The Watauga Power Company, which built a dam across the historic Watauga River, and began operating in December, 1911, was probably the first to produce hydroelectric power commercially in Tennessee. Other dams had been built before that time, and electricity produced by steam power had been used earlier.

In 1926, the Tennessee Electric Company, headed by Jo Conn Guild, was the largest company in Tennessee. It was only a few years later that the TVA was established and private power in Tennessee became a thing of the past.

President Roosevelt often spoke about his plans not only for the TVA, but also of six other "authorities" which would cover the entire United States. Thus far, the Tennessee Valley Authority is the only one of its kind, although the National Government has engaged in public power and river-improvement projects elsewhere.

E. H. CRUMP, POLITICAL BOSS

At the conclusion of his second term, Governor McAlister did not run for reelection. In the 1936 Democratic primary, the McAlister forces and Senator Kenneth D. McKellar supported Burgin E. Dossett, who had made a reputation for himself in public affairs particularly in the field of education. During the last weeks of the campaign, powerful political "Boss" E. H. Crump, of Memphis, suddenly threw his support to Gordon Browning. This support determined

Dossett's defeat and Browning's victory in the Democratic primary.

Governor Browning, immediately after his inauguration on January 15, 1937, began a vigorous program for the reorganization of various state departments, as well as enactment of legislation for improvement and expansion of the public school system, conservation of natural resources, and revision of the state's financial system. Before Browning had been in office very long, he antagonized Boss Crump. When he was a candidate to succeed himself, the full force of the "Crump machine" was put in motion against him. Browning was defeated by Prentice Cooper.

There is no doubt that during these years Mr. Crump was the most powerful man on the state political scene and was able to control elections in any way he chose. That he was an able and likable man and a genius at manipulating politics, his friends and large following proved beyond a doubt. That he also had a genius for making enemies and bringing harsh criticism upon himself, is also proved by the many articles, speeches, and books written by his antagonists.

PRENTICE COOPER

The next governor, Prentice Cooper of Shelbyville, served three consecutive terms, the last governor of Tennessee to have this honor. Governor Cooper, had served in World War I, graduated from law school, and practiced law with his father in Shelbyville. He also served as a member of the state House of Representatives and, from 1925-26, was attorney-general of the Eighth Judicial District.

During his administration, a payment of $49 million dollars was made on the State

TVA steam plants also generate electricity.

debt and a $25 million surplus accumulated in the State Treasury. It also saw reform of the state's administrative system by abolishing overlapping agencies; an increase of 60 percent in educational appropriations; introduction of free textbooks and equal pay for Negro and white teachers; the construction of many new buildings for state institutions; an increase in the number and areas of state parks; and procurement of over a billion dollars in new industries established in the state.

In 1953, ex-Governor Cooper was elected president of Tennessee's Constitutional Convention, the first convention to amend successfully the state Constitution of 1870. He also served as United States Ambassador to Peru.

WORLD WAR II

The great event of the Cooper administration was the outbreak of World War II, with an attack by the Japanese Air Force on the

Birthplace of Cordell Hull. Because of his devotion to world unity he won the Nobel Peace Prize in 1945.

U.S. fleet at Pearl Harbor on December 7, 1941. Tennessee, like the rest of the nation, was shocked and saddened. Secretary of State, Cordell Hull of Tennessee, was engaged in a series of conferences with President Roosevelt and two high-ranking members of the Japanese government at the time the attack was made. Though the Secretary knew that the situation was tense, he had no idea that the attack would be made. The effect upon the country and its President, also its Commander-in-Chief, was startling.

When, in 1939, Adolf Hitler had begun his invasions of smaller European countries, there was no desire on the part of Americans to become involved. But now the great nations of the world were engaged in the most terrible warfare yet known to man. In spite of their desires the Americans were drawn into it.

Of all the states, Tennessee would be heavily involved, for on her soil the deadliest weapon of all was to be developed. The citi-zens of Tennessee had no idea that their state would play such a vital part in the war. Nor did they or the rest of the nation realize that such a weapon could be developed. Tennesseans joined the armed forces by the thousands. On land, on the sea and in the air, they threw their might into the war. In the European theater of war, they took an important part in the invasion of Normandy; in turning back the first German counter-attack at Mortain, France; and in repulsing the Germans at the Battle of the Bulge, near Bastogne. They fought in the Pacific theater of war in naval battles; on the islands of Guadalcanal, Guam, Saipan, the Marianas, Okinawa, and Iwo Jima.

ATOMIC WARFARE

The possible production of an atom bomb was considered seriously by President Roosevelt in 1941, when he appointed a committee composed of General George C. Marshall,

Aerial view of the Oak Ridge National Laboratory, selected by the government for the first nuclear reactor to be put in operation during World War II.

Dr. Vannevar Bush, Dr. James B. Conant, and Secretary of War, Henry L. Stimson, to advise him on policy related to the study of nuclear fission. Major-General Leslie R. Groves, was placed in charge of the project, and Secretary Stimson served as senior advisor on the military employment of atomic energy. Oak Ridge, Tennessee was selected for the project because of the availability of electrical power through the TVA.

The development of this weapon was probably the best-kept secret in history. Only the few men actually responsible for it had an idea of the purpose of projects involved in its development. Not even the people of Oak Ridge, Tennessee, where the Manhattan Project was located, had any idea of what was happening. Neither, for that matter, did officials of TVA, which was furnishing the tremendous amount of electric power necessary for the project.

As the war gained momentum in Europe and the Pacific, research at Oak Ridge for a new and more powerful weapon continued. Great progress was made during the last months of President Roosevelt's life. When he died suddenly on April 12, 1945, final responsibility for use of this awesome weapon fell to his successor, President Harry Truman. Less than a month after he took office, President Truman announced Germany's unconditional surrender. The atom bomb was not yet ready, so the war in the Pacific continued with conventional weapons. Finally, the hour of decision came.

And then the event which had been in the making in the Tennessee Valley occurred. A Superfortress carrying one bomb flew over the Japanese city of Hiroshima on August 6, 1945 and dropped its deadly load. A mountain of smoke with a mushroom-like stem rose, and a whole city was destroyed. On

*Gas-cooled reactor at
Oak Ridge National Laboratory.*

August 9, another bomb was dropped on Nagasaki. As the great mushroom cloud passed away, another city had been destroyed. These two bombings brought death to approximately 100,000 Japanese and injury from after-effects to a large number of survivors.

GOVERNORS McCORD AND BROWNING

In 1945, Tennessee's chief executive was Governor James McCord, who had succeeded Governor Cooper. It was during Governor McCord's first administration that Tennessee, with the rest of the world, saw the end of World War II. With the end of hostilities, Governor McCord made plans to meet the needs of returning servicemen; to improve public schools, which had suffered from wartime overcrowding, lack of equipment and repairs, teacher shortages, and other serious problems; and to speed the state's return to peacetime economy.

During this period, Senator Kenneth McKellar remained Tennessee's senior senator in Congress, and Tom A. Stewart was junior senator. Following the death of Senator Nathan L. Bachman during the first administration of Gordon Browning, Governor Browning had appointed George L. Berry, nationally-known figure in printing pressmen's and labor organizations, to fill the vacancy. Senator Berry served until January 16, 1939, when Stewart became senator.

In 1946, Senator McKellar and Governor McCord were renominated in the Democratic primary and elected in November. Ex-Governor Browning's name was introduced into the race, and, although still on military duty in the European theater of war, he received 120,535 votes.

The situation was reversed in 1948, when Browning won over Governor McCord and returned to the governor's chair which he had vacated ten years earlier. Through part of this interval he had served as a judge. With the outbreak of World War II, he resigned and volunteered for military duty overseas, the only governor of Tennessee to have served in foreign countries during two world wars. Re-elected in 1950, Browning had the distinction of serving three terms.

Like all recent governors, Browning was faced with mounting demands for increasing services in every phase of government; education, highways, health, institutions, aid for dependent children, the aged and physically handicapped. At the same time he was called upon to reduce taxes and state expenditures.

During his administration, the Korean War, which began in 1950, commanded the attention of the state and the nation. During this conflict, Tennessee increased its enrollment of men in the armed forces and units of the Air National Guard, Army National Guard, Army Reserve Corps and Marines Corps furnished more than 10,000 officers and men—fighter pilots, infantrymen, marines, engineers, artillerymen, and supply and support units.

CURRENT POLITICS

In 1952, Governor Browning became a candidate for his fourth term, the third consecutive term to which he was entitled under the existing state constitution. While his opponent, thirty-two-year-old Frank Clement, of Dickson, was expected to run a good race, there was some doubt that he could beat the veteran Browning. However, Clement was the victor, and when he was inaugurated in

Governor Frank Clement.

1953 at the age of thirty-three, he became the youngest governor in the United States.

Another political upset that year was the defeat of Senator Kenneth McKellar by his young opponent, Congressman Albert Gore of the Fourth District. Senator Gore had served previously in the House of Representatives and had already attracted national attention. Well-informed and a good speaker, Gore had a keen mind and a pleasing personality. During his first years in the Senate, he did not enjoy the prestige which Senator McKellar's long years of service had won for him. Senator Gore has since overcome that handicap and is today one of the most powerful men in the Senate. He was re-elected in 1958 and again in 1964.

Currently serving as junior U.S. Senator from Tennessee is Howard H. Baker, Jr., a Republican. His father, the late Howard H. Baker, represented Tennessee's Second Congressional District for many years. His wife's father is Senator Everett Dirksen, of Illinois. Senator Baker, elected in 1966, is the first Tennessee Republican to be elected to this office by popular vote, although the party, by an effective coalition with States Rights Democrats, had carried the state in the presidential elections of 1952, 1956, and 1960.

While Governor Clement was serving his first term, the 1953 Constitutional Convention changed the governor's term of office from two to four years, with the provision that he could not succeed himself. This did not apply to the two-year term he was then serving. In 1954, he campaigned for reelection and was returned to the governor's chair for four years. Thus, Clement was the last governor to serve a two-year term and the first to serve a four-year term.

In 1958, Buford Ellington, who had managed Clement's campaign and had served under him as Commissioner of Agriculture, was elected governor. At the end of his four-year term, former Governor Clement was again a candidate and, for the third time, was elected. At the conclusion of Clement's third term, a total of ten years of service as chief executive, Governor Ellington was elected to succeed him. Thus, these two men will have served as governor for a total of eighteen years.

Tennessee's present govern▪ Buford Ellington, delivering his inaugural address.

Climate, Agriculture and Industry

CLIMATE

The climate of Tennessee is as varied as its topography. It is affected not only by moisture, sunlight, and temperature, but also by latitude, elevation of its mountains and hills, prevailing winds, soils and the nature of vegetation they produce, and the proximity to bodies of water. Before the present system of man-made lakes was built, approximately 300 square miles of Tennessee's area were covered by water. Today, millions of acres of land lie under the waters of twenty-four lakes that have a shoreline of more than 10,000 miles. To some extent, these lakes have altered the climate, as well as the life of the people in the immediate areas affected by them.

Tennessee's temperature ranges from zero (and sometimes sub-zero weather in winter) to over one hundred degrees during summer heat waves. Like the topography and climate, the temperature varies greatly.

However, the mean temperature varies very little. From east to west, on a line through the center of the state, the variation is only three degrees. The mean average in the Great Valley of East Tennessee is 57°; in Middle Tennessee, 58°; and in West Tennessee, 59°. North of this line, along the northern border, the mean temperature is about one degree higher. South of this line, along the southern border, the mean temperature is about one degree lower.

The rainfall of Tennessee is as variable as its other natural features, but it contributes toward making a pleasant climate and to the production of crops.

AGRICULTURE

Tennessee's great diversity in soils and climate is reflected in its widely varied farm crops, grasses, and forests. Farmers of the state are producing many large cash crops successfully and profitably, as well as smaller crops either for market or for home con-

Reelfoot Lake was once the hunting ground of the Chickasaws. Flooded during an earthquake in 1811, it is now a favorite place for fishing.

A long growing season and
an abundance of fertile land
make Tennessee a fine agricultural state.
Above, fodder being cut.
Below, tobacco and corn grow on a hillside.

sumption. A large number of vegetables, grain crops, and fruits which grow in states south of Tennessee, grow well in its climate, as do many other crops which are cultivated as far north as Canada.

Since pioneer days, corn, or Indian maize, has been not only one of the state's largest crops, but one of its most important. As early as 1840, Tennessee ranked first in the production of this important crop. The opening of vast western territory suitable for growing corn made it less profitable for corn to be shipped to distant markets. This resulted in no serious loss, because corn kept on the farm where it was raised and fed to cattle, hogs, and poultry, was more profitable than that shipped directly to market.

From the time it first develops in early summer, until it is harvested in late autumn, corn is the most versatile and most important crop raised in Tennessee. Although its cash value is lower than those of cotton and tobacco; its value to men and animals cannot be estimated in dollars and cents. Progress has been made in developing strains of corn suited to its many uses and to the seasons in which it is to be grown. The State Department of Agriculture, in cooperation with the University of Tennessee and various state and national agencies, has gone far in developing scientific methods for producing this important plant.

Tennessee's largest cash crop is cotton, its second, tobacco. Both require expert cultivation, fertilizing, and harvesting care to become profitable. Both require a great deal of skilled labor, as well as much that is unskilled. Scientific progress in the control of insects and plant diseases, invention of machinery tractors, cotton pickers and spraying equipment — and "dusting" crops from low-flying planes, have helped to replace

Men bargaining for choice Tennessee tobacco, a leading cash product.

much manpower once demanded for the cultivation of these crops. Many of the displaced agricultural workers, once employed in raising these and other crops, have migrated to the cities in Tennessee, other parts of the South, and other parts of the country.

Progress has also been made in the production of other crops by farmers and truck gardeners, as well as in the cattle-raising and poultry businesses. In recent years, poultry raising has grown from a small enterprise into one of the state's most important businesses. Scientific progress has lent an important hand, not only in the feeding and general care of poultry, but also in the control of disease and in marketing.

Cattle raising for the dairy farming and meat-packing industries is practiced successfully in Tennessee. Fine grazing lands, well-watered by small streams, creeks, and rivers, produce the finest grasses and, except in cases of drought, afford plenty of water for the herds. The climate is neither too hot nor too cold for raising fine animals.

Another important agricultural enterprise is the breeding, raising, and training of the famous Tennessee walking horse, known the world over for its beauty. In this day of almost complete mechanization, the walking horse is a luxury, whether raised as a hobby, or as a profit-making business. The walking horse thrives in the Tennessee blue-grass country and perpetuates one of Tennessee's oldest traditions, the raising of fine horses.

Farm workers pick cotton by hand, as they did over a hundred years ago.

Despite the general trend toward reduction of the number of farms and movement of much of the farm population to cities, the farms of the state are prosperous and attractive. One of the interesting developments of the last quarter century has been the "half-way-back to the farm movement." This encourages families to continue operating their farms, but, when necessary or desirable, to supplement their incomes by work in the constantly increasing number of small factories, or other "public works" which have sprung up throughout the countryside.

INDUSTRY

From pioneer days, when men established crude ironworks and built primitive mills along its mountain streams, Tennesseans have been aware of the value of the state's natural resources. As technological advances and mechanical inventions have developed, Tennesseans have utilized them.

Today, Tennessee's varied resources have reached a high state of development, and each year the number of new plants, as well as expansion of existing plants, is increasing.

"Tennessee has long since passed from an agricultural state to an industrial economy," states the Division for Industrial Development of the Governor's Staff, "yet its scenic beauty, pleasant climate and rich historical background enable it to preserve a certain graciousness of living that is quickly apparent to those who visit our cities and talk with business leaders."

Among the products of Tennessee's major industries are: processed foods; textiles; apparel; lumber; furniture and fixtures; pulp and paper; petroleum and coal; rubber; leather and leather goods; stone; clay, and glass; fabricated metal; transportation equipment; and instruments.

Among the printing and publishing establishments of the state are the nationally-known Kingsport Press, Kingsport; Methodist Publishing House and Baird-Ward printing establishment, of Nashville. These, and many others, produce literature which is distributed throughout the nation and the world.

Harnessing the power of Tennessee's streams, first, by primitive mills, and, later, by water-powered turbines and generators, has long been an important part of Tennessee's development. Today many of these streams, impounded by a great system of dams, furnish hydroelectric power. When it became apparent that hydroelectric power was not sufficient to meet the needs of Ten-

This ironworks is an example of another of Tennessee's profitable industries.

Sawmills are in operation most of the year. Tennessee is a leader in the production of hardwood lumber.

nessee and the nation, a great system of steam plants was added. Today, the production of electricity by use of nuclear power is being developed. Beyond that lies the possibilities offered by direct conversion of heat into electricity through thermionic conversion and other methods.

In regard to the production of electric power, the Division for Industrial Development points out:

"New additions under construction or on order, will increase the present 18-million-kilowatt capacity of the TVA system to more than 24 million kilowatts by 1972. Most of this new capacity is in unusually large and economical steam units. Among them is the Browns Ferry Nuclear Plant with nearly 3½ million kilowatts in three units, and two very large coal-fired units. Others are Cordell Hull, Percy Priest, Barkley, Elk River and Tim's Fork."

With the transition of Tennessee from an agricultural to a predominantly industrial state, many problems have arisen. New machinery, the development of effective insecticides and fertilizers, and other improve-

Industrial plants such as this one show that Tennessee is indeed a progressive state.

*Both private and public financing help to promote Tennessee's
industrial growth and economy. Plants such as this copper refinery (left)
and this TVA toolshop provide employment for many Tennesseans.*

ments in the operation of farms, have displaced thousands of unskilled workers, most of whom have migrated to the cities of Tennessee and the nation seeking employment. To seek solutions for these and other problems, as well as to bring in new industries, the state in 1953, launched its Industrial Development Program, which has proven effective and has grown with the rapid industrial development of the state.

Mineral Industry   Tennessee's minerals, like its other natural resources, are rich and varied. They range from a small amount of gold and a few precious stones, chiefly garnets found in East Tennessee, mostly in connection with the mining of copper, to the more profitable deposits of coal, zinc, phosphate rock, and others.

Varieties of Tennessee marble, quarried chiefly in the area of Knoxville, along the Holston, French Broad, and Tennessee rivers, have long been recognized for their beauty and used in many important buildings, including Tennessee's own capitol and, among others, in the great National Art Gallery, said to be the largest marble building in the world.

Major Cities

The three natural divisions of Tennessee were settled in the order of their location in relation to the colonies: the closest, East Tennessee, first, then Middle Tennessee and, finally, West Tennessee. The major towns and cities, most of which still stand on the original sites chosen by the pioneers, grew from forts or clusters of cabins built by the early settlers. The four largest cities, Memphis, Nashville, Knoxville, and Chattanooga, are situated on major waterways which are as important today as they were to the first settlers. These sites were first chosen, not only for the fertility of the land surrounding the rivers, but also for the valuable transportation and communication system the river itself provided.

Today a great four-way system of airways, highways, railways, and greatly improved waterways, offers swift, efficient transportation, while television, radio, telephone, and telegraph make it possible for the people of Tennessee to communicate with each other as fast as light and sound can travel. Both the urban and rural sections have benefited from this progress. There is no longer a "backwoods" where many citizens lived in isolated communities out of touch with the rest of the state. Tennessee is now a great alert commonwealth with a population within easy reach of the modern world.

MEMPHIS

Memphis, on the east side of the Mississippi River, with a population of 769,800, is Tennessee's largest city. It is located on the fourth of the Chickasaw Bluffs which take their name from the aboriginal inhabitants of the region, the Chickasaw Indians. These bluffs were known to the early Spanish and French explorers, but actual settlement by white men did not take place until 1819. It was not until after the treaty negotiated in 1818 with the Chickasaws by Andrew Jackson and Isaac Shelby that the section now known as West Tennessee was opened and the city of Memphis was founded.

The original tract of land on which the city stands was granted to John Rice who was killed by the Indians in the Cumberland settlements. Elisha Rice, John's brother, sold the land, a total of 5,000 acres, to Andrew Jackson and John Overton in 1794. Jackson later sold his part to General James Winchester who is credited with selecting the name of Memphis, the historic Egyptian city on the Nile Delta. The new town was also situated in the rich alluvial lands of a great river. Plans for the city were laid out by John Overton, whose efforts in promoting its settlement won for him the title "Father of Memphis."

Between the year of its founding and the outbreak of the Civil War in 1861, Memphis made great progress and was recognized as a leading southern city. In the 1850's it was the scene of great conventions and other gatherings for the discussion of southern problems and the promotion of southern commerce. Memphis was the western terminus of the Memphis and Charleston Railroad, the completion of which was celebrated in 1857 by the picturesque ceremony, the "Wedding of the Waters," when a barrel of

Cotton bales are loaded on wagons in this view of Memphis in the 1800's.

water from the Atlantic Ocean was poured into the Mississippi River.

On June 6, 1862, Memphis was captured by a large Federal fleet, after a hard-fought battle with Union gunboats. It was occupied by the Union Army throughout the Civil War, with the exception of a brief interval on August 21, 1864, when it was recaptured in an early morning surprise attack and held for a few hours by the daring Confederate general, Nathan Bedford Forrest. After the war Memphis was the home of many ex-Confederates, including General Forrest and the Honorable Isham G. Harris, who turned their energies toward rebuilding Tennessee and the South. Jefferson Davis also lived here for a short time.

Today Memphis is one of the greatest cotton markets in the United States and the world's largest hardwood center. Located, as it is, on the borders of the Deep South, it exerts as much influence on bordering states as it does on Tennessee. It is the commercial capital of the mid-South and a great indus-

trial center. Its wealth and progress are reflected in its many handsome private residences, its gay social life, its excellent educational institutions, churches, libraries, parks, and business establishments. And yet, memories remain of W. C. Handy, who made Beale Street famous for the "blues" and of "Boss" Ed Crump who controlled Tennessee politics to such an extent during the late 1920's and 1930's that no candidate for office, regardless of his supposed majority, could consider himself elected until the decision of Crump's Shelby County votes was announced. These things, and many others, give Memphis an individual personality. In spite of its material progress and cosmopolitan air, the city still retains much of its graciousness and Southern charm.

Among the many attractions in Memphis are the magnificent Memphis-Arkansas Bridge, which spans the Mississippi River and connects the South with the Southwest; the magnificent Fontaine House and other historic homes; the University of Tennessee

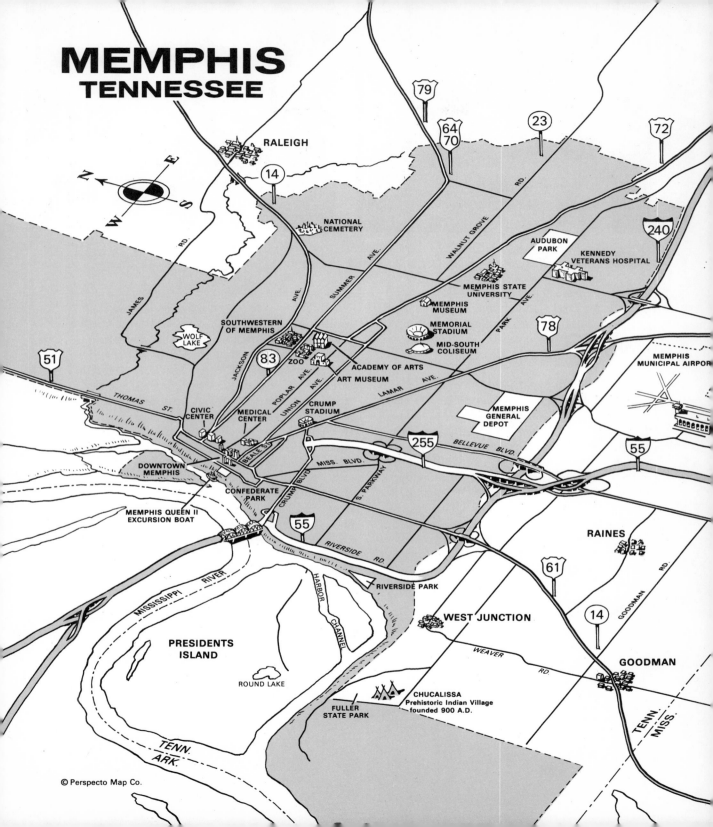

Examples of furnishings in an early period of Tennessee history. Left, the kitchen of Cragfont, home of General Winchester, near Gallatin. Right, the parlor of the Fontaine house, Memphis.

Medical Center; the Overton Park Zoo; and the famous Beale Street bands, which still keep authentic jazz music alive.

NASHVILLE, THE CAPITAL

Nashville, located on the bluffs of the Cumberland River, has a population of 518,000 and is second to Memphis in size. It was named in honor of the Revolutionary hero, General Francis Nash. Nashville was the first permanent settlement in Middle Tennessee. For some three-quarters of a century before, it was known to French traders. A great spring, salt-bearing rocks, and luxuriant vegetation, attracted every species of wildlife found in the section. Frenchmen found it a hunter's paradise and a pleasant and convenient residence during their long hunting expeditions. The Cumberland River and its tributaries, leading to the Mississippi and to the Gulf of Mexico, provided easy access to markets for pelts and furs.

Nashville was founded soon after the landing of the Donelson flotilla, on August 24, 1780. It was first known as Nashborough, but in 1784 it officially became Nashville.

None of the pioneer stories surpass in interest and historical importance that of the Donelson flotilla and the settlement of Nashville. It was a strange fleet that landed at the site. The boats were not trim craft built by experts in a shipyard, although they proved seaworthy enough. Many were crude in appearance, but they had the rugged strength necessary for carrying their burden through nearly a thousand miles of wilderness, through swift currents, and over treacherous shoals. Their sturdy timbers withstood the fire of hostile Indians as they passed through the Chickamauga Towns and the dangerous "Suck" of the Tennessee River. The flagship of the fleet was the "The Good Boat *Adventure*," commanded by Colonel Donelson. Like the other boats, it was built at Fort Patrick Henry—site of the present city of Kingsport—to accommodate several families and carry their household goods and supplies to set up housekeeping in a new land. The fleet carried a large number of women and children, including the families of James Robertson and several other members of the advance party which had left by land to make preparations for them. Robertson had explored the area earlier, and in 1779 led the first party of settlers there from the Watauga Settlements.

The Donelson flotilla consisted of some

NASHVILLE
TENNESSEE

© Perspecto Map Co.

Fort Nashborough stands as a monument to the men and women who founded Nashville in 1780.

thirty or forty boats—flats, dugouts, and other craft. Because smallpox had developed on board, one boat dropped behind and was captured by the Indians. A few others were lost. Some left the fleet at the mouth of the Ohio River and dropped down south, rather than to attempt to stem the current of the Ohio. However, a major portion of the fleet was successful in reaching its destination on the Cumberland.

Among the women of the party were Mrs. James Robertson and her five children; Mrs. Ephriam Peyton and her mother, Mrs. Jennings; Nancy Gower, who is said to have piloted the *Adventure* while the men of the party were fighting the hostile Indians as they passed by the Chickamauga towns; and many others who played heroic parts in the journey and in the founding of Nashville. Another passenger, Mrs. Ann Johnson, sister of James Robertson, taught school during the voyage and later, in the settlements.

Colonel Donelson's own family, including women, children and approximately thirty slaves, were among the emigrants. With them was the vivacious, bright-eyed Rachel Donelson who was to become the wife of Andrew Jackson. That Colonel Donelson felt a deep responsibility for his cargo is shown throughout the diary he kept during the voyage. His final entry, on Monday, April 24, 1780, expressed his satisfaction at being able to reunite families which had almost given up hope of ever being together again.

"This day we arrived at our journey's end at the Big Salt Lick, where we have the pleasure of finding Captain Robertson and his company. It is a source of satisfaction to us to be enabled to restore to him and others their families and friends, who were entrusted to our care, and who, some time since, perhaps, despaired of ever meeting."

On the seventh day after the docking of the *Adventure* at the Great Salt Lick, the Cumberland Compact, which had been prepared by Richard Henderson and others, was considered, adopted, and signed by 256 of the settlers. Only one signer was forced to make his mark, indicating an unusually high degree of literacy among the settlers.

Immediately after the adoption of the compact, a land office was opened, the militia was organized with James Robertson as colonel, and "The Court and Government of Notables" began to operate with Robertson as the presiding officer. In this capacity, Colonel Robertson performed the first marriage ceremony in the settlement in the summer of 1780. James Robertson, for his labors and his contributions to the growth and development of all three grand divisions of the state deserves to be called "Father of Tennessee."

Following quickly in the footsteps of the older settlers was another group of younger men who had come West to seek their fortunes and to take part in the building of the country. Among these men was Andrew Jackson who helped keep Nashville in the forefront of national affairs from 1815 to his death in 1845. With the passing of the Jackson period, Nashville's growth and prominence continued during the Mexican War. President James K. Polk, and Texas hero Sam Houston both claimed Nashville for their home.

During the Civil War Nashville was the first of Tennessee's major cities to be captured by Union forces. Its defense was made impossible by the fall of Fort Donelson and the presence of Federal gunboats on the Cumberland River, and on February 23, 1862 it was occupied by the Union Army. From that day forward the city's defenses were strengthened and Fort Negley, the largest and strongest fortification built by the Union Army during the war, was erected on St. Cloud's Hill. It was while General U. S. Grant was in Nashville that he was called to Washington by the President to be made commander-in-chief of the Federal armies; and it was in Nashville that General W. T. Sherman made his preparations and assembled supplies for his "March to the Sea." After the war, General Nathan Bedford Forrest was a frequent visitor to Nashville and here, in a room of the old Maxwell House Hotel, organized the Ku Klux Klan. During the Reconstruction years the state capitol was the scene of bitter battles between the reconstruction governor, William G. Brownlow and the disfranchised ex-Confederates.

As the Reconstruction years passed, Nashville made great progress in re-establishing business organizations, and in re-

The Country Music Hall of Fame houses both pictures and personal objects of famous country stars.

The Municipal Auditorium at Nashville combines both modern charm and classic beauty in its design.

storing or rebuilding factories and private residences damaged or destroyed during the years of occupation. Along with its efforts to restore material progress, Nashville turned its attention to its school system. Attention to education and the presence of many buildings of classical Greek style popularized by William Strickland, architect of the state capitol, has earned Nashville the title of "Athens of the South."

Music City, U.S.A. In recent years, however, Nashville has won for itself an entirely different name—"Music City, U.S.A." Through years of making records and radio and television broadcasting, a style of country music has developed known nationally and internationally as "The Nashville Sound." This unique style has brought most of the large recording companies of the United States to the city and has made music in Nashville a multi-million dollar business. Recently a country music museum has been built which boasts a great collection of music, musical instruments, histories, and photographs of popular performers. Nashville is also the home of the "Grand Ole Opry," the oldest continuous radio program in existence.

The city has many other points of interest such as Fort Nashborough, the Old City Cemetery, the replica of the Parthenon, Belle Meade Mansion, the Botanical Gardens and Fine Arts Center at Cheekwood, Ellington Agricultural Center, the War Memorial Building, the State Museum, the State Supreme Court Building, the State Library, and, of course, the historic capitol building of the State of Tennessee which crowns the highest hill in the city.

KNOXVILLE

Knoxville, the third largest city with 392,800 inhabitants is important not only in the formation and early history of the state, but also for the significant part which it plays in the world of today. It is the western gateway of the Great Smoky Mountain National Park, and is in the center of the TVA region with its many electric power plants, lakes, and recreational facilities. However, it is more than an important center for vacation-minded tourists, it is a region noted for its great scientific developments. Nearby is Oak Ridge, selected as the site of the Manhattan Project for the development of atomic energy.

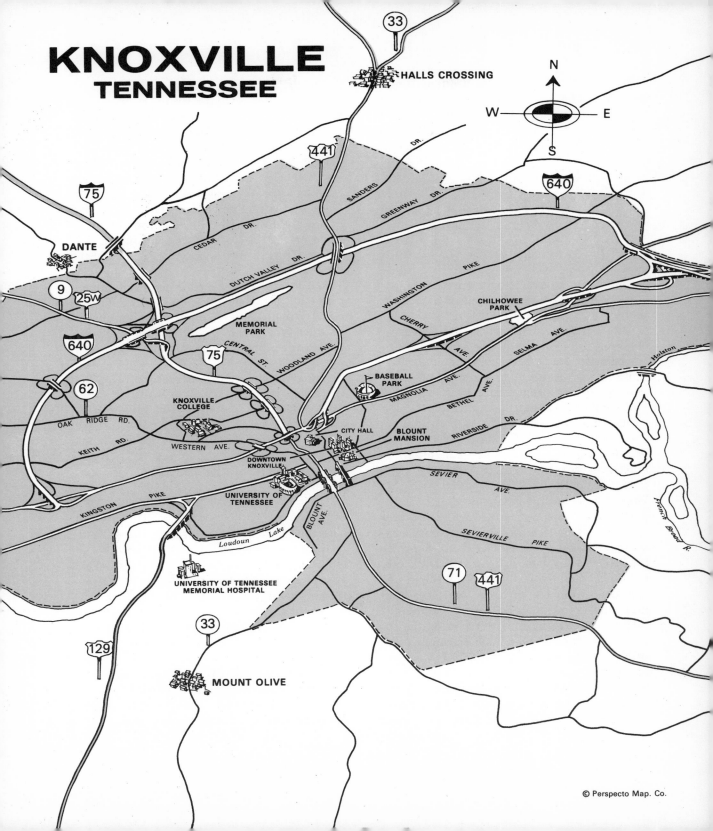

The First Capital When William Blount first assumed the duties of the Territory South of the River Ohio, his business was conducted from the home of William Caobb, near Jonesborough. He soon chose as the site of his home the fort and settlement formed by James White in 1786 near the point where the French Broad and Holston rivers come together, forming the Tennessee River. Here the first official capital was set up, and the town of Knoxville founded. It was named for Henry Knox, Secretary of War during the Revolution. General White, in 1792, drew up the original plan of the town and promoted its settlement.

In 1791, this settlement was the scene of the important Treaty of the Holston, negotiated with the Cherokee Indians, and in 1798 it was established as a supply and repair depot for wagon trains going West. Knoxville served as the capital of the territory and the state almost continuously from 1792 until 1817, with the exception of the session of 1807, which met briefly in Kingston, but returned to Knoxville after two days, and the sessions from 1813 to 1817, which met in Nashville.

During the Civil War, Knoxville was occupied by both armies. First, it was the headquarters of the Confederate Army in East Tennessee, but, in June, 1863, the city was occupied by General William P. Sanders, of the Union Army, who was later succeeded by General Ambrose Burnside. Like other parts of East Tennessee, Knoxville had large numbers of Union sympathizers throughout the war, and was torn between the contending factions. With the rest of the state, it finally emerged from the devastation of war and again took a leading part in the development of East Tennessee.

Today, Knoxville is the center of East Tennessee's rich agricultural region from which it draws an extensive trade in livestock, dairy products, poultry, and tobacco. The city continues to participate in the development of the natural resources of the area. Nearby are deposits of coal and iron; sand and gravel are also in great abundance. Deposits of Tennessee marble, an exceptional building material, surround the area, and some of the quarries are within the city limits. The city has many important plants for the refining and processing of minerals. Textiles are Knoxville's major manufactured item, but furniture, electrical porcelain, cement, and steel products are also produced in great quantities and new industries are being constantly added to the list.

Knoxville has many attractions, such as Governor Blount's mansion built in 1792, the Confederate Memorial Hall, and Market House built in 1897. The four TVA dams in the area make many lakes available for fishing, boating and swimming. The city is also the home of the University of Tennessee.

CHATTANOOGA

Chattanooga is the youngest and smallest (population 308,100) of Tennessee's four major cities. The name, Chattanooga, officially adopted in 1838, comes from the Creek Indian word Chat-to-to-noo-gee, meaning "rock coming to a point." Long before the present city was dreamed of this site was the meeting place of several major Indian trails, including the Great War Path and the Shawnee trail into the Cumberland Valley. The natural surroundings of the area attracted the earliest travelers in the western country; Lookout Mountain, Nickajack

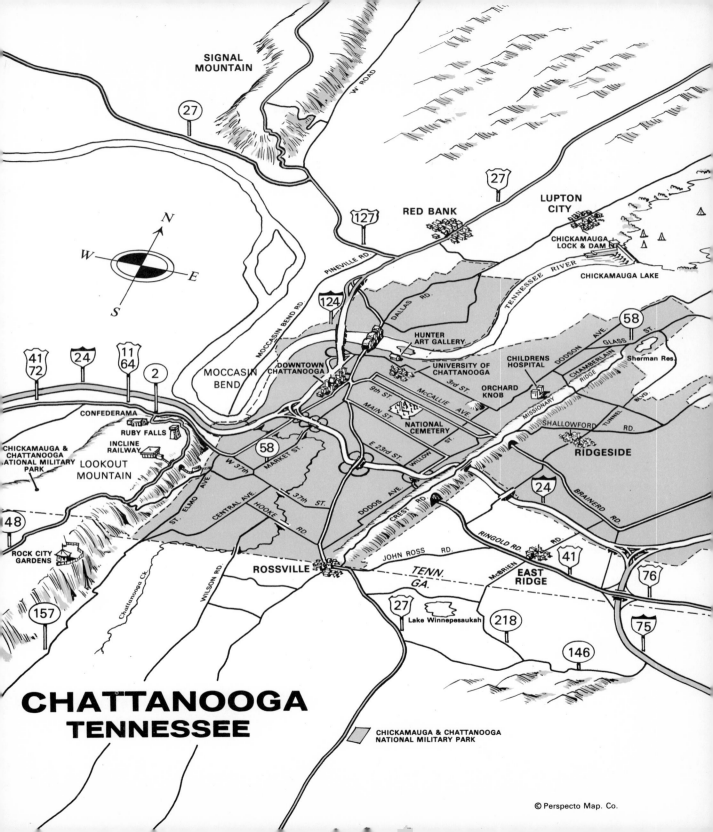

SIGNAL MOUNTAIN

W ROAD

27

27

RED BANK

LUPTON CITY

127

PINEVILLE RD.

CHICKAMAUGA LOCK & DAM

TENNESSEE RIVER

CHICKAMAUGA LAKE

N
W E
S

124

DALLAS RD.

HUNTER ART GALLERY

CHILDRENS HOSPITAL

58

DODSON AVE.

GLASS ST.

Sherman Res.

CHAMBERLAIN

41 72

24

11 64

2

MOCCASIN BEND RD.

MOCCASIN BEND

DOWNTOWN CHATTANOOGA

UNIVERSITY OF CHATTANOOGA

3rd ST.

9th ST.

McCALLIE AVE.

ORCHARD KNOB

RIDGE

MISSIONARY

TUNNEL RD.

RIDGESIDE

CONFEDERAMA

RUBY FALLS

INCLINE RAILWAY

58

MAIN ST.

NATIONAL CEMETERY

SHALLOWFORD

CHICKAMAUGA & CHATTANOOGA NATIONAL MILITARY PARK

LOOKOUT MOUNTAIN

W 37th AVE.

MARKET ST.

ST. ELMO AVE.

37th ST.

E 23rd ST.

WILLOW ST.

DODOS AVE.

CREST RD.

24

BRAINERD RD.

48

CENTRAL AVE.

HOOKE RD.

WILSON RD.

ROSSVILLE

JOHN ROSS RD.

RINGOLD RD.

RD.

41

McBRIEN RD.

EAST RIDGE

76

ROCK CITY GARDENS

Chattanooga Ck.

TENN. GA.

75

157

27

Lake Winnepesaukah

218

146

CHATTANOOGA
TENNESSEE

CHICKAMAUGA & CHATTANOOGA NATIONAL MILITARY PARK

© Perspecto Map. Co.

Broad Street in Chattanooga during the late nineteenth century.

Cave, the Suck (or Boiling Pot) in the Tennessee River, the Muscle Shoals, and other impediments to navigation, inspired not only interest but fear. Located here were the towns of the hostile Chickamaugas, the base of Indian expeditions against the Cumberland settlements and other attacks on travelers who dared go down the river through their country.

It was not until the year 1837 that the Indian title to the lands of this section were extinguished and the Cherokees, treading their heartbreaking "Trail of Tears" to Oklahoma, made way for the white settlements. A post office was established in that year at Ross' Landing, home of the Cherokee chief, John Ross, who fought bitterly against the removal of his people but who eventually led them to the West.

Some of the most important battles of the Civil War were fought at Chattanooga. The Confederates, under General Bragg, in September, 1863, won a decisive victory here, but the Union Army, under the command of General Grant, reversed the situation in the battles of Chattanooga, Lookout Mountain, and Missionary Ridge. Following these victories, the Federal troops strengthened their position in the city and in late May and early June, 1864, it was from this well-stocked base that General Sherman launched his "March to the Sea." Now, its battlefields are well marked and have many monuments dedicated to units and individual heroes of both the Union and Confederate armies who fought upon them.

Chattanooga was rebuilt with the aid of many northern men who invested large amounts of capital in this area. Today Chattanooga processes iron ore and produces farm implements, machinery, structural steel and other items. Among the city's attractions are the Rock City Gardens, Fairyland Caverns, Ruby Falls and Lookout Mountain. Chickamauga Lake, formed by the Chickamauga Dam, provides many recreational facilities. There are also art galleries, museums, parks, and golf courses.

Education in Tennessee

EARLY SCHOOLS

The southwestern frontier had scarcely been settled when men and women began to make plans for the education of the children of this new and undeveloped country. Schools were established as rapidly as possible, but there were many delays. Homes had to be built, settlements protected against the Indians, and governments formed. Meanwhile the children received their educations by family firesides, or in one of the early schools conducted by such men as Samuel Doak, Samuel Carrick, and Thomas Craighead.

The Reverend Doak, first of the three to found an important institution, became president of the first school, Martin Academy, later named Washington College. Craighead was elected president of Davidson Academy, which was provided for in the North Carolina Act of 1785. Carrick became president of Blount College, established by the territorial legislature in 1794, which later became the University of Tennessee.

As settlements grew, other schools were established. But, it was many years before an adequate school system could be developed. The country was sparsely populated and the danger from Indian attacks made it impossible for children to go even small distances to school. Thus, the schools had to be confined to pioneer cabins or to groups which had gathered in forts or stations along the frontier. Parents were most often the teachers, although other members of the family or community frequently taught. Sometimes there were private schools such as the "seminary" which Reverend Samuel Carrick advertised in the *Knoxville Gazette* in 1792.

Classes for young children were taught by mothers and other women of the households. Fathers and other men in the settlements helped, particularly with the more advanced education of young men. In those days it was rare for a woman to have more than the simplest education, if she could read and write at all. Many of the men who were leaders in the settlements were well educated.

In pioneer days, children received their education at home. Scenes such as this, with the family gathered around the table, while the head of the house read passages from the Bible, were common.

Children who received their educations at home were well prepared for school, in case they were fortunate enough to be near one. If they did not have this opportunity, they had been given the tools for self-education which could continue for the remainder of their lives.

If the boys received some training in reading, writing, and arithmetic and, had average ability and ambition, they could be successful. Even a meager knowledge of the "three R's" was sufficient, for ability and ambition were often more important than book learning. As for the girls, their great need was a knowledge of homemaking. All other learning beyond the ability to read and write was generally looked upon as unnecessary for women.

In spite of this general attitude, however, Tennessee became a leader in the field of education for women. The group of girls who, with Barbara Blount, attended Blount College during 1804-1806, were the first "co-eds" in the country.

While the Blount College experiment in coeducation was not permanent, many academies and colleges for young women were established. Eventually, colleges and universities became coeducational, admitting women as full-fledged students on an equal footing with men. As early as 1806, the Fisk Female Academy was established by Moses Fisk and his friend, Sampson Williams. Soon after its establishment other institutions for young women were organized: East Tennessee Female Academy; Nashville Female Academy; Mary Sharp College; Ward Seminary; Belmont College; and, later Ward-Belmont College. As both private and public education developed in Tennessee, the training of young women began to assume its rightful place in the state school system.

SECONDARY EDUCATION

The history of secondary education in Tennessee is not a story of high schools or of preparatory schools as they exist today. In the beginning, a number of so-called colleges taught subjects which later were included in the curricula of secondary schools. Academies, or early equivalent of the present secondary school, taught subjects now taught in elementary schools. Therefore, it is impossible to separate the early history of secondary education from either that of the elementary school or that of the college.

During colonial days, the New England colonies because of their compact settlements and corresponding unity of interests, found it convenient to support schools by the creation of common funds, by private subscription or, occasionally, by taxation. Support of public education by taxation was not yet established in Tennessee, although many important steps were taken for the support of institutions of higher learning and academies by the sale of public lands.

An effort was made in 1806 when, by a joint agreement of the governments of the United States, North Carolina and Tennessee, certain public lands were set apart for the support of a system of public education. Academies were established in twenty-seven counties under this arrangement. The funds acquired from the sale of lands were not adequate and the movement did not achieve its expected goals.

Most of the early attempts to create an adequate public school system were far from effective. Proposals to supplement the common schools fund by direct taxation were so strongly opposed that most of them were withdrawn. These efforts failed for a number of reasons. The most important was the fact that the "common schools" were charitable institutions. This idea dated back to the time when provision was made for the orphans of men who fought in the War of 1812. Another reason was that literacy was not yet considered a requirement for good citizenship, nor was it necessary for making a living. Most progressive men believed in the importance of education, but were satisfied to let it remain limited to the few.

Effective legislation for the support of public schools began as early as 1815. While progress was made before the 1830's, it was not until the 1834 state Constitutional Convention that a sound foundation was laid for the establishment of a public school system. Many years later a satisfactory system began to emerge. This progress, halted by the Civil War, resumed with the 1870 Constitutional Convention. Through this period the academy system, supported by the traditional one-room school, provided improved educational advantages for the boys and girls of Tennessee.

The year 1899 was an important one in Tennessee's secondary-school history. The fifty-first General Assembly passed the High School Act which provided that county school funds could be legally expended in the support of high schools. Tiptonville High

The library at Rugby, an experimental community founded by Thomas Hughes in 1879.

School in Lake County was the first school established in accordance with the provisions of this act.

The growth of the free public high school movement in Tennessee was slow. By 1910, there were fewer than fifty four-year high schools. That year only 1008 pupils were graduated. Since the establishment of the first high school, great changes have taken place in Tennessee's elementary and secondary schools as well as in its institutions of higher learning.

Two major wars and the nation's involvement in Vietnam and Korea, have necessitated not only accelerated programs for advanced education in science, but also

Christ Church at Rugby. Based on philosophical and theological principles of Christian stoicism, the community eventually dissolved because it could not support itself.

Age-old handicrafts are kept alive today throughout Tennessee. The arts of weaving and rug-making are handed down from generation to generation. The Cumberland Mountain Craft Center and Gatlinburg, the "Craft Capital," produce fine handmade products.

social sciences, economics, and other fields affected by world and local problems. The "Sputnik," put into orbit by the Russians in November, 1957, accentuated this necessity for scientific education and resulted in rapid, high-pressure expansion of an advanced space program and a new and urgent emphasis on scientific education.

Tennessee's educators have established highly-developed programs for scientific education and social studies, as well as for mathematics, languages, reading, writing, public speaking, and many other subjects designed to produce well-informed and well-rounded students. Construction of new buildings utilizing the latest and most modern designs and renovation of older buildings continues in order to relieve crowded classrooms and provide adequate quarters and instruction for the state's rapidly increasing school population.

Progressive legislation for the support and improvement of Tennessee's public schools has been enacted since 1873, when the first act establishing a program of public education for primary grades was passed. In 1909 and in 1925, the General Assembly passed additional legislation for the purpose of reorganizing the framework of the state educational system.

Provision for the establishment of a state-owned and state-operated system of area schools for vocational and technical training of out-of-school boys and adults and for regional institutes providing technical training at a post-high school level, was made by legislation enacted in 1963.

The educational activities of Tennessee are carried on under the direction of the State Board of Education, with the exception of the University of Tennessee, which operates under its own Board of Trust.

Higher education is important to Tennessee. George Peabody (left), a noted teachers' college, Vanderbilt University (right) and Scarritt College form the University Center at Nashville.

The Scopes Trial   In 1925 the Tennessee General Assembly passed a law forbidding the teaching of evolution in the public schools. Education, science, and religion came into immediate conflict, and there were bitter arguments between "fundamentalists" who believed in a literal interpretation of the Biblical passages on the origin of man, and the "radicals" who sought to teach what they considered sound theories of certain scientists.

Soon after the passage of the law, John T. Scopes, a young teacher at the Rhea County High School in Dayton, decided to challenge the law by openly teaching his ideas on the theory of evolution to his pupils. He was charged with violation of the law and brought to trial. His chief counsel was the brilliant lawyer, Clarence Darrow. The equally famous William Jennings Bryan presented the cause of the fundamentalists.

All of the great news services and many nationally known newspapers and magazines had writers on the scene. The press throughout the country carried screaming headlines over their daily accounts of the trial. Scopes was found guilty and fined one hundred dollars. A newspaper of the period called it the most famous misdemeanor case in the State's history. The law was finally repealed in 1967.

COLLEGES AND UNIVERSITIES

Tennessee's interest in education is seen in the many great public and private universities and colleges located within the state. Vanderbilt University and Fisk University in Nashville, the University of the South at Sewanee, and the University of Tennessee at Knoxville are only a few of the outstanding examples.

Originally Central University in its charter, Vanderbilt changed its name in 1873 when a large donation was made by Cornelius Vanderbilt for the development of the university. First affiliated with the Methodist Episcopal Church, the State Supreme Court in 1914 ruled against complete control of the university by the church and since that time, Vanderbilt has considered itself non-sectarian and independent. Today, Vanderbilt has a strong College of Arts and Sciences, a graduate school, and independent schools of engineering, religion, law, and medicine.

The University of the South, popularly known as Sewanee, was founded in 1857. Protestant Episcopal in affiliation it is an all male institution with an enrollment of about 1,000. Henry Horton, governor of Tennessee in 1928, attended school here. Sewanee is a school with a tradition of rigorous liberal arts training and most of its students graduate in the social sciences and English. The school also has programs in forestry and engineering.

The University of Tennessee, which began during the territorial period as Blount College, is no longer confined to its original campus in Knoxville, but has extended its activities to such an extent that it utilizes the entire state as its campus. It is not only a teaching institution, but a research center and public service agency which meets varied needs of the people, from remote farms to complicated science laboratories and the aerospace center at Tullahoma.

Its headquarters and largest campus are still located in Knoxville, where courses are offered by all of its colleges, except the Medical and Dental Units, which are located in Memphis. Recent expansion, including acquisition of the University of Chattanooga, now provides four-year university courses at Nashville, Martin, and Chattanooga, as well as an evening school and the School of Social Work in Nashville.

The University's twenty colleges are: Liberal Arts and Science; Engineering; Law;

The beautiful campus of the University of the South at Sewanee.

Teacher Education; Home Economics; Agriculture; Business Administration; Journalism; Architecture; Health, Physical Education and Recreation; Social Work; Medicine; Dentistry; Pharmacy; Nursing; Basic Medical Science; Graduate School; Urban and Regional Planning; Biomedical Studies; and the Space Institute.

Institutions of higher learning governed by the State Board of Education are: Austin Peay State University, Clarksville; East Tennessee State University, Johnson City; Memphis State University, Memphis; Middle Tennessee State University, Murfreesboro; Tennessee Agricultural and Industrial State University, Nashville; Tennessee Technological University, Cookeville; Columbia State Community College; Jackson State Community College; and Cleveland State Community College.

In addition, there are three special schools: Alvin C. York Agricultural Institute, Jamestown; Tennessee School for the Blind, Donelson; Tennessee School for the Deaf, Knoxville.

Dr. Robert H. White, State Historian, author of Messages of the Governors *and other important works on Tennessee history.*

The University of Tennessee was founded in 1794 at Knoxville. Below, a drawing of the "Old College."

State Government

THE LEGISLATIVE DEPARTMENT

In 1796, having attended to defining the basic rights of the individual, the framers of Tennessee's original Constitution turned their attention to providing for details of putting the government into operation. To accomplish this, they set up three major departments separate and distinct from each other: the Legislative; the Executive; and the Judicial.

The Legislative Department was created to make laws designed to implement the provisions of the Constitution and to provide for the many details of putting the state's government into operation. These laws must be in harmony with the provisions of the Constitution and may not in any way interfere with individual rights guaranteed by that document.

One of the most important types of legislation provided for by the Constitution deals with the levying of taxes, not only by the state government, but also by cities, towns, and counties. On this and other phases of state and local government, there are many laws which regulate the different branches of the government.

The passage of these laws is carefully set forth in the Constitution, which makes detailed provisions for the introduction, passage, rejection, or repeal of bills proposed to the General Assembly. A bill may originate in either house, but it may be amended, altered, or rejected by the other house. Every bill must be read in the house in which it originated for three successive days and be passed each day, before it can be submitted for consideration by the other house.

After a bill has been passed upon favorably by both houses, it is submitted to the governor for his signature. If he signs the bill, it becomes a law. If he disapproves and vetoes it, the bill may then be resubmitted to the house in which it originated. If the bill then receives a majority of the votes in both houses, it is passed over the governor's veto and becomes a law.

There are other details demanded for the passage of legislation which should be studied by citizens who may consider serving in the legislature and by those who are interested in securing the passage of legislation. Many organizations originate bills and work for their passage by the General Assembly. Corporations, educational institutions, women's clubs, civic organizations, and other important groups often participate actively in securing passage of important laws.

Regular sessions of the General Assembly are held once every two years, beginning the first Monday in January of odd-numbered years. In accord with legislation enacted in 1967, the General Assembly now also meets, in adjourned session, in even-numbered years for a total of thirty days. The first of such adjourned sessions was that which convened in February, 1968.

After a session of the General Assembly convenes, in its first order of business is the election of Speakers for the Senate and House of Representatives. The Speaker of the Senate, who also serves as Lieutenant-Governor, is an especially important person. In case of a vacancy in the governor's chair, he becomes the state's chief executive. Next in succession, for the governorship are: the

Secretary of State, Comptroller of the Treasury, and Treasurer.

The Senate, called the "upper house," is composed of thirty-three members. A senator must be at least thirty years of age, an American citizen, a resident of the state for three years, and a resident of the county or district he represents for at least one year immediately preceding his election. In addition to its other important duties the Senate has the power to try impeachment proceedings.

The House of Representatives, called the "lower house," has ninety-nine members. A member of the House of Representatives must be at least twenty-one years of age, a resident of the state for three years and a resident of the county or district he represents for one year immediately preceding his election. The House of Representatives, in addition to its other duties, has the sole power to originate impeachment proceedings against public officials.

Among the important functions of the General Assembly are: to make or repeal laws; to appropriate all money paid out of the state treasury; to make laws concerning the levying and collection of taxes; and to authorize counties and incorporated towns and cities to levy taxes.

THE EXECUTIVE DEPARTMENT

The most powerful person in the state government is the governor, its chief executive. The Executive Department is distinctly separate from the legislative and the judicial departments. The governor has no power to pass laws, although his influence and recommendations have an important effect in shaping legislation. He cannot try cases, make judicial decisions, or appoint judges, except in cases where he is authorized to appoint judges and chancellors to fill vacancies caused by death or resignation. He does have the power to pardon people convicted of crimes or to commute their sentences.

His chief duties are of a broader nature. He represents the state and its people to the nation and the world. He promotes its welfare at home and abroad and seeks to improve the services of the various welfare departments and state institutions. The governor insists upon rigid enforcement of laws and punishment of crime, and also promotes measures for the rehabilitation of criminals. He makes every effort to see that inmates of jails and penitentiaries have humane treatment, health care, and education during the period they are confined.

Since the business of the state has become so complex that one man cannot handle it, the governor has been given the power to name commissions and staff members of the state departments. These major departments are: Finance and Taxation, Administration, Personnel, and Purchasing. The present governor has also five special assistants: William L. Barry and S. H. Roberts, executive assistants; H. T. Lockard, Administrative Assistant; Hudley Crockett, News Secretary and Special Assistant; Dr. Hyram Plass, Director of Urban and Federal Affairs; James H. Alexander, Governor's Staff Director; and Claude Armour, Special Assistant to the Governor on Law and Order.

Constitutional Officers In the Executive Department there are three constitutional officers elected by the General Assembly: the Secretary of State, Comptroller of the Treasury, and State Treasurer. The Secretary of State is elected for a four-year term.

The iris (left), Tennessee's state flower; the tulip poplar (right), the state tree, in bloom.

Among the most important of his varied duties is that of keeping an official register of all official acts and proceedings of the governor and when called upon to do so, to ". . . lay same, all papers, minutes, and vouchers relative thereto, before the General Assembly . . ." Others include the filing of original acts and resolutions of the General Assembly, recording of all commissions issued by the governor, recording of applications for corporate charters, and filing the rules and regulations of the various state department boards. The Secretary of State is also responsible for preparation of the *Tennessee Blue Book* which gives information on how the state of Tennessee operates, the personnel of its departments, historical information, and other facts.

Both the Comptroller of the Treasury and the State Treasurer are elected by the General Assembly for a two-year term. Although the state Constitution does not prescribe the duties of the state comptroller, his function in government is prescribed by a number of legislative enactments. He serves as staff to

the General Assembly and its various committees and as auditor and in other financial activities of the government.

The State Treasurer is custodian of all state funds. He receives tax money collected by the Department of Revenue, deposits the money in banks throughout the state, and performs other important acts connected with the state financial system.

Special Departments and Commissions
Other departments also assist the governor in the administration of state affairs: Agriculture, Conservation, Correction, Education, Employment Security, Finance and Administration, Highways, Insurance and Banking, Labor, Mental Health, Military, Personnel, Public Health, Public Welfare, Revenue, Standards and Purchases, and Veterans' Affairs.

THE JUDICIAL DEPARTMENT

Creation of the Judicial Department of Tennessee was preceded by several unique forms of courts which administered justice and promoted the establishment of law and order from the first days of settlement.

Today the Judicial Department of the state of Tennessee, by terms of the Constitution, is composed of ". . . one Supreme Court and . . . such Circuit, Chancery, and other inferior Courts as the Legislature shall from time to time, ordain and establish."

Under this provision, many courts have been established to carry the increasing load of cases which population growth and complexities of modern life are placing upon the dockets of the courts. To help relieve the overburdened docket of the State Supreme Court, the Court of Appeals, which has jurisdiction over most civil cases, was established. It has nine judges who are elected by

Members of the governor's staff. From left to right: H. T. Lockard, S. H. (Bo) Roberts, Hudley Crockett, and W. L. Barry.

the people for terms of eight years. Under the provision of the law, only three of these judges may come from each of the three divisions of the state. In order to expedite business, the court is authorized to sit in sections with three judges each at Knoxville, Nashville, and Jackson.

The highest court, the State Supreme Court, is composed of five members. The present judges are: Chief Justice Hamilton S. Burnett and Associate Justices Chester C. Chattin, Larry Barkley Creson, Ross W. Dyer, and Allison B. Humphreys.

An Attorney General and Reporter for the state are also in the Judicial Department, as well as a district attorney for each circuit for which a judge having criminal jurisdiction is provided by law.

TENNESSEE'S DELEGATION IN THE CONGRESS

From the time that the legislature selected William Blount and William Cocke to represent the new state of Tennessee in the United States Senate, men of unusual ability have represented the state. The caliber of men elected by the people to serve in the

U.S. House of Representatives has also been equally high, as was shown when Andrew Jackson became Tennessee's first representative in the lower house.

This tradition has been maintained through the years. Three Tennesseans who became President of the United States—Jackson, Polk, and Johnson—served in the Congress, as did Sam Houston who became President of the Texas Republic. The late Joseph W. Byrns, representative from the Hermitage District for many years, served as speaker of the House of Representatives during the administration of Franklin D. Roosevelt. Cordell Hull, who had served both as a Representative and as a Senator was named Secretary of State by President Roosevelt in 1933. He served until ill health forced his retirement in 1944, having remained in that office longer than any other man in the nation's history. Hull did outstanding work in the negotiation of reciprocal trade agreements which contributed to cooperation between the nations. Especially known for his efforts to bring the North and South American nations into closer contact with each other, he was the author of the famous "Good Neighbor" policy.

Tennessee's present delegation in Congress maintains the high standards for which the state has been noted through the years.

Ranking member of the present delegation is Senator Albert Gore, Democrat, born at Carthage, Tennessee, on December 26, 1907. First serving as a member of the House of Representatives, he was elected to the United States Senate in 1952 and was re-elected in 1958 and 1964. He has held important chairmanships and for many years has taken an important place among the leaders in national affairs.

The junior United States Senator, Howard H. Baker, Jr., is a Republican, who was elected to that office in 1966. He has made progress in establishing himself as a member of the Senate and will undoubtedly assume a more important place in the Senate as he grows in experience and in seniority.

Present members of the United States House of Representatives are: James H. Quillen, of the First District, one of the two Republicans in the delegation; John J. Duncan, Second District; William E. Brock, Third District; Joe L. Evins, Fourth District; Richard H. Fulton, Fifth District; William R. Anderson, Sixth District; Ray

Blanton, Seventh District; Robert A. Everett, Eighth District; and Dan Kuykendall, Republican, Ninth District.

In addition to his excellent record as a member of the House of Representatives, Representative William R. Anderson has another distinction. He is a veteran of submarine warfare and, from 1957 to 1959 was skipper of the *Nautilus*. Returning to Tennessee, he was first elected to membership in the House of Representatives in 1964.

CURRENT PROBLEMS OF GOVERNMENT

Both governors and legislators have sponsored many important measures for the benefit of the state and have managed the steadily increasing problems of government. Taxes have been increased because mounting costs of operating the state government and increasing demands for new and improved services have necessitated the raising of additional funds.

One of the problems which legislators and governors of all states have faced during the twentieth century is the continually increasing influence of the federal government which accompanies the expenditure of Fed-

With dignified majesty the capitol building at Nashville is a fitting tribute to a great state.

eral funds in the states. This expenditure is authorized by Congressional legislation and decisions by the United States Supreme Court and lower Federal courts. These decisions and steadily increasing amounts demanded by federal taxation, have posed serious problems. The states are also affected by directives issued by the President himself, as well as directives and "guide lines" made by lesser officials of the federal government.

Other serious problems also plague Tennessee and the nation. Increases in the population of large cities, as well as smaller towns, by unskilled laborers have caused concentrations of low-income groups in slum areas. These have created problems which cause great concern throughout the nation. Local, state, and federal authorities are making all possible efforts to find solutions. Yet, while solutions are being sought, riots have broken out, great areas of many cities have been looted and burned, and the people whom the governments were seeking to help have had their homes and businesses destroyed. In some cases, lives have been lost.

Riots and "sit-ins" in some institutions of learning have resulted in millions of dollars of damage to buildings and equipment which public funds and private philanthropy had provided for the education of the students who destroyed them. Some of these incidents have occurred in Tennessee. Fortunately, they have been brought under control by the faculties of the institutions, public law enforcement officials and, often, by the law-abiding students.

Today, as in the past, Tennesseans are solving their problems and, in the forefront, as they were on the fields of battle, are the men who served the state and the nation in both World Wars, Korea and Vietnam. Speaking to them—and for them—on the occasion of the Golden Anniversary of the Tennessee American Legion (1968), James G. Stahlman, publisher of *The Nashville Banner*, veteran of both world wars, and recipient of the Legion's Fiftieth Anniversary Award, warned of the dangers which are confronting the nation today. In a powerful, characteristically fearless speech, Mr. Stahlman reminded his hearers of their proud heritage, told them of their obligation to use their collective influence to counteract the dangerous influences which threaten to destroy the nation, and made an eloquent appeal to the youth of the state.

"This is the time of all times for the youth of the nation to accent for themselves a redemptive recognition of their individual and collective responsibilities; to revere the Lord, God Almighty, love this nation, respect its flag, obey its laws and serve it faithfully and honorably wherever military and civil duty may call.

"May God give an overwhelming majority of them the wisdom and the courage to take this stand. They are not only the last best hope of America, they are also the last best hope of Earth."

The Sweep of History in Tennessee

1492 Spain claims territory as a result of Columbus' discovery of America

1497 England claims territory after John Cabot's voyage

1524 France claims territory as a result of Verrazano's voyage

1540 De Soto enters what is now Tennessee

1673 James Needham and Gabriel Arthur are first Englishmen to enter Tennessee

Marquette and Joliet stop at Chickasaw Bluffs on the Mississippi River

1682 La Salle claims Mississippi Valley for France and builds Fort Prud'homme on first Chickasaw Bluff near mouth of Hatchie River

1715 Cherokees and Chickasaws drive Shawnees out of Tennessee country

1730 Cherokee chiefs go to England; Sir Alexander Cuming negotiates first treaty between English and Cherokees

1739 French build Fort Assumption at site of Memphis

1748 Dr. Thomas Walker explores vicinity of present Kingsport

1750 Dr. Thomas Walker and party discover Cumberland Gap

1754 French and Indian War begins

1757 Fort Loudoun, first Anglo-American fort in Tennessee, completed on Little Tennessee River

1760 Cherokees capture Fort Loudoun

Richard Henderson commissions Daniel Boone to find desirable sites for settlements in East Tennessee and Kentucky

1761 Peace made between English and Cherokees

Elisha Walden and his Long Hunters explore East Tennessee and Cumberland area

1763 Treaty of Paris: France surrenders to England all claims to region east of the Mississippi River

1763 English establish Proclamation Line forbidding settlement west of Appalachians

1769 William Bean builds cabin on Boone's Creek, near its junction with Watauga River

1770 James Robertson settles on Watauga River

1772 Watauga Association adopts first written constitution in America

1775 Revolutionary War begins

Transylvania Company buys Cherokee land between Kentucky and Cumberland rivers

Boone opens Wilderness Road to Kentucky

1776 Declaration of Independence signed

Washington District supersedes Watauga Association; first political unit in U.S. named for George Washington

1777 Washington District becomes Washington County, with boundaries coextensive with present State of Tennessee

1779 James Robertson, "Father of Middle Tennessee," reaches Cumberland Settlement

1780 *Adventure* lands at site of Nashville

Cumberland Compact signed

Battle of King's Mountain

Sevier defeats Cherokees at Boyd's Creek

1784 State of Franklin established and constitution adopted; lasts until 1788

1786 Franklin and North Carolina claim jurisdiction in East Tennessee

James White settles White's Fork, now Knoxville

1790 Congress creates Territory of the United States of America South of the River Ohio, with William Blount as governor; first U.S. census shows population of 35,691

1791 White's Fork (Knoxville) becomes capital of Southwest Territory

1796 Tennessee becomes the sixteenth state of the U.S. on June 1
First State Constitution adopted
Tennessee County abolished to establish Robertson and Montgomery counties and the name Tennessee given to state
First General Assembly meets at Knoxville
First state governor, John Sevier, inaugurated

1806 Congress grants sale of lands for support of academies and for Blount and Cumberland colleges

1807 Bank of Nashville, first in Tennessee, chartered
East Tennessee College established at Knoxville, succeeding Blount College

1810 Population: 261,727

1811 Reelfoot Lake formed by earthquake

1812 War declared with Great Britain

1815 Jackson defeats British forces at Battle of New Orleans on January 8

1819 First steamboat, *General Jackson,* arrives at Nashville
John Overton lays out city of Memphis

1826 Davy Crockett elected to United States Congress

1827 Sam Houston becomes governor

1828 Jackson defeats John Quincy Adams for presidency of the United States

1832 Andrew Jackson re-elected president of the United States

1834 New state constitution adopted

1836 Sam Houston and other Tennesseans lead Texans to independence from Mexico
Davy Crockett killed at the Alamo

1838 Removal of the Cherokees from Tennessee

1839 Chattanooga established

1842 First train in Tennessee

1843 Nashville becomes permanent capital

1844 James K. Polk elected president

1846 Mexican War begins

1848 Governor Brown calls for volunteers for the Mexican War. Tennessee's quota is 2,800 but 30,000 respond and Tennessee confirms reputation as "Volunteer State"

1853 Andrew Johnson becomes governor

1854 General Assembly passes bill for support of schools by direct taxation

1855 State Capitol completed
First Biennial State Fair, forerunner of annual State Fair, held in Nashville

1861 Civil War begins; Tennessee secedes from the Union

1862 Forts Henry and Donelson surrender
Federal troops occupy Nashville
Andrew Johnson appointed military governor of Tennessee
Memphis surrenders
General Nathan Bedford Forrest captures Murfreesboro on July 13

1863 Siege of Knoxville
Bragg defeats Rosecrans at Battle of Chickamauga on September 19 and 20
Battle of Chattanooga

1864 Andrew Johnson elected vice-president
Battles of Franklin and Nashville

1865 Slaves freed by state constitutional amendment
Andrew Johnson becomes president on April 15, day after Lincoln's assassination

1866 Tennessee restored to the Union on July 24

1870 Tennessee's third constitution adopted

1875 First state board of education

1897 Tennessee Centennial Exposition

1909 General education bill passed by the General Assembly
Statewide prohibition law passed

1913	One-third of gross revenues of state appropriated for education
1917	United States enters World War I
1918	World War I ends on November 11
1919	State ratifies the Eighteenth Amendment (prohibition) to U.S. Constitution State women's suffrage bill enacted
1920	State ratifies Nineteenth Amendment (women's suffrage) to U.S. Constitution
1922	First commercial radio station in Tennessee begins operation in Nashville Scopes trial
1931 1935	Tennessee votes for repeal of Eighteenth Amendment (prohibition) to U.S. Constitution
1933	Tennessee Valley Authority established
1934	Great Smoky Mountain National Park established
1935	General Assembly establishes Tennessee State Planning Commission

1941	United States enters World War II
1942	Oak Ridge chosen as sight for Manhattan Project
1945	World War II ends
1947	Atomic Energy Commission takes over Oak Ridge
1950	Population: 3,291,718
1953	Tennessee's first constitutional convention in eighty-three years
1956	Senator Estes Kefauver selected as Democratic nominee for vice-president
1960	Population: 3,567,089 Extensive repair and renovation of state Capitol completed
1962	Frank G. Clement elected governor
1963	Estes Kefauver dies August 10
1966	Buford Ellington elected governor Amendments to Tennessee Constitution passed

Tennessee Information Roundup

Area—42,244 square miles (including 482 miles of inland water). Ranks 34th in size among all states and 8th in size among Southern States
Extreme Length—(east to west) 480 miles
Extreme Width—(north to south) 115 miles
Highest Point—6,642 (Clingmans Dome)
Lowest Point—182 feet (along the Mississippi River in Shelby County)
Principal Rivers—Mississippi, Tennessee, and Cumberland
Temperature Extremes—High: 113° F. at Perryville; Low: −32° F. at Mountain City

State Motto—*Agriculture and Commerce*
State Slogan—*America at Its Best*
State Nicknames—"The Volunteer State" and "Big Bend State"
Great Seal of Tennessee—Authorized in 1796; first used in 1802
State Flag—Designed by LeRoy Reeves, became official in 1905
State Symbols—Tree: Tulip Poplar
                        Flower: Iris
                        Bird: Mockingbird
State Songs—"When It's Iris Time in Tennessee" (adopted in 1935), Words and music by
    Willa Mae Ward and "Tennessee Waltz" adopted in 1965), Words by Pee Wee King and
    music by Redd Stewart
Public School Song—"My Tennessee," Words and music by Francis Hannah Tranum

Statehood—16th State, June 1, 1796
Counties—95
U.S. Senators—2
U.S. Representatives—9
Electoral votes—11
State Legislature—33 senators; 99 representatives

Capital—Nashville, settled 1779
Major Cities (1960 Census)
    Memphis, 527,492   Chattanooga, 130,009
    Nashville, 250,887   Knoxville, 111,827
Population—3,567,089 (1960 census)
Population Density—84 persons per square mile

Principal Manufacturing Industries—Chemicals, metals and metal products; food products;
    textiles and related products; lumber and wood products; stone, clay, glass products; elec-
    trical machinery
Principal Minerals—Coal (bituminous), copper, limestone, marble, phosphate, zinc, stone
Principal Agriculture Products—Beef cattle, corn, cotton, dairy products, horses, strawberries,
    tobacco, vegetables, wheat

    Growing Season—East: 150 to 210 days; West: 180 to 230 days

CONSTITUTION OF THE

State of Tennessee

From its adoption February 23, 1870, Tennessee's Constitution remained unamended—the oldest such document in the world—until 1953, at which time a Limited Constitutional Convention assembled in Nashville to consider revision. The revisions adopted by the Convention were approved by the voters of Tennessee at a special election held November 3, 1953. Governor Frank G. Clement issued a Proclamation November 19, 1953 proclaiming the amendments to be a part of the Constitution. A second Limited Constitutional Convention assembled in Nashville in 1959 to consider three proposed amendments to the Constitution, only one of which was approved. The revision adopted by the Convention was approved by the voters of Tennessee on November 8, 1960. Governor Buford Ellington issued a Proclamation on December 1, 1960, proclaiming the amendment to be a part of the Constitution. A third Limited Convention was held in 1965 and nine amendments dealing with the Legislative branch of government were adopted by the Convention; all were approved by the voters at the November, 1966 General election. Governor Frank G. Clement issued a Proclamation on December 2, 1966 proclaiming these Amendments to be a part of the Constitution. The amendments of 1953, 1960, and 1965 are embodied in the following document.

PREAMBLE AND DECLARATION OF RIGHTS

Whereas, The people of the territory of the United States south of the river Ohio, having the right of admission into the General Government as a member State thereof, consistent with the Constitution of the United States, and the act of Cession of the State of North Carolina, recognizing the ordinance for the government of the territory – of the United States northwest of the Ohio River, by their Delegates and Representatives in Convention assembled, did on the sixth day of February, in the year of our Lord one thousand seven hundred and ninety-six, ordain and establish a Constitution, or form of government, and mutually agreed with each other to form themselves into a free and independent State by the name of the State of Tennessee, and,

Whereas, The General Assembly of the said State of Tennessee, (pursuant to the third section of the tenth article of the Constitution,) by an act passed on the Twenty-seventh day of November, in the year of our Lord one thousand eight hundred and thirty-three, entitled, "An Act" to provide for the calling of a Convention, passed in obedience to the declared will of the voters of the State, as expressed at the general election of August, in the year of our Lord one thousand eight hundred and thirty-three, did authorize and provide for the election by the people of delegates and representatives, to meet at Nashville, in Davidson county, on the third Monday in May, in the year of our Lord one thousand eight hundred and thirty-four, for the purpose of revising and amending, or changing, the Constitution, and said Convention did accordingly meet and form a Constitution, which was submitted to the people, and was ratified by them, on the first Friday in March, in the year of our Lord one thousand eight hundred and thirty-five, and,

Whereas, The General Assembly of said State of Tennessee, under and in virtue of the first section of the first article of the declaration of Rights, contained in and forming a part of the existing Constitution of the State, by an act passed on the fifteenth day of November, in the year of our Lord one thousand eight hundred and sixty-nine, did provide for the calling of a Convention by the people of the State, to meet at Nashville, on the second Monday in January, in the year of our Lord one thousand eight hundred and seventy, and for the election of delegates for the purpose of amending or revising the present Constitution, or forming and making a new Constitution; and,

Whereas, The people of the State, in the mode provided by said Act, have called said Convention, and elected Delegates to Represent them therein; Now, therefore,

We, the Delegates and Representatives of the people of the State of Tennessee, duly elected, and in Convention assembled, in pursuance of said Act of Assembly, have ordained and established the following constitution and form of government for this State, which we recommended to the people of Tennessee for their ratification: That is to say—

ARTICLE I

DECLARATION OF RIGHTS

SECTION 1. *All power inherent in the people—Government under their control.*—That all power is inherent in the people, and all free governments are founded on their authority, and instituted for their peace, safety, and happiness; for the advancement of those ends they have at all times, an unalienable and indefeasible right to alter, reform, or abolish the government in such manner as they may think proper.

SEC. 2. *Doctrine of nonresistance condemned.*—That government being instituted for the common benefit, the doctrine of non-resistance against arbitrary power and oppression is absurd, slavish, and destructive of the good and happiness of mankind.

SEC. 3. *Freedom of Worship.*—That all men have a natural and indefeasible right to worship Almighty God according to the dictates of their own conscience; that no man can of right be compelled to attend, erect, or support any place of worship, or to maintain any minister against his consent; that no human authority can, in any case whatever, control or interfere with the rights of conscience; and that no preference shall ever be given, by law, to any religious establishment or mode of worship.

SEC. 4. *No religious or political test.*—That no political or religious test, other than an oath to support the Constitution of the United States and of this State, shall ever be required as a qualification to any office or public trust under this state.

SEC. 5. *Elections to be free and equal—right of Suffrage.* The elections shall be free and equal, and the right of suffrage, as hereinafter declared, shall never be denied to any person entitled thereto, except upon a conviction by a jury of some infamous crime, previously ascertained and declared by law, and judgment thereon by court of competent jurisdiction.

SEC. 6. *Trial by jury—Qualifications of jurors.*—That the right of trial by jury shall remain inviolate, and no religious or political test shall ever be required as a qualification for jurors.

SEC. 7. *Unreasonable Searches and Seizures—General warrants.*—That the people shall be secure in their persons, houses, papers and possessions, from unreasonable searches and seizures; and that general warrants, whereby an officer may be commanded to search suspected places, without evidence of the fact committed, or to seize any person or persons not named, whose offenses are not particularly described and supported by evidence, are dangerous to liberty and ought not to be granted.

SEC. 8. *No man to be disturbed but by law.*—That no man shall be taken or imprisoned, or disseized of his freehold, liberties or privileges, or outlawed, or exiled, or in any manner destroyed or deprived of his life, liberty or property, but by the judgment of his peers or the law of the land.

SEC. 9. *Right of the accused in criminal prosecutions.*—That in all criminal prosecutions, the accused hath the right to be heard by himself and his counsel; to demand the nature and cause of the accusation against him, and to have a copy thereof, to meet the witness face to face, to have compulsory process for obtaining witnesses in his favor, and in prosecutions by indictment or presentment, a speedy public trial, by an impartial jury of the County in which the crime shall have been committed, and shall not be compelled to give evidence against himself.

SEC. 10. *Double jeopardy prohibited.*—That no person shall, for the same offense, be twice put in jeopardy of life or limb.

SEC. 11. *No ex post facto laws.*—That laws made for the punishment of acts committed previous to the existence of such laws, and by them only declared criminal, are contrary to the principles of a free Government; wherefore no EX POST FACTO law shall be made.

SEC. 12. *No corruption of blood or forfeiture of estates.*—That no conviction shall work corruption of blood or forfeiture of estate. The estate of such persons as shall destroy their own lives shall descend or vest as in case of natural death. If any person be killed by casualty, there shall be no forfeiture in consequence thereof.

SEC. 13. *Treatment after arrest.*—That no person arrested and confined in jail shall be treated with unnecessary rigor.

SEC. 14. *Prerequisites to criminal charge.*—That no person shall be put to answer any criminal charge but by presentment, indictment or impeachment.

SEC. 15. *Bailable offenses—Habeas corpus.*—That all prisoners shall be bailable by sufficient sureties, unless for capital offenses, when the proof is evident, or the presumption great. And the privilege of the writ of HABEAS CORPUS shall not be suspended, unless when in case of rebellion or invasion, the General Assembly shall declare the public safety requires it.

SEC. 16. *Restrictions on bail, fines and punishment.*—That excessive bail shall not be required, nor excessive fines imposed, nor cruel and unusual punishments inflicted.

SEC. 17. *Open courts—Redress of injuries—Suits against the State.*—That all courts shall be open; and every man, for an injury done him in his lands, goods, person or reputation, shall have remedy by due course of law, and right and justice administered without sale, denial, or delay. Suits may be brought against the State in such manner and in such courts as the Legislature may by law direct.

SEC. 18. *No imprisonment for debt.*—The Legislature shall pass no law authorizing imprisonment for debt in civil cases.

SEC. 19. *Freedom of speech and press.*—That the printing presses shall be free to every person to examine the proceedings of the Legislature; or of any branch or officer of the government, and no law shall ever be made to restrain the right thereof. The free communication of thoughts and opinions, is one of the invaluable rights of man, and every citizen may freely speak, write, and print on any subject, being responsible for the abuse of that liberty. But in prosecutions for the publication of papers investigating the official conduct of officers, or men in public capacity, the truth thereof may be given in evidence; and in all indictments for libel, the jury shall have a right to determine the law and the facts, under the direction of the court, as in other criminal cases.

SEC. 20. *No retrospective laws.*—That no retrospective law, or law impairing the obligations of contracts, shall be made.

SEC. 21. *No man's services or property taken without consent or compensation.*—That no man's particular services shall be demanded, or property taken, or applied to public use, without the consent of his representatives, or without just compensation being made therefor.

SEC. 22. *No perpetuities or monopolies.*—That perpetuities and monopolies are contrary to the genius of a free State, and shall not be allowed.

SEC. 23. *Right of assembly.*—That the citizens have a right, in a peaceable manner, to assemble together for their common good, to instruct their representatives, and to apply to those invested with the powers of government for redress of grievances, or other proper purposes, by address or remonstrance.

SEC. 24. *Militia—Civil authority.*—That the sure and certain defense of a free people, is a well regulated militia; and, as standing armies in time of peace are dangerous to freedom, they ought to be avoided as far as the circumstances and safety of the community will admit; and that in all cases the military shall be kept in strict subordination to the civil authority.

SEC. 25. *Martial law—Punishment.*—That no citizen of this State, except such as are employed in the army of the United States, or militia in actual service, shall be subjected to punishment under the martial or military law. That martial law, in the sense of the unrestricted power of military officers, or others, to dispose of the persons, liberties or property of the citizen, is inconsistent with the principles of free government, and is not confided to any department of the government of this State.

SEC. 26. *Right to bear arms—Regulations.*—That the citizens of this State have a right to keep and to bear arms for their common defense; but the Legislature shall have power, by law, to regulate the wearing of arms with a view to prevent crime.

SEC. 27. *Quartering soldiers*—That no soldier shall, in time of peace, be quartered in any house without the consent of the owner; nor in time of war, but in a manner prescribed by law.

SEC. 28. *No one compelled to bear arms.*—That no citizen of this State shall be compelled to bear arms, provided he will pay an equivalent, to be ascertained by law.

SEC. 29. *Navigation of the Mississippi.*—That an equal participation in the free navigation of the Mississippi, is one of the inherent rights of the citizens of this State; it cannot, therefore, be conceded to any prince, potentate, power, person or persons whatever.

SEC. 30. *No hereditary honors.*—That no hereditary emoluments, privileges, or honors, shall ever be granted or conferred in this State.

SEC. 31. *Boundaries of the State.*—That the limits and boundaries of this State be ascertained, it is declared they are as hereinafter mentioned, that is to say: Beginning on the extreme height of the Stone mountain, at the place where the line of Virginia intersects it, in latitude thirty-six degrees and thirty minutes north; running thence along the extreme height of the said mountain, to the place where Watauga river breaks through it; thence a direct course to the top of the Yellow Mountain, where Bright's road crosses the same; thence along the ridge of said mountain, between the waters of Doe river and the waters of Rock creek, to the place where the road crosses the Iron Mountain; from thence along the extreme height of said mountain, to the place where Nolichucky river runs through the same; thence to the top of the Bald Mountain; thence along the extreme height of said mountain to the Painted Rock, on French Broad river; thence along the highest ridge of said mountain, to the place where it is called the Great Iron or Smoky Mountain; thence along the extreme height of said mountain to the place where it is called Unicoi or Unaka Mountain, between the Indian towns of Cowee and Old Chota; thence along the main ridge of the said mountain to the southern boundary of this State, as described in the act of cession of North Carolina to the United States of America; and that all the territory, lands and waters lying west of said line, as before mentioned, and contained within the chartered limits of the State of North Carolina, are within the boundaries and limits of this State, over which the people have the right of exercising sovereignty, and the right of soil, so far as is consistent with the Constitution of the United States, recognizing the Articles of Confederation, the Bill of Rights and Constitution of North Carolina, the cession act of the said State, and the ordinance of Congress for the government of the territory northwest of the Ohio; Provided, nothing herein contained shall extend to affect the claim or claims of individuals to any part of the soil which is recognized to them by the aforesaid cession act; And provided also, That the limits and jurisdiction of this State shall extend to any other land and territory now acquired, or that may hereafter be acquired, by compact or agreement with other States, or otherwise, although such land and territory are not included within the boundaries herein before designated.

SEC. 32. *Prisons and prisoners.*—That the erection of safe and comfortable prisons, the inspection of prisons, and the humane treatment of prisoners, shall be provided for.

SEC. 33. *Slavery prohibited.*—That slavery and involuntary servitude, except as a punishment for crime, whereof the party shall have been duly convicted, are forever prohibited in this State.

SEC. 34. *Right of property in man.*—The General Assembly shall make no law recognizing the right of property in man.

ARTICLE II

DISTRIBUTION OF POWERS

SECTION 1. *Division of powers.*—The powers of the Government shall be divided into three distinct departments: the Legislative, Executive, and Judicial.

SEC. 2. *Limitation of Powers.*—No person or persons belonging to one of these departments shall exercise any of the powers properly belonging to either of the others, except in the cases herein directed or permitted.

LEGISLATIVE DEPARTMENT

SEC. 3. *Legislative authority—Term of office.*—The Legislative authority of this State shall be vested in a General Assembly, which shall consist of a Senate and House of Representatives, both dependent on the people. Representatives shall hold office for two years

and Senators for four years from the day of the general election, except that the Speaker of the Senate and the Speaker of the House of Representatives, each shall hold his office as Speaker for two years or, until his successor is elected and qualified, provided however, that in the first general election after adoption of this amendment Senators elected in districts designated by even numbers shall be elected for four years and those elected in districts designated by odd numbers shall be elected for two years. In a county having more than one senatorial district, the districts shall be numbered consecutively.

SEC. 4. *Census.*—The apportionment of Senators and Representatives shall be substantially according to population. After each decennial census made by the Bureau of Census of the United States is available the General Assembly shall establish senatorial and representative districts. Nothing in this Section nor in this Article II shall deny to the General Assembly the right at any time to apportion one House of the General Assembly using geography, political subdivisions, substantially equal population and other criteria as factors; provided such apportionment when effective shall comply with the Constitution of the United States as then amended or authoritatively interpreted. If the Constitution of the United States shall require that Legislative apportionment not based entirely on population be approved by vote of the electorate, the General Assembly shall provide for such vote in the apportionment act.

SEC. 5. *Apportionment of representatives.*—The number of Representatives shall be ninety-nine and shall be apportioned by the General Assembly among the several counties or districts as shall be provided by law. Counties having two or more Representatives shall be divided into separate districts. In a district composed of two or more counties, each county shall adjoin at least one other county of such district; and no county shall be divided in forming such a district.

SEC. 5a. Each district shall be represented by a qualified voter of that district.

SEC. 6. *Apportionment of senators.*—The number of Senators shall be apportioned by the General Assembly among the several counties or districts substantially according to population, and shall not exceed one-third the number of Representatives. Counties having two or more Senators shall be divided into separate districts. In a district composed of two or more counties, each county shall adjoin at least one other county of such district; and no county shall be divided in forming such a district.

SEC. 6a. Each district shall be represented by a qualified voter of that district.

SEC. 7. *Time of elections.*—The first election for Senators and Representatives shall be held on the second Tuesday in November, one thousand eight hundred and seventy; and forever thereafter, elections for members of the General Assembly shall be held once in two years, on the first Tuesday after the first Monday in November. Said elections shall terminate the same day.

SEC. 8. *Legislative sessions—Governor's inauguration.*—The General Assembly shall meet in organizational session on the first Tuesday in January next succeeding the election of the members of the House of Representatives, at which session, if in order, the Governor shall be inaugurated, and it shall remain in session for not longer than fifteen consecutive calendar days during which session no legislation shall be passed on third and final reading. Thereafter, the General Assembly shall meet on the fourth Tuesday in February next, and may by joint resolution recess or adjourn until such time or times as it shall determine. It shall be convened at other times by the Governor as provided in Article III, Section 9, or by the presiding officers of both Houses at the written request of two-thirds of the members of each House.

SEC. 9. *Qualifications of representatives.*—No person shall be a Representative unless he shall be a citizen of the United States, of the age of twenty-one years, and shall have been a citizen of this State for three years, and a resident in the county he represents one year, immediately preceding the election.

SEC. 10. *Senators—Qualifications.*—No person shall be a Senator unless he shall be a citizen of the United States, of the age of thirty years, and shall have resided three years in this State, and one year in the county or district, immediately preceding the election. No Senator or Representative shall, during the time for which he was elected, be eligible to any office or place of trust, the appointment to which is vested in the Executive or the General Assembly, except to the office of trustee of a literary institution.

SEC. 11. *Election of officers—Quorum—Adjournments.*—The Senate and House of Representatives, when assembled, shall each choose a speaker and its other officers; be judges of the qualifications and election of its members, and sit upon its own adjournments from day to day. Not less than two-thirds of all the members to which each house shall be entitled shall constitute a quorum to do business; but a smaller number may adjourn from day to day, and may be authorized, by law, to compel the attendance of absent members.

SEC. 12. *Each house to make its own rules.*—Each House may determine the rules of its proceedings, punish its members for disorderly behavior, and, with the concurrence of two-thirds, expel a member, but not a second time for the same offense; and shall have all other powers necessary for a branch of the Legislature of a free State.

SEC. 13. *Privilege of members.*—Senators and Representatives shall, in all cases, except treason, felony, or breach of the peace, be privileged from arrest during the session of the General Assembly, and in going to and returning from the same; and for any speech or debate in either House, they shall not be questioned in any other place.

SEC. 14. *Power to punish other than members.*—Each House may punish by imprisonment, during its session, any person not a member, who shall be guilty of disrespect to the House, by any disorderly or any contemptuous behavior in its presence.

SEC. 15. *Vacancies.*—When the seat of any member of either House becomes vacant his successor shall be elected by the Legislative body of the county of his residence at a meeting duly called for such purpose. Only a qualified voter of the district from which such member was elected may be eligible to succeed him. The term of any Senator so elected shall expire at the next general election, at which his successor shall be elected.

SEC. 16. *Limitation upon power of adjournment.*—Neither House shall, during its session, adjourn without the consent of the other for more than three days, nor to any other place than that in which the two Houses shall be sitting.

SEC. 17. *Origin and frame of bills.*—Bills may originate in either House; but may be amended, altered or rejected by the other. No bill shall become a law which embraces more than one subject, that subject to be expressed in the title. All acts which repeal, revive or amend former laws, shall recite in their caption, or otherwise, the title or substance of the law repealed, revived or amended.

SEC. 18. *Passage of bills.*—Every bill shall be read once, on three different days, and be passed each time in the House where it originated, before transmission to the other. No bill shall become a law, until it shall have been read and passed, on three different days in each house, and shall have received, on its final passage in each house, the assent of a majority of all the members to which that house shall be entitled under this constitution; and shall have been signed by the respective speakers in open session, the fact of such signing to be noted on the Journal; and shall have received the approval of the Governor, or shall have been otherwise passed under the provisions of this constitution.

SEC. 19. *Rejection of a bill.*—After a bill has been rejected, no bill containing the same substance shall be passed into a law during the same session.

SEC. 20. *Style of laws—Effective date.*—The style of the laws of this State shall be, *"Be it enacted by the*

General Assembly of the State of Tennessee." No law of a general nature shall take effect until forty days after its passage unless the same or the caption thereof shall state that the public welfare requires that it should take effect sooner.

SEC. 21. *Journal of proceedings.*—Each House shall keep a journal of its proceedings, and publish it, except such parts as the welfare of the State may require to be kept secret; the ayes and noes shall be taken in each House upon the final passage of every bill of a general character, and bills making appropriations of public moneys; and the ayes and noes of the members on any question, shall, at the request of any five of them, be entered on the journal.

SEC. 22. *Open sessions and meetings—Exception.*— The doors of each House and of committees of the whole shall be kept open, unless when the business shall be such as ought to be kept secret.

SEC. 23. *Compensation of members of General Assembly.*—Each member of the General Assembly shall receive an annual salary of $1,800.00 per year payable in equal monthly installments from the date of his election, and in addition, such other allowances for expenses in attending sessions or committee meetings as may be provided by law. The Senators, when sitting as a Court of Impeachment, shall receive the same allowances for expenses as have been provided by law for the members of the General Assembly. The compensation and expenses of the members of the General Assembly may from time to time be reduced or increased by laws enacted by the General Assembly; however, no increase or decrease in the amount thereof shall take effect until the next general election for Representatives to the General Assembly. Provided, further, that the first General Assembly meeting after adoption of this amendment shall be allowed to set its own expenses. However, no member shall be paid expenses, nor travel allowances for more than ninety Legislative days of a regular session, excluding the organizational session, nor for more than thirty Legislative days of any extraordinary session.

This amendment shall take effect immediately upon adoption so that any member of the General Assembly elected at a general election wherein this amendment is approved shall be entitled to the compensation set herein.

SEC. 24. *Appropriations of public moneys.*—No money shall be drawn from the treasury but in consequence of appropriations made by law; and an accurate statement of the receipts and expenditures of the public money shall be attached to and published with the laws at the rise of each stated session of the General Assembly.

SEC. 25. *Defaulters ineligible.*—No person who heretofore hath been, or may hereafter be, a collector or holder of Public Moneys, shall have a seat in either House of the General Assembly, or hold any other office under the state government, until such person shall have accounted for, and paid into the Treasury, all sums for which he may be accountable or liable.

SEC. 26. *Ineligibility—Lucrative offices.*—No judge of any Court of law or equity, Secretary of State, Attorney General, Register, Clerk of any court of Record, or person holding any office under the authority of the United States, shall have a seat in the General Assembly; nor shall any person in this State hold more than one lucrative office at the same time; provided, that no appointment in the Militia, or to the office of Justice of the Peace, shall be considered a lucrative office, or operative as a disqualification to a seat in either House of the General Assembly.

SEC. 27. *Right of protest.*—Any member of either House of the General Assembly shall have liberty to dissent from and protest against, any act or resolve which he may think injurious to the Public or to any individual, and to have the reasons for his dissent entered on the journals.

SEC. 28. *Taxable property—Valuation—Rates.*—All property real, personal or mixed shall be taxed, but the Legislature may except such as may be held by the State, by Counties, Cities or Towns, and used exclusively for public or corporation purposes, and such as may be held and used for purposes purely religious, charitable, scientific, literary or educational, and shall except one thousand dollars worth of personal property in the hands of each taxpayer, and the direct product of the soil in the hands of the producer, and his immediate vendee. All property shall be taxed according to its value, that value to be ascertained in such manner as the Legislature shall direct, so that taxes shall be equal and uniform throughout the State. No one species of property from which a tax may be collected, shall be taxed higher than any other species of property of the same value, but the Legislature shall have power to tax Merchants, Peddlers, and privileges, in such manner as they may from time to time direct. The portion of a Merchants Capital used in the purchase of Merchandise sold by him to nonresidents and sent beyond the State, shall not be taxed at a rate higher than the *ad valorem* tax on property. The Legislature shall have power to levy a tax upon incomes derived from stocks and bonds that are not taxed *ad valorem*.

All male citizens of this State over the age of twenty-one years, except such persons as may be exempted by law on account of age or other infirmity shall be liable to a poll tax of not less than fifty cents nor more than one dollar per annum. Nor shall any County or Corporation levy a poll tax exceeding the amount levied by the state.

SEC. 29. *Counties and towns—Power to tax—Credit.—* The General Assembly shall have power to authorize the several counties and incorporated towns in this State, to impose taxes for County and Corporation purposes respectively, in such manner as shall be prescribed by law; and all property shall be taxed according to its value, upon the principles established in regard to state taxation. But the credit of no County, City or Town shall be given or loaned to or in aid of any person, company, association, or corporation, except upon an election to be first held by the qualified voters of such county, city or town, and the assent of three-fourths of the votes cast at said election. Nor shall any county, city or town become a stockholder with others in any company, association or corporation except upon a like election, and the assent of a like majority. But the counties of Grainger, Hawkins, Hancock, Union, Campbell, Scott, Morgan, Grundy, Sumner, Smith, Fentress, VanBuren, and the new County herein authorized to be established out of fractions of Sumner, Macon and Smith counties, White, Putnam, Overton, Jackson, Cumberland, Anderson, Henderson, Wayne, Cocke, Coffee, Macon, Marshall, and Roane shall be excepted out of the provisions of this section so far that the assent of a majority of the qualified voters of either of said counties voting on the question shall be sufficient when the credit of such county is given or loaned to any person, association or corporation; Provided, That the exception of the counties above named shall not be in force beyond the year one thousand eight hundred and eighty; and after that period they shall be subject to the three-fourths majority applicable to the other counties of the State.

SEC. 30. *Articles not taxable—Inspection fees.—*No article manufactured of the produce of this State, shall be taxed otherwise than to pay inspection fees.

SEC. 31. *Acts forbidden the State.—*The credit of this State shall not be hereafter loaned or given to or in aid of any person, association, company, corporation or municipality: nor shall the State become the owner in whole or in part of any bank or a stockholder with others in any association, company, corporation or municipality.

SEC. 32. *Amendments to Constitution of United States.—*No convention or General Assembly of this State shall act upon any amendment of the constitution of the United States proposed by Congress to the several States; unless such Convention or General Assembly shall have been elected after such amendment is submitted.

SEC. 33. *No State bonds to defaulting railroads.—* No bonds of the State shall be issued to any Railroad company which at the time of its application for the same shall be in default in paying the interest upon the State bonds previously loaned to it or that shall

hereafter and before such application sell or absolutely dispose of any State bonds loaned to it for less than par.

ARTICLE III

Executive Department

SECTION 1. *Governor's executive power.—*The Supreme Executive power of this State shall be vested in a governor.

SEC. 2. *Election of Governor.—*The Governor shall be chosen by the electors of the members of the General Assembly, at the time and places where they shall respectively vote for the members thereof. The returns of every election for Governor shall be sealed up, and transmitted to the seat of Government, by the returning officers, directed to the Speaker of the Senate, who shall open and publish them in the presence of a majority of the members of each House of the General Assembly. The person having the highest number of votes shall be Governor; but if two or more shall be equal and highest in votes, one of them shall be chosen Governor by joint vote of both houses of the General Assembly. Contested elections for governor shall be determined by both Houses of the General Assembly, in such manner as shall be prescribed by law.

SEC. 3. *Governor's qualifications.—*He shall be at least thirty years of age, shall be a citizen of the United States, and shall have been a citizen of this State seven years next before his election.

SEC. 4. *Governor's term of service.—*The Governor hereafter elected shall hold office for four years, and until his successor shall be elected and qualified. One succeeding to the vacated office during the first eighteen calendar months of such term shall hold office until his successor to such vacated office is elected at the following election for members of the General Assembly and qualified for the remainder of the term, as provided in Section 2 of this Article and Section 8 of Article II; and one succeeding to said vacated office subsequent to the first eighteen months of the term shall continue to hold office for the remainder of the full term. No Governor elected and qualified for a four year term shall be eligible for the succeeding term.

SEC. 5. *Governor as commander-in-chief—Calling out Militia.—*He shall be commander-in-chief of the Army and Navy of this State, and of the Militia, except when they shall be called into the service of the United States: But the Militia shall not be called into service except in case of rebellion or invasion, and then only when the General Assembly shall declare, by law, that the public safety requires it.

SEC. 6. *Pardons and reprieves.*—He shall have power to grant reprieves and pardons, after conviction, except in cases of impeachment.

SEC. 7. *Governor's compensation.*—He shall, at stated times, receive a compensation for his services, which shall not be increased or diminished during the period for which he shall have been elected.

SEC. 8. *Governor may require information.*—He may require information in writing, from the officers in the executive department, upon any subject relating to the duties of their respective offices.

SEC. 9. *Governor may convene the legislature.*—He may, on extraordinary occasions, convene the General Assembly by proclamation, in which he shall state specifically the purposes for which they are to convene; but they shall enter on no legislative business except that for which they were specifically called together.

SEC. 10. *Governor to execute laws.*—He shall take care that the laws be faithfully executed.

SEC. 11. *Governor to give information to the legislature.*—He shall, from time to time, give to the General Assembly information of the state of the government, and recommend for their consideration such measures as he shall judge expedient.

SEC. 12. *Vacancy in office of governor.*—In case of the removal of the Governor from office, or of his death, or resignation, the powers and duties of the office shall devolve on the Speaker of the Senate; and in case of the death, removal from office, or resignation of the Speaker of the Senate, the powers and duties of the office shall devolve on the Speaker of the House of Representatives.

SEC. 13. *Ineligibility for governorship.*—No member of Congress, or person holding any office under the United States, or this State, shall execute the office of Governor.

SEC. 14. *Governor to make temporary appointments.*—When any officer, the right of whose appointment is by this Constitution vested in the General Assembly, shall, during the recess, die, or the office, by the expiration of the term, or by other means, become vacant, the Governor shall have the power to fill such vacancy by granting a temporary commission, which shall expire at the end of the next session of the legislature.

SEC. 15. *Seal of State.*—There shall be a seal of this State, which shall be kept by the Governor, and used by him officially, and shall be called the Great Seal of the State of Tennessee.

SEC. 16. *Grants and commissions to be sealed and signed by the governor.*—All grants and commissions shall be in the name and by the authority of the State of Tennessee, be sealed with the State Seal, and signed by the Governor.

SEC. 17. *Secretary of state.*—A Secretary of State shall be appointed by joint vote of the General Assembly and commissioned during the term of four years; he shall keep a fair register of all the official acts and proceedings of the Governor; and shall, when required, lay the same, and all papers, minutes and vouchers relative thereto, before the General Assembly; and shall perform such other duties as shall be enjoined by law.

SEC. 18. *Bills to be approved by the governor—Governor's veto—Bills passed over governor's veto.*—Every Bill which may pass both Houses of the General Assembly shall, before it becomes a law, be presented to the Governor for his signature. If he approve, he shall sign it, and the same shall become a law; but if he refuse to sign it, he shall return it with his objections thereto, in writing, to the house in which it originated; and said House shall cause said objections to be entered at large upon its journal, and proceed to reconsider the Bill. If after such reconsideration, a majority of all the members elected to that House shall agree to pass the Bill, notwithstanding the objections of the Executive, it shall be sent, with said objections, to the other House, by which it shall be likewise reconsidered. If approved by a majority of the whole number elected to that House, it shall become a law. The votes of both Houses shall be determined by yeas and nays, and the names of all the members voting for or against the Bill shall be entered upon the journals of their respective Houses.

If, while the General Assembly remains in session, the Governor shall fail to return any bill, with his objections within five days (Sundays excepted) after it shall have been presented to him, the same shall become a law without his signature. The Governor may approve, sign, and file in the office of the Secretary of State within ten days after the adjournment of the General Assembly any bill presented to him for signature during the last five days of the session, and when thus approved the same shall become a law. If the General Assembly, by its adjournment, prevents the return of any bill within said five-day period it shall become a law, unless disapproved by the Governor and filed by him, with his objections, in the office of the Secretary of State within ten days after such adjournment.

Every joint resolution or order (except on question of adjournment and proposals of specific amendments to the Constitution) shall likewise be presented to the Governor for his signature, and on being disapproved by him shall in like manner, be returned with his objections; and the same before it shall take effect shall be repassed by a majority of all the members elected to both houses in the manner and according to the rules prescribed in case of a bill.

The Governor may reduce or disapprove the sum of money appropriated by any one or more items, or parts of items, in any bill appropriating money, while approving other portions of the bill, and the portions so approved shall become law, and the item or parts of items disapproved or reduced shall be void to the extent that they have been disapproved or reduced, but any such reduction or disapproval with respect to bills presented to the Governor five (5) or more days before final adjournment of the General Assembly shall not be effective unless the Governor shall, not less than three (3) whole days prior to final adjournment, and not more than five (5) days (Sundays excepted) after presentation of the bill, give written notice to the House in which the bill originated setting out the items or parts of items disapproved or reduced and the reasons therefor, and, with respect to bills presented to the Governor within five (5) days before such final adjournment, any such reduction or disapproval of any item or parts of items shall not be effective unless the Governor shall not later than the following day give such written notice and the reasons for such disapproval or reduction of such items or parts of items to the House in which the bill originated, unless prevented from so doing by final adjournment of the General Assembly. Any such items or parts of items so disapproved or reduced shall be restored to the bill in the original amount and become law if repassed by the General Assembly according to the rules and limitations prescribed for the passage of other bills over the executive veto.

ARTICLE IV

ELECTIONS

SECTION 1. *Right to vote—Election precincts—Military duty.*—Every person of the age of twenty-one years, being a citizen of the United States, and a resident of this State for twelve months, and of the county wherein such person may offer to vote for three months, next preceding the day of election, shall be entitled to vote for electors for President and Vice-President of the United States, members of the General Assembly and other civil officers for the county or district in which such person resides; and there shall be no other qualification attached to the right of suffrage.

The General Assembly shall have power to enact laws requiring voters to vote in the election precincts in which they may reside, and laws to secure the freedom of elections and the purity of the ballot box.

All male citizens of this State shall be subject to the performance of military duty, as may be prescribed by law.

SEC. 2. *Right of suffrage may be excluded for crime.*—Laws may be passed excluding from the right of suffrage persons who may be convicted of infamous crimes.

SEC. 3. *Privileges of voters.*—Electors shall, in all cases, except treason, felony, or breach of the peace, be privileged from arrest or summons, during their attendance at elections, and in going to and returning from them.

SEC. 4. *Mode of voting.*—In all elections to be made by the General Assembly, the members thereof shall vote *viva voce,* and their votes shall be entered on the journal. All other elections shall be by ballot.

ARTICLE V

IMPEACHMENTS

SECTION 1. *Impeachment.*—The House of Representatives shall have the sole power of impeachment.

SEC. 2. *Trial of impeachments—*All impeachments shall be tried by the Senate. When sitting for that purpose the Senators shall be upon oath or affirmation, and the Chief Justice of the Supreme Court, or if he be on trial, the Senior Associate Judge, shall preside over them. No person shall be convicted without the concurrence of two-thirds of the Senators sworn to try the officer impeached.

SEC. 3. *How prosecuted.*—The House of Representatives shall elect from their own body three members, whose duty it shall be to prosecute impeachments. No impeachments shall be tried until the Legislature shall have adjourned *sine die,* when the Senate shall proceed to try such impeachment.

SEC. 4. *Who may be impeached.*—The Governor, Judges of the Supreme Court, Judges of the Inferior Courts, Chancellors, Attorneys for the Senate, Treasurer, Comptroller and Secretary of State, shall be liable to impeachment, whenever they may, in the opinion of the House of Representatives, commit any crime in their official capacity which may require disqualification; but judgment shall only extend to removal from office, and disqualification to fill any office thereafter. The party shall, nevertheless, be liable to indictment, trial, judgment and punishment according to law. The Legislature now has, and shall continue to have, power to relieve from the penalties imposed, any person disqualified from holding office by the judgment of a Court of Impeachment.

SEC. 5. *Officers liable to indictment and removal from office.*—Justices of the Peace, and other civil officers, not hereinbefore mentioned, for crimes or misdemeanors in office, shall be liable to indictment in such courts as the Legislature may direct; and upon conviction, shall be removed from office by said court, as if found guilty on impeachment; and shall be subject to such other punishment as may be prescribed by law.

ARTICLE VI

JUDICIAL DEPARTMENT

SEC. 1. *Judicial power.*—The judicial power of this State shall be vested in one Supreme Court and in such Circuit, Chancery and other inferior Courts as the Legislature shall from time to time, ordain and establish; in the Judges thereof, and in Justices of the Peace. The Legislature may also vest such jurisdiction in Corporation courts as may be deemed necessary. Courts to be holden by Justices of the Peace may also be established.

SEC. 2. *Supreme court.*—The Supreme Court shall consist of five judges, of whom not more than two shall reside in any one of the grand divisions of the State. The Judges shall designate one of their own number who shall preside as Chief Justice. The concurrence of three of the judges shall in every case be necessary to a decision. The jurisdiction of this Court shall be appellate only, under such restrictions and regulations as may from time to time be prescribed by law; but it may possess such other jurisdiction as is now conferred by law on the present Supreme Court. Said Court shall be held at Knoxville, Nashville and Jackson.

SEC. 3. *Supreme court judges.*—The Judges of the Supreme Court shall be elected by the qualified voters of the State. The Legislature shall have power to prescribe such rules as may be necessary to carry out the provisions of section two of this article. Every Judge of the Supreme Court shall be thirty-five years of age, and shall before his election have been a resident of the State for five years. His term of service shall be eight years.

SEC. 4. *Judges of inferior courts.*—The Judges of the Circuit and Chancery Courts, and of other inferior Courts, shall be elected by the qualified voters of the district or circuit to which they are to be assigned. Every Judge of such Courts shall be thirty years of age, and shall before his election, have been a resident of the State for five years and of the circuit or district one year. His term of service shall be eight years.

SEC. 5. *Attorney-general and reporter.*—An Attorney General and Reporter for the State, shall be appointed by the Judges of the Supreme Court and shall hold his office for a term of eight years. An Attorney for the State for any circuit or district, for which a Judge having criminal jurisdiction shall be provided by law, shall be elected by the qualified voters of such circuit or district, and shall hold his office for a term of eight years, and shall have been a resident of the State five years, and of the circuit or district one year. In all cases where the Attorney for any district fails or refuses to attend and prosecute according to law, the Court shall have power to appoint an Attorney *pro tempore.*

SEC. 6. *Removal of judges and attorneys.*—Judges and Attorneys for the State may be removed from office by a concurrent vote of both Houses of the General Assembly, each House voting separately; but two-thirds of the members to which each House may be entitled must concur in such vote. The vote shall be determined by ayes and noes, and the names of the members voting for or against the Judge or Attorney for the State together with the cause or causes of removal, shall be entered on the Journals of each House respectively. The Judge or Attorney for the State, against whom the Legislature may be about to proceed, shall receive notice thereof accompanied with a copy of the causes alleged for his removal, at least ten days before the day on which either House of the General Assembly shall act thereupon.

SEC. 7. *Compensation of judges.*—The Judges of the Supreme or Inferior Courts, shall, at stated times, receive a compensation for their services, to be ascertained by law, which shall not be increased or diminished during the time for which they are elected. They shall not be allowed any fees or perequisites of office nor hold any other office of trust or profit under this State or the United States.

SEC. 8. *Jurisdiction of inferior courts.*—The jurisdiction of the Circuit, Chancery and other Inferior Courts, shall be as now established by law, until changed by the Legislature.

SEC. 9. *Judge's charge.*—The Judges shall not charge juries with respect to matters of fact, but may state the testimony and declare the law.

SEC. 10. *Certiorari.*—The Judges or Justices of the Inferior Courts of Law and Equity, shall have power in all civil cases, to issue writs of *certiorari* to remove any cause or the transcript of the record thereof, from any inferior jurisdiction, into such court of law, on sufficient cause, supported by oath or affirmation.

SEC. 11. *Incompetency of judges—Special judges.*—No Judge of the Supreme or Inferior Courts shall preside on the trial of any cause in the event of which he may be interested, or where either of the parties shall be connected with him by affinity of consanguinity, within such degrees as may be prescribed by law, or in which he may have been a counsel, or in which he may have presided in any inferior Court, except by consent of all the parties. In case all or any of the Judges of the Supreme Court shall thus be disqualified from presiding on the trial of any cause or causes, the Court, or the judges thereof, shall certify the same to the Governor of the State, and he shall forthwith specially commission the requisite number of men, of law knowledge, for the trial and determination thereof. The Legislature may by general laws make provision that special Judges may be appointed, to hold any Courts the Judge of which shall be unable or fail to attend or sit; or to hear any cause in which the Judge may be incompetent.

SEC. 12. *Requisites of writs and process.*—All writs and other process shall run in the name of the State of Tennessee and bear test and be signed by the respective clerks. Indictments shall conclude, "against the peace and dignity of the State."

SEC. 13. *Clerks of courts.*—Judges of the Supreme Court shall appoint their clerks who shall hold their offices for six years. Chancellors shall appoint their clerks and masters, who shall hold their offices for six years. Clerks of The Inferior Courts holden in the respective Counties or Districts, shall be elected by the qualified voters thereof for the term of four years. Any Clerk may be removed from office for malfeasance, incompetency or neglect of duty, in such manner as may be prescribed by law.

SEC. 14. *Fines exceeding fifty dollars to be assessed by jury.*—No fine shall be laid on any citizen of this State that shall exceed fifty dollars, unless it shall be assessed by a jury of his peers, who shall assess the fine at the time they find the fact, if they think the fine should be more than fifty dollars.

SEC. 15. *Districts in counties—Justices and Constables — Number — Term — Removal from District.*— The different Counties of this State shall be laid off, as the General Assembly may direct, into districts of convenient size, so that the whole number in each County shall not be more than twenty-five, or four for every one hundred square miles. There shall be two Justices of the peace and one Constable elected in each district by the qualified voters therein, except districts including County towns, which shall elect three Justices and two Constables. The Jurisdiction of said officers shall be co-extensive with the County. Justices of the Peace shall be elected for the term of six, and Constables for the term of two years. Upon the removal of either of said officers from the district in which he was elected, his office shall become vacant

from the time of such removal. Justices of the Peace shall be commissioned by the Governor. The Legislature shall have power to provide for the appointment of an additional number of Justices of the Peace in incorporated towns.

ARTICLE VII

STATE AND COUNTY OFFICERS

SECTION 1. *County Officers—Their Election—Terms —Removal.*—There shall be elected in each county, by the qualified voters therein, one Sheriff, one Trustee, one Register; the Sheriff for two years, the Trustee for four years, and the Register for four years; but no person shall be eligible to the office of Sheriff more than six years in any term of eight years, provided that the first four year term of the trustee shall begin on or after September 1, 1962. There shall be elected for each county by the Justices of the Peace, one coroner, and one ranger who shall hold their offices for two years; said officers shall be removed for malfeasance, or neglect of duty, in such manner as may be prescribed by law.

SEC. 2. *Vacancies—How filled.*—Should a vacancy occur, subsequent to an election, in the office of Sheriff, Trustee or Register, it shall be filled by the Justices; if in that of the clerks to be elected by the people, it shall be filled by the Courts; and the person so appointed shall continue in office until his successor shall be elected and qualified; and such office shall be filled by the qualified voters at the first election for any of the County Officers.

SEC. 3. *Treasurer and comptroller.*—There shall be a Treasurer or Treasurers and a Comptroller of the Treasury appointed for the State, by the joint vote of both houses of the General Assembly, who shall hold their offices for two years.

SEC. 4. *Other elections and vacancies.*—The election of all officers, and the filling of all vacancies not otherwise directed or provided by this Constitution, shall be made in such manner as the Legislature shall direct.

SEC. 5. *Civil officers — Election — Vacancies.* — Elections for Judicial and other civil officers shall be held on the first Thursday in August, one thousand eight hundred and seventy, and forever thereafter on the first Thursday in August next preceding the expiration of their respective terms of service. The term of each officer so elected shall be computed from the first day of September next succeeding his election. The term of office of the Governor and of other executive officers shall be computed from the fifteenth of January next after the election of the Governor. No appointment or election to fill a vacancy shall be made for a period extending beyond the unexpired term. Every officer shall hold his office until his successor is elected or appointed, and qualified. No special election shall be held to fill a vacancy in the office of Judge or District Attorney, but at the time herein fixed for the biennial election of civil officers; and such vacancy shall be filled at the next Biennial election recurring more than thirty days after the vacancy occurs.

ARTICLE VIII

MILITIA

SECTION 1. *Militia officers to be elected.*—All militia officers shall be elected by persons subject to military duty, within the bounds of their several companies, battalions, regiments, brigades and divisions, under such rules and regulations as the Legislature may from time to time direct and establish.

SEC. 2. *Staff officers to be appointed.*—The Governor shall appoint the Adjutant-General and his other staff officers; the Major-Generals, Brigadier-Generals, and commanding officers of regiments, shall respectively appoint their staff officers.

SEC. 3. *Exemptions from attending musters.*—The Legislature shall pass laws exempting citizens belonging to any sect or denomination of religion, the tenets of which are known to be opposed to the bearing of arms, from attending private and general musters.

ARTICLE IX

DISQUALIFICATIONS

SECTION 1. *Ineligibility of ministers and priests to seats in legislature.*—Whereas Ministers of the Gospel are by their profession, dedicated to God and the care of souls, and ought not to be diverted from the great duties of their functions; therefore, no Minister of the Gospel, or priest of any denomination whatever, shall be eligible to a seat in either House of the Legislature.

SEC. 2. *No atheist shall hold a civil office.*—No person who denies the being of God, or a future state of rewards and punishments, shall hold any office in the civil department of this State.

SEC. 3. *Duelists shall hold no office.*—Any person who shall, after the adoption of this Constitution, fight a duel, or knowingly be the bearer of a challenge to fight a duel, or send or accept a challenge for that purpose, or be an aider or abettor in fighting a duel, shall

be deprived of the right to hold any office of honor or profit in this State, and shall be punished otherwise, in such manner as the Legislature may prescribe.

ARTICLE X

OATHS, BRIBERY OF ELECTORS, NEW COUNTIES

SECTION 1. *Oath of office.*—Every person who shall be chosen or appointed to any office of trust or profit under this Constitution, or any law made in pursuance thereof, shall, before entering on the duties thereof, take an oath to support the Constitution of this State, and of the United States, and an oath of office.

SEC. 2. *Oath of members of the general assembly.*—Each member of the Senate and House of Representatives, shall before they proceed to business take an oath or affirmation to support the Constitution of this State, and of the United States and also the following oath: I . . . . do solemnly swear (or affirm) that as a member of this General Assembly, I will, in all appointments, vote without favor, affection, partiality, or prejudice; and that I will not propose or assent to any bill, vote or resolution, which shall appear to me injurious to the people, or consent to any act or thing, whatever, that shall have a tendency to lessen or abridge their rights and privileges, as declared by the Constitution of this State.

SEC. 3. *Punishment of electors and candidates for bribery.*—Any elector who shall receive any gift or reward for his vote, in meat, drink, money or otherwise, shall suffer such punishment as the law shall direct. And any person who shall directly or indirectly give, promise or bestow any such reward to be elected, shall thereby be rendered incapable, for six years, to serve in the office for which he was elected, and be subject to such further punishment as the Legislature shall direct.

SEC. 4. *New counties—Approach of county lines to courthouse — Limit to reduction of counties — Exceptions—Vote necessary to detach fractions for formation of new counties or to remove a county seat—Liability for existing debt.*—New Counties may be established by the Legislature to consist of not less than two hundred and seventy-five square miles, and which shall contain a population of seven hundred qualified voters; no line of such County shall approach the Court House of any old County from which it may be taken nearer than eleven miles, nor shall such old County be reduced to less than five hundred square miles. But the following exceptions are made to the foregoing provisions, viz.: New Counties may be established by the present or any succeeding Legislature out of the following Territory to wit: Out of that portion of Obion county which lies west of low water mark of

Reel Foot Lake: Out of fractions of Sumner, Macon and Smith Counties; but no line of such new County shall approach the Court House of Sumner or of Smith counties nearer than ten miles, nor include any part of Macon County lying within nine and a half miles of the Court House of said County nor shall more than twenty square miles of Macon County nor any part of Sumner County lying due west of the western boundary of Macon County, be taken in the formation of said new County: Out of fractions of Grainger and Jefferson Counties but no line of such new County shall include any part of Grainger County north of the Holston River; nor shall any line thereof approach the Court House of Jefferson County nearer than eleven miles. Such new County may include any other Territory which is not excluded by any general provision of this Constitution: Out of fractions of Jackson and Overton Counties but no line of such new County shall approach the Court House of Jackson or Overton Counties nearer than ten miles, nor shall such County contain less than four hundred qualified voters, nor shall the area of either of the old Counties be reduced below four hundred and fifty square miles: Out of the fractions of Roane, Monroe, and Blount Counties, around the town of Loudon; but no line of such new County shall ever approach the towns of Maryville, Kingston, or Madisonville, nearer than eleven miles, except that on the south side of the Tennessee River, said lines may approach as near as ten miles to the Court House of Roane county.

The Counties of Lewis, Cheatham, and Sequatchie, as now established by Legislative enactments are hereby declared to be Constitutional Counties. No part of Bledsoe County shall be taken to form a new County or a part thereof or be attached to any adjoining County. That portion of Marion County included within the following boundaries, beginning on the Grundy and Marion County line at the Nickajack trace and running about six hundred yards west of Ben Poseys, to where the Tennessee Coal Rail Road crosses the line, running thence southeast through the Pocket near William Summars crossing the Battle Creek Gulf at the corner of Thomas Wootons field, thence running across the Little Gizzard Gulf at Raven Point, thence in a direct line to the Bridge crossing the Big Fiery Gizzard, thence in a direct line to the mouth of Holy Water Creek, thence up said Creek to the Grundy County line, and thence with said line to the beginning; is hereby detached from Marion County, and attached to the County of Grundy. No part of a County shall be taken off to form a new County or a part thereof without the consent of two-thirds of the qualified voters in such part taken off; and where an old County is reduced for the purpose of forming a new one, the Seat of Justice in said old County shall not be removed without the concurrence of two-thirds of both branches of the Legislature, nor shall the seat of Justice of any County be removed without the concurrence of two-thirds of the qualified

voters of the County. But the foregoing provision requiring a two-thirds majority of the voters of a County to remove its County seat shall not apply to the Counties of Obion and Cocke. The fractions taken from old Counties to form new Counties or taken from one County and added to another shall continue liable for their *pro rata* of all debts contracted by their respective Counties prior to the separation, and be entitled to their proportion of any stocks or credits belonging to such old Counties.

SEC. 5. *To vote with old county.*—The citizens who may be included in any new County shall vote with the County or Counties from which they may have been stricken off, for members of Congress, for Governor and for members of the General Assembly until the next apportionment of members to the General Assembly after the establishment of such new County.

ARTICLE XI

MISCELLANEOUS PROVISIONS

SECTION 1. *Existing laws not affected by this constitution.*—All laws and ordinances now in force and use in this State, not inconsistent with this Constitution, shall continue in force and use until they shall expire or be altered or repealed by the Legislature; but ordinances contained in any former Constitution or schedule thereto are hereby abrogated.

SEC. 2. *No impairment of rights.*—Nothing contained in this Constitution shall impair the validity of any debts or contracts, or affect any rights of property or any suits, actions, rights of action or other proceedings in Courts of Justice.

SEC. 3. *Amendments to Constitution.*—Any amendment or amendments to this Constitution may be proposed in the Senate or House of Representatives, and if the same shall be agreed to by a majority of all the members elected to each of the two houses, such proposed amendment or amendments shall be entered on their journals with the yeas and nays thereon, and referred to the general assembly then next to be chosen; and shall be published six months previous to the time of making such choice; and if in the general assembly then next chosen as aforesaid, such proposed amendment or amendments shall be agreed to by two-thirds of all the members elected to each house, then it shall be the duty of the general assembly to submit such proposed amendment or amendments to the people at the next general election in which a Governor is to be chosen. And if the people shall approve and ratify such amendment or amendments by a majority of all the citizens of the State voting for Governor, voting in their favor, such amendment or amendments shall become a part of this Constitution. When any amendment or amendments to the Constitution shall be proposed in pursuance of the foregoing provisions the same shall at each of said sessions be read three times on three several days in each house.

The Legislature shall have the right by law to submit to the people, at any general election, the question of calling a convention to alter, reform, or abolish this Constitution, or to alter, reform, or abolish any specified part or parts of it; and when, upon such submission, a majority of all the voters voting upon the proposal submitted shall approve the proposal to call a convention, the delegates to such convention shall be chosen at the next general election and the convention shall assemble for the consideration of such proposals as shall have received a favorable vote in said election, in such mode and manner as shall be prescribed. No change in, or amendment to, this Constitution proposed by such convention shall become effective, unless within the limitations of the call of the convention, and unless approved and ratified by a majority of the qualified voters voting separately on such change or amendment at an election to be held in such manner and on such date as may be fixed by the convention. No such convention shall be held oftener than once in six years.

SEC. 4. *Power to grant divorces.*—The Legislature shall have no power to grant divorces; but may authorize the Courts of Justice to grant them for such causes as may be specified by law; but such laws shall be general and uniform in their operation throughout the State.

SEC. 5. *Lotteries.*—The Legislature shall have no power to authorize lotteries for any purpose, and shall pass laws to prohibit the sale of lottery tickets in this State.

SEC. 6. *Changing names—Adoption—Legitimation.*— The legislature shall have no power to change the names of persons, or to pass acts adopting or legitimatizing persons; but shall, by general laws, confer this power on the Courts.

SEC. 7. *Interest rates.*—The Legislature shall fix the rate of interest, and the rate so established shall be equal and uniform throughout the State; but the Legislature may provide for a conventional rate of interest, not to exceed ten per centum per annum.

SEC. 8. *General laws only to be passed.*—The Legislature shall have no power to suspend any general law for the benefit of any particular individual, nor to pass any law for the benefit of individuals inconsistent with the general laws of the land; nor to pass any law granting to any individual or individuals, rights, privileges, immunitie, [immunities] or exemptions other than such as may be, by the same law extended to any member of the community, who may be able to bring himself within the provisions of such law. No corpora-

tion shall be created or its powers increased or diminished by special laws but the General Assembly shall provide by general laws for the organization of all corporations, hereafter created, which laws may, at any time, be altered or repealed. And no such alteration or repeal shall interfere with or divest rights which have become vested.

SEC. 9. *Power over local affairs—Home rule for cities and counties—Consolidation of functions.*—The Legislature shall have the right to vest such powers in the Courts of Justice, with regard to private and local affairs, as may be expedient.

The General Assembly shall have no power to pass a special, local or private act having the effect of removing the incumbent from any municipal or county office or abridging the term or altering the salary prior to the end of the term for which such public officer was selected, and any act of the General Assembly private or local in form or effect applicable to a particular county or municipality either in its governmental or its proprietary capacity shall be void and of no effect unless the act by its terms either requires the approval by a two-thirds vote of the local legislative body of the municipality or county, or requires approval in an election by a majority of those voting in said election in the municipality or county affected.

Any municipality may by ordinance submit to its qualified voters in a general or special election the question: "Shall this municipality adopt home rule?"

In the event of an affirmative vote by a majority of the qualified voters voting thereon, and until the repeal thereof by the same procedure, such municipality shall be a home rule municipality, and the General Assembly shall act with respect to such home rule municipality only by laws which are general in terms and effect.

Any municipality after adopting home rule may continue to operate under its existing charter, or amend the same, or adopt and thereafter amend a new charter to provide for its governmental and proprietary powers, duties and functions, and for the form, structure, personnel and organization of its government, provided that no charter provision except with respect to compensation of municipal personnel shall be effective if inconsistent with any general act of the General Assembly and provided further that the power of taxation of such municipality shall not be enlarged or increased except by General act of the General Assembly. The General Assembly shall by general law provide the exclusive methods by which municipalities may be created, merged, consolidated and dissolved and by which municipal boundaries may be altered.

A charter or amendment may be proposed by ordinance of any home rule municipality, by a charter commission provided for by Act of the General Assembly and elected by the qualified voters of a home rule municipality voting thereon or, in the absence of such act of the General Assembly, by a charter commission of seven (7) members, chosen at large not more often than once in two (2) years, in a municipal election pursuant to petition for such election signed by qualified voters of a home rule municipality not less in number than ten (10%) per cent of those voting in the then most recent general municipal election.

It shall be the duty of the legislative body of such municipality to publish any proposal so made and to submit the same to its qualified voters at the first general state election which shall be held at least sixty (60) days after such publication and such proposal shall become effective sixty (60) days after approval by a majority of the qualified voters voting thereon.

The General Assembly shall not authorize any municipality to tax incomes, estates, or inheritances, or to impose any other tax not authorized by Sections 28 or 29 of Article II of this Constitution. Nothing herein shall be construed as invalidating the provisions of any municipal charter in existence at the time of the adoption of this amendment.

The General Assembly may provide for the consolidation of any or all of the governmental and corporate functions now or hereafter vested in municipal corporations with the governmental and corporate functions now or hereafter vested in the counties in which such municipal corporations are located; provided, such consolidations shall not become effective until submitted to the qualified voters residing within the municipal corporation and in the county outside thereof, and approved by a majority of those voting within the municipal corporation and by a majority of those voting in the county outside the municipal corporation.

SEC. 10. *Internal Improvements to be Encouraged.*—A well regulated system of internal improvement is calculated to develop the resources of the State, and promote the happiness and prosperity of her citizens; therefore it ought to be encouraged by the General Assembly.

SEC. 11. *Homestead exemption.*—A homestead in the possession of each head of a family and the improvements thereon, to the value, in all of one thousand dollars shall be exempt from sale under legal process, during the life of such head of a family, to inure to the benefit of the widow, and shall be exempt during the minority of their children occupying the same. Nor shall said property be alienated without the joint consent of husband and wife, when that relation exists. This exemption shall not operate against public taxes, nor debts contracted for the purchase money of such homestead or improvements thereon.

SEC. 12. *Education to be cherished—Common school fund—Poll tax—Whites and negroes.*—Knowledge, learning, and virtue, being essential to the preservation of republican institutions, and the diffusion of the opportunities and advantages of education throughout the different portions of the State, being highly conducive to the promotion of this end, it shall be the duty of the General Assembly in all future periods of this Government, to cherish literature and science. And the fund called common school fund, and all the lands and proceeds thereof, dividends, stocks, and other property of every description whatever, heretofore by law appropriated by the General Assembly of this State for the use of common schools, and all such as shall hereafter be appropriated, shall remain a perpetual fund, the principal of which shall never be diminished by Legislative appropriations; and the interest thereof shall be inviolably appropriated to the support and encouragement of common schools throughout the State, and for the equal benefit of all the people thereof; and no law shall be made authorizing said fund or any part thereof to be divested to any other use than the support and encouragement of common schools. The State taxes derived hereafter from polls shall be appropriated to educational purposes, in such manner as the General Assembly shall from time to time direct by law. No school established or aided under this section shall allow white and negro children to be received as scholars together in the same school. The above provisions shall not prevent the Legislature from carrying into effect any laws that have been passed in favor of the Colleges, Universities or Academies, or from authorizing heirs or distributees to receive and enjoy escheated property under such laws as may be passed from time to time.

SEC. 13. *Game and fish.*—The General Assembly shall have power to enact laws for the protection and preservation of Game and Fish, within the State, and such laws may be enacted for and applied and enforced in particular Counties or geographical districts, designated by the General Assembly.

SEC. 14. *Intermarriage between whites and negroes.*—The intermarriage of white persons with negroes, mullattos, or persons of mixed blood, descended from a negro to the third generation inclusive or their living together as man and wife in this State is prohibited. The legislature shall enforce this section by appropriate legislation.

SEC. 15. *Religious holidays.*—No person shall in time of peace be required to perform any service to the public on any day set apart by his religion as a day of rest.

SEC. 16. *Bill of rights to remain inviolate.*—The declaration of rights hereto prefixed is declared to be a part of the Constitution of this State, and shall never be violated on any pretence whatever. And to guard against transgression of the high powers we have delegated, we declare that everything in the bill or rights contained, is excepted out of the General powers of the government, and shall forever remain inviolate.

SEC. 17. *County offices.*—No County office created by the Legislature shall be filled otherwise than by the people or the County Court.

SCHEDULE

SECTION 1. *Terms of public officers—Appointments—Exceptions.*—That no inconvenience may arise from a change of the Constitution, it is declared that the Governor of the State, the members of the General Assembly and all officers elected at or after the general election of March one thousand eight hundred and seventy, shall hold their offices for the terms prescribed in this Constitution.

Officers appointed by the courts shall be filled by appointment, to be made and to take effect during the first term of the court held by Judges elected under this Constitution.

All other officers shall vacate their places thirty days after the date fixed for the election of their successors under this Constitution.

The Secretary of State, Comptroller and Treasurer shall hold their offices until the first session of the present General Assembly occurring after the ratification of this Constitution and until their successors are elected and qualified.

The officers then elected shall hold their offices until the fifteenth day of January, one thousand eight hundred and seventy-three.

SEC. 2. *Supreme court judges—Vacancies—Attorney-general and reporter.*—At the first election of Judges under this Constitution there shall be elected six Judges of the Supreme Court, two from each grand division of the State who shall hold their offices for the term herein prescribed.

In the event any vacancy shall occur in the office of either of said Judges at any time after the first day of January one thousand eight hundred and seventy-three, it shall remain unfilled and the Court shall from that time be constituted to five Judges. While the Court shall consist of six Judges they may sit in two sections, and may hear and determine causes in each at the same time, but not in different grand divisions at the same time.

When so sitting, the concurrence of two Judges shall be necessary to a decision.

The Attorney General and Reporter for the State shall be appointed after the election and qualification of the Judges of the Supreme Court herein provided for.

SEC. 3. *Oath of office mandatory.*—Every Judge and every officer of the executive department of this State

and every Sheriff holding over under this Constitution, shall, within twenty days after the ratification of this Constitution is proclaimed, take an oath to support the same, and the failure of any officer to take such oath shall vacate his office.

SEC. 4. *Statute of limitations.*—The time which has elapsed from the sixth day of May one thousand eight hundred and sixty one until the first day of January one thousand eight hundred and sixty seven shall not be computed, in any case affected by the statutes of limitation, nor shall any writ of error be affected by such lapse of time.

Done in Convention at Nashville the twenty-third day of February in the year of our Lord one thousand eight hundred and seventy, and of the Independence of the United States, the ninety fourth.

AMENDMENTS TO THE 1870 CONSTITUTION

The 1870 Tennessee Constitution was ratified and proclaimed by the Governor on May 5, 1870. Thereafter this Constitution remained unchanged for eighty-three (83) years and was the oldest unamended Constitution in existence. The Tennessee General Assembly in 1959 authorized a limited Constitutional Convention. This limited Convention was approved by the voters of the State of Tennessee in 1952 and delegates were chosen in a special election held on November 4, 1952. The Convention met and recommended back to the electorate eight amendments which were in turn submitted to the voters of Tennessee on November 3, 1953. All eight amendments were approved by the people and proclaimed a part of the Constitution by Governor Frank G. Clement on the 9th day of November 1953.

In 1957 the Tennessee General Assembly authorized another limited Constitutional Convention and the voters approved the holding of this Convention in 1959. Following election of the delegates thereto at the November 4, 1958 election, the Convention assembled July 1, 1959. This Convention referred only one proposition back to the voters which would change the term of office of the County Trustee from two to four years. This amendment was approved by the voters on the 8th day of November, 1960.

The General Assembly again in 1962 in extraordinary session authorized the third limited Constitutional Convention. The voters approved the calling of the Convention at the November, 1962 general election and delegates were elected at the August general election of 1964 and convened on July 26, 1965. This Convention proposed nine amendments all dealing with Article 2 of the Constitution and all nine were approved by the voters at the November election of 1966. *All amendments ratified as a result of the three limited Constitutional Conventions set out above are incorporated in the text of the foregoing Constitution.*

Index